I0824756

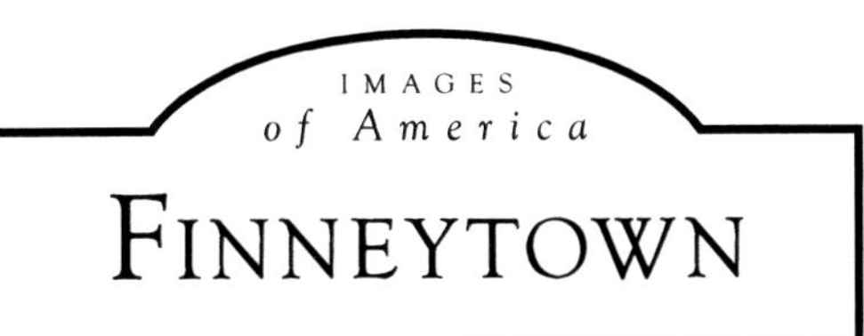
IMAGES
of America
FINNEYTOWN

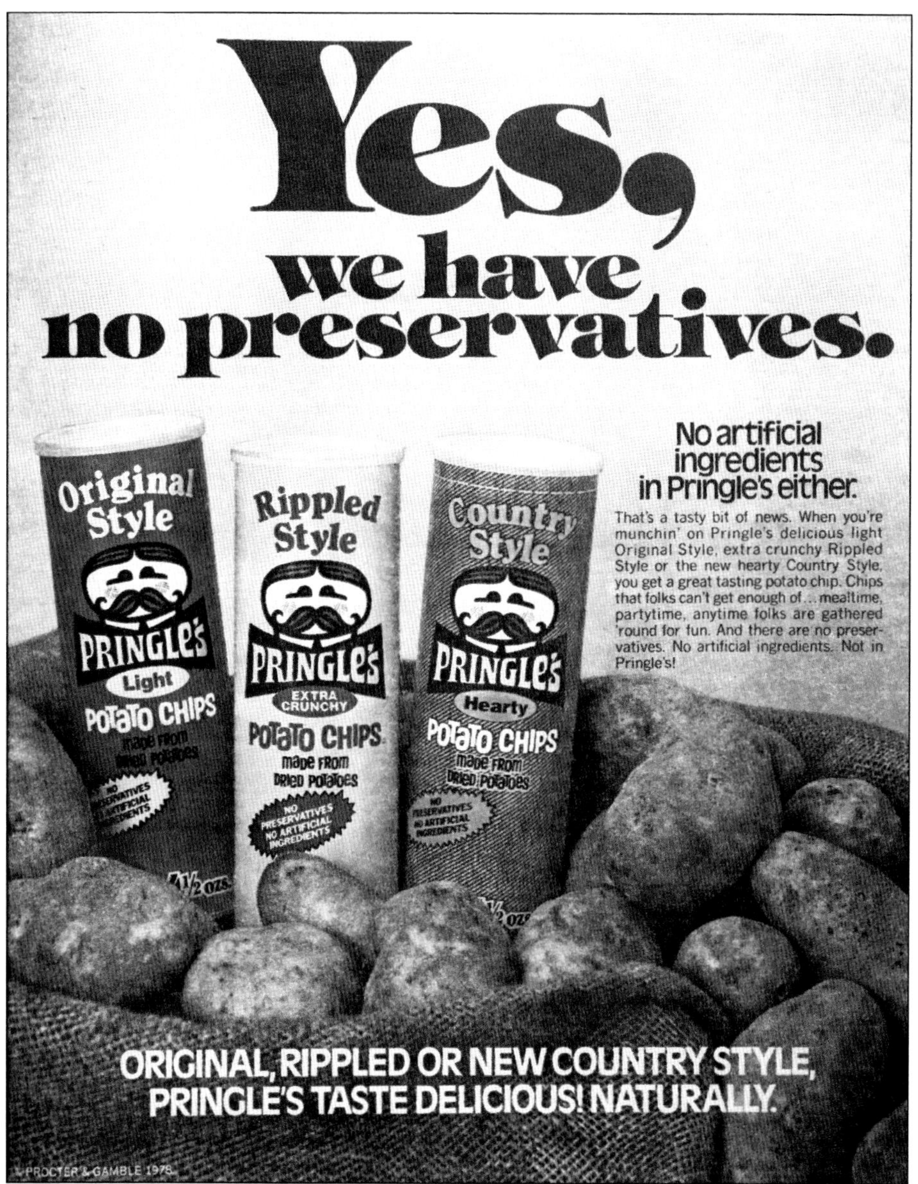

The name "Pringles" originated from Pringle Drive, a quiet, half-mile street in Finneytown. Procter & Gamble (P&G) developed the potato chip in the 1950s and early 1960s. When P&G's advertising agency proposed "Wrinkles" as the product name, "My dad insisted on an alliteration," said David Gendell, son of P&G brand manager Gerard Gendell. In 1968, P&G test-marketed "Pringle's Newfangled Potato Chips" in Evansville, Indiana, with a cartoon image of a mustached Mr. Pringle. This advertisement is from 1978. (Author's collection.)

On the Cover: On September 6, 1957, school leaders and 68 eighth-grade students who would be the first graduating class of the new Finneytown High School, held a groundbreaking ceremony at the construction site. H. Ray Noe, Finneytown school board president, tossed the first shovel of dirt. He led the community's building campaign to finance the new secondary school campus. (Courtesy of Steve Battistone.)

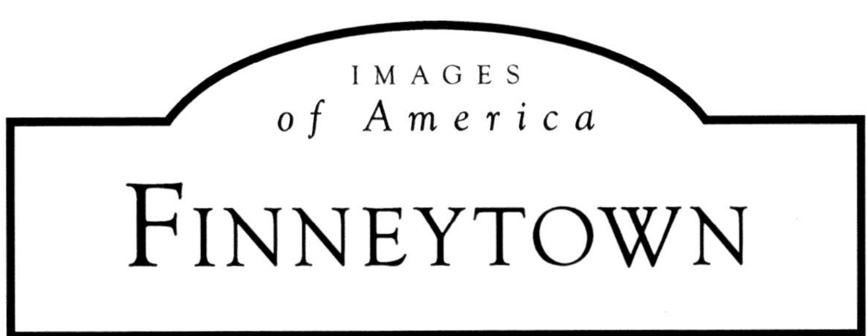

FINNEYTOWN

Rick Kennedy and Mark Evans
Foreword by Jeff Immelt

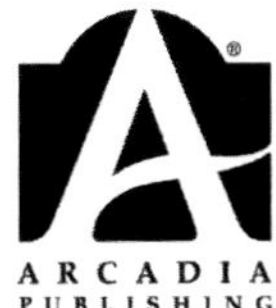

Copyright © 2025 by Rick Kennedy and Mark Evans
ISBN 9781-4671-6233-3

Published by Arcadia Publishing
Charleston, South Carolina

Printed in the United States of America

Library of Congress Control Number: 2024952318

For all general information, please contact Arcadia Publishing:
Telephone 843-853-2070
Fax 843-853-0044
E-mail sales@arcadiapublishing.com

Visit us on the Internet at www.arcadiapublishing.com

This book is dedicated to Steve Battistone, president of Finneytown High School's class of 1973. His research, photographs, and encouragement were invaluable to this book.

Contents

Foreword

After experiencing my "wonder years" growing up in Finneytown, I left the community in 1974. I furthered my education, embarked on an exciting business career, raised a family, traveled the world, and collaborated with industry leaders on projects of global significance.

When I return to Finneytown, I know that I have come home.

I've been blessed with loving parents who lived a long time and stayed in the Cincinnati area. And my visits with them over the years always involved a welcomed trip down Winton Road to the haunts of my youth. I would swing by our old home on Cotillion Drive, and around the corner to the McNulty family's house. It was the scene of our neighborhood "Olympics"—Wiffle ball, touch football, and basketball. I'd always end this sentimental journey by strolling the walkways of Finneytown High School, where, as a bushy-haired teenager, I strode confident and optimistic about my life ahead.

When visiting Finneytown, I always feel warmth and thankfulness for my friends, teachers, and a supportive community. As kids, we didn't know if we were rich or poor. We were always encouraged and taught to believe in ourselves.

Now many decades later, Finneytown looks different. The population is more diverse. The neighborhoods are older. Some streets have never looked better, and some are in disrepair. From a business standpoint, Springfield Township has helped to keep Finneytown vibrant. The community is building new public schools. And I am encouraged when I feel the spirit and pride of today's Finneytown.

In 2020, Finneytown Local School District superintendent Laurie Banks reached out to outline her vision for the school community. She promoted strong ideas on how to rebuild the physical space for learning in order to give students better opportunities and to support teachers in their mission. I am "all in" to support this vision.

Finneytown has a wonderful past, as celebrated in this book, and I was lucky to be part of it. Without a doubt, the enthusiasm that I remember is still there today. May Finneytown always be a place where people can be inspired to live out their dreams.

—Jeff Immelt

ACKNOWLEDGMENTS

The Finneytown community rallied around this book. A special thanks goes to Steve Battistone, Gail Hafer Hauer, Leslie Weisner, Donald Burck, Rob Leininger, and Jeff Immelt. Other important contributors include Brett Harper; William and Janet Swartzel; Susan Rissover; Chip Doyle; Kim Flamm; Dwight Weber; Nick Kemper and Jennifer Donahue at St. Xavier High School; Grant Anderson, Finneytown Local School District; Rocky Merz, the Cincinnati Park Board; Kenny Burck; Chris Smith, the Cincinnati Public Library; Mike Arnold and Stephen Heck, Baroque Violin Shop; Merce Hershey; Steve Lang; Mike Frye; Nancy Thyberg; Janet Boling; Karen Kuhlmann; Bradley Mattes; Tyson Hermes, Chris Glass; Rick Henthorn; Judith O'Rourke; John Kiesewetter; Don Bahr; Alicia Bourbeau; Clay Mizelle; Jeff Kobberdahl; Rick Payne; Christopher Riley; Nancy McGuire; William Neidermeyer; Tom Nieman; Randy McNutt; Matt Angert; Elizabeth Garber; Chris Hoeweler; Stanley Mark; Mike Steel; Jeff Steel; Jean Lubker; Jeff New; Holt & Reichard; Beth Johnson; Bob Muro; Tim Dutton; Amy Flesher; Tomasz Grelak; Dave Whitehead; and Mark Besserman.

INTRODUCTION

From the 1800s until World War II, Finneytown was a farm community atop the wooded hills above Cincinnati. However, after the war ended, and the US troops came home, sleepy Finneytown transformed.

This book details its early days through the postwar boom of 1946–1969, when Finneytown's population more than tripled, and young families filled its new subdivisions, schools, and churches. Seemingly overnight, the farms and open fields disappeared, replaced by streets carved out for small, cookie-cutter houses, as well as custom-built, stately homes, several with mid-century modern designs.

Nestled in a small area, this diversity of housing for a wide range of incomes created a close-knit, economically inclusive community, which continues to influence Finneytown's ethos. Moreover, the best of its mid-century modern houses are now desirable architectural timepieces.

Still, defining Finneytown gets complicated. It was never annexed into Cincinnati or incorporated as a village in Springfield Township. The only public institution bearing its name is Finneytown Local School District, though the community has both public and private schools. And yet, Finneytown appears on local TV weather maps, and news stories describe Finneytown people and events.

Technically, Finneytown is an unincorporated "census-designated place" bordered by a school district. But it feels like a town, and residents tell you they live in one. Some people put it this way: Finneytown is simply a state of mind.

Whatever you call it, Finneytown is old. It's named after Revolutionary War veteran Ebenezer Finney, who led his family and in-laws in 1800 from New York State to forestland, which he inherited from his grandfather, near today's North Bend and Winton Roads. Ohio was still three years away from becoming a state. Soon after arriving, the settlers built a church on Finney's property. Around 1801, Finney designated a half-acre of his farm near the church for a cemetery (today's Old Finneytown Cemetery) where the original settlers, and a striking number of their young children, are buried. For several years, these settlers coexisted with nearby Native American tribes.

In the early 19th century, the focal point for the farm community was at the intersection of unpaved North Bend and Winton Roads, where a smattering of businesses included a general store, saloon, and blacksmith shop. The community was informally known as "Finneytown," and the name began to appear in local newspapers by the 1860s.

Finneytown's strong association with education dates to the same era. In 1860, William Cummings built a schoolhouse near his farm on Winton Road, and an elementary school operated there for 162 years. In 1870, the Catholic Sisters of the Good Shepherd established a school for white and black girls in troubled circumstances to the east of the community along North Bend Road. Later called Girls Town, it operated in Finneytown for a century. In 1905, a Springfield Township judge designated Finneytown as an independent public school district, and it has remained that way ever since.

In the early 20th century, two large nurseries were added to Finneytown's pastoral landscape. In 1919, the Nieman family created a nursery (later developed into subdivisions) along Winton Road. A decade later, the Cincinnati Park Board created Warder Nursery to support the city parks. In the late 1930s, Finneytown created its first residential subdivision—a cluster of small tract homes near Warder Nursery called Parkview Heights. The subdivision's children trekked to Finneytown School, which slowly grew and added buildings. Catholics in Parkview Heights established St. Vivian Church. For social events, civic meetings, dancing, and a little whiskey drinking, the community had the Finneytown Inn on North Bend Road, a longtime roadhouse that began as a mid-19th-century saloon. In the mid-1940s, a handful of local men formed a volunteer fire department. But all in all, Finneytown was still a sleepy town.

Then, the postwar boom arrived. Facing housing shortages, the government offered favorable home loans to veterans and tax benefits for home ownership. Developers swarmed Finneytown, bought up farmland, and sold their houses to young couples with kids. Many of the adults worked for nearby GE and P&G. (P&G developed and named the iconic Pringles potato chip after Finneytown's Pringle Drive.) Hollyhock Farms Inc. built stately homes off Compton Road, while Lang Brothers built tract houses in the Greenfield Village subdivision. By the mid-1950s, Modern Builders and Lang Brothers had created Brentwood Village, and O.O. Thompson & Sons created Brentwood Acres and Thompson Acres. The View Place subdivision overlooked Mill Creek Valley.

As a patchwork of subdivisions sprouted up, Finneytown voted on what the community should be. Two questions arose: Should rural Finneytown be incorporated as a village within Springfield Township or annexed into the neighboring city of Cincinnati? In 1952, citizens voted against incorporating as a village by seven votes—403 to 396. The next year, they again voted against incorporation, 731 to 561. Meanwhile, Cincinnati pursued annexation, calling Finneytown a "gateway" to annexing other communities. By 1954, the debate intensified. Finneytown Citizens Committee for City Annexation pitted against Citizens' Committee for Northern Hills, which opposed annexation. The groups solicited door-to-door and held rallies. Cincinnati newspapers supported annexation while the influential Finneytown Civic Club opposed it. In the end, residents voted against annexation, and Finneytown's confusing identity prevailed.

Into the 1960s, the newer subdivisions ranged from tiny tract houses in Wintondale to large, custom-built houses in Greenfield Village and North Hill Estates. The swelling population filled the pews of expanding neighborhood churches, such as Northminster Presbyterian, Faith Lutheran, St. Vivian, Christian Reform, and Central Baptist. (In the 1970s, two large congregations located in Finneytown: Holy Trinity-St. Nicholas Greek Orthodox Church and Emanuel Apostolic Church, resulting from a merger of Emanuel Tabernacle Church of Avondale and First Apostolic Church of Lincoln Heights.)

Residential growth in the 1960s drove commercial development: Brentwood Shopping Center (opened in 1958 as one of the region's largest outdoor malls), professional offices, retail strip malls, a swim club, a bowling alley, lounges, and restaurants. As fast-food chain restaurants sprouted up across America, fast-growing Finneytown was often one of the first places in Cincinnati to open for business.

Dramatic post-war growth coincided with an American architectural movement now called mid-century modern, which enhanced Finneytown's visual aesthetic. "In the early 1950s, there was a big push to bring the modern architecture of the West Coast to the Midwest," said Susan Rissover, co-owner of CincinnatiModern, a real estate agency focused on mid-century modern homes. Local architects and architecture professors at the nearby University of Cincinnati's College of Design, Architecture, Art and Planning (DAAP) created designs in Cincinnati that were described at the time as "futuristic" residential homes. "Several streets created in Finneytown had the perfect topography of hills and wooded areas for constructing mid-century modern homes," Rissover added. As a result, some of the region's leading modernist architects, such as Rudy Hermes, Benjamin Dombar, Richard Calef, and James Alexander, left enduring designs within Finneytown. While mid-century modern architecture was mostly unappreciated by homebuyers in the late 20th century, the homes today are highly valued.

As Finneytown's population continued to grow in the baby boomer era, the community's educational choices dramatically upgraded. Until the late 1950s, Finneytown had no high school—only public Finneytown School (later called Whitaker Elementary) and St. Vivian Catholic School, both on Winton Road. These schools educated students up through eighth grade. However, by 1958, nearly half of Finneytown's 9,000 residents were under 19 years of age, and something had to be done. Between 1957 and 1964, the community financed Finneytown High School and the adjoining secondary school campus, as well as Cottonwood and Brent Elementary Schools. Later, Central Baptist opened a private school. At the same time Finneytown High School was being built in the late 1950s, historic St. Xavier High School, which had operated downtown since 1831, pulled up stakes and constructed a large campus on open land along North Bend near the View Place subdivision. The all-male, private high school, among the region's largest private high schools, would continue to bring considerable positive attention to Finneytown.

During the 1960s, prominent Cincinnatians raised families in Finneytown, including businessman Charlie Keating, physician and activist Dr. John Willke, TV news anchor Al Schottelkotte, and Cincinnati Reds player and broadcaster Gordie Coleman. Later, many kids who grew up in Finneytown attained great success, such as GE chairman Jeff Immelt, Olympic champions Amanda Borden and Joe Hudepohl, local TV anchor Tanya O'Rourke, and Ohio Supreme Court Justice Joe Deters.

Finneytown's most culturally significant resident is Charley Harper (1922–2007). During his half-century living in the community, he became one of America's most recognizable illustrators, and his reputation continues to grow worldwide.

Today, more than a half-century after its transformation during an era of unprecedented birth rates, Finneytown continues to thrive. Typical of America's "first-ring" suburbs, the demographics changed dramatically over time. A hallmark of Finneytown in the 1950s and 1960s was its economic diversity. Today, the community's diversity also includes an older and more ethnically diverse population. Finneytown now finds itself in the center of an expanding Greater Cincinnati. As a result, convenience is a prime attraction for residents of all ages. However, while Finneytown is busier and more urban, it retains the splendid reminders of its past. They speak to its colorful history – and to its special "state of mind."

One

Settling the Frontier

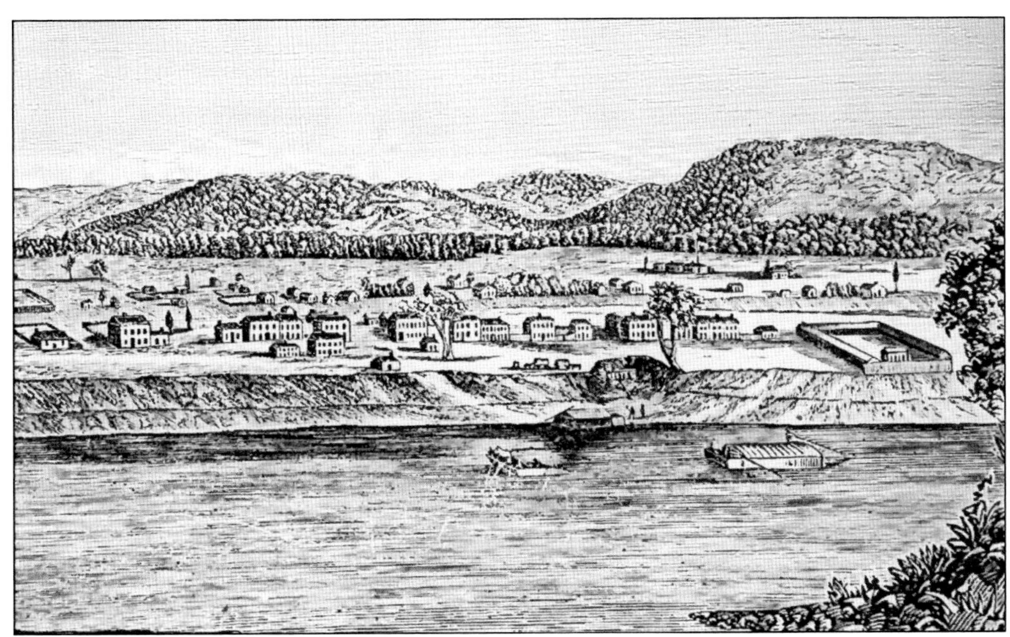

Ebenezer Ward Finney was 45 years old in 1800 when he led his family and other relatives from Rensselaer, New York, to the new village of Cincinnati, Ohio. Arriving by flatboat on the Ohio River shore, they journeyed nine miles uphill into the wilderness and settled near today's Winton and North Bend Roads in Springfield Township. Their frontier outpost was informally known as "Finneytown." (Author's collection.)

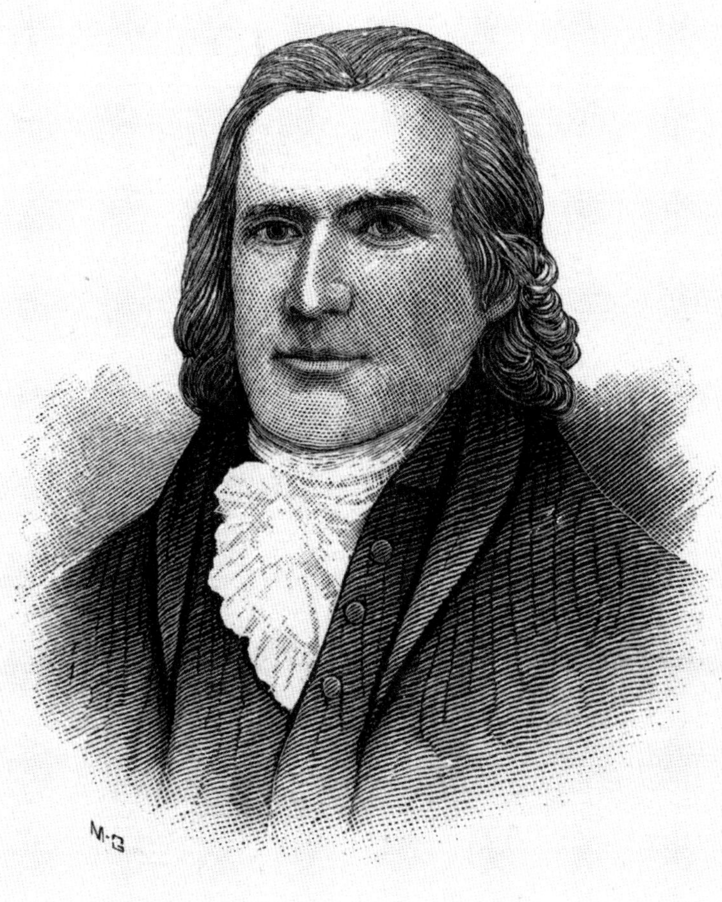

Tumultuous years in southwest Ohio preceded Finney's arrival. For centuries, indigenous tribes had fought each other within the territory. After the Revolutionary War (1776–1783), the tribes grew hostile to arriving settlers in the "Northwest Territory," a region north of the Ohio River claimed by the new nation as spoils of war. While many settlers received land grants for their military service, John Cleves Symmes (pictured), Chief Justice of New Jersey, purchased vast wilderness north of the Ohio River and between the two Miami Rivers in 1788. Shortly thereafter, General Anthony Wayne, directing campaigns from Cincinnati's Fort Washington, put an end to the native hostilities, resulting in the Treaty of Greenville in 1795. That year, Rev. Ebenezer Ward of New York purchased from Symmes a block of land in the newly formed Springfield Township. Ward's grandson, Ebenezer Ward Finney, inherited much of this land and settled there. (New York City Library.)

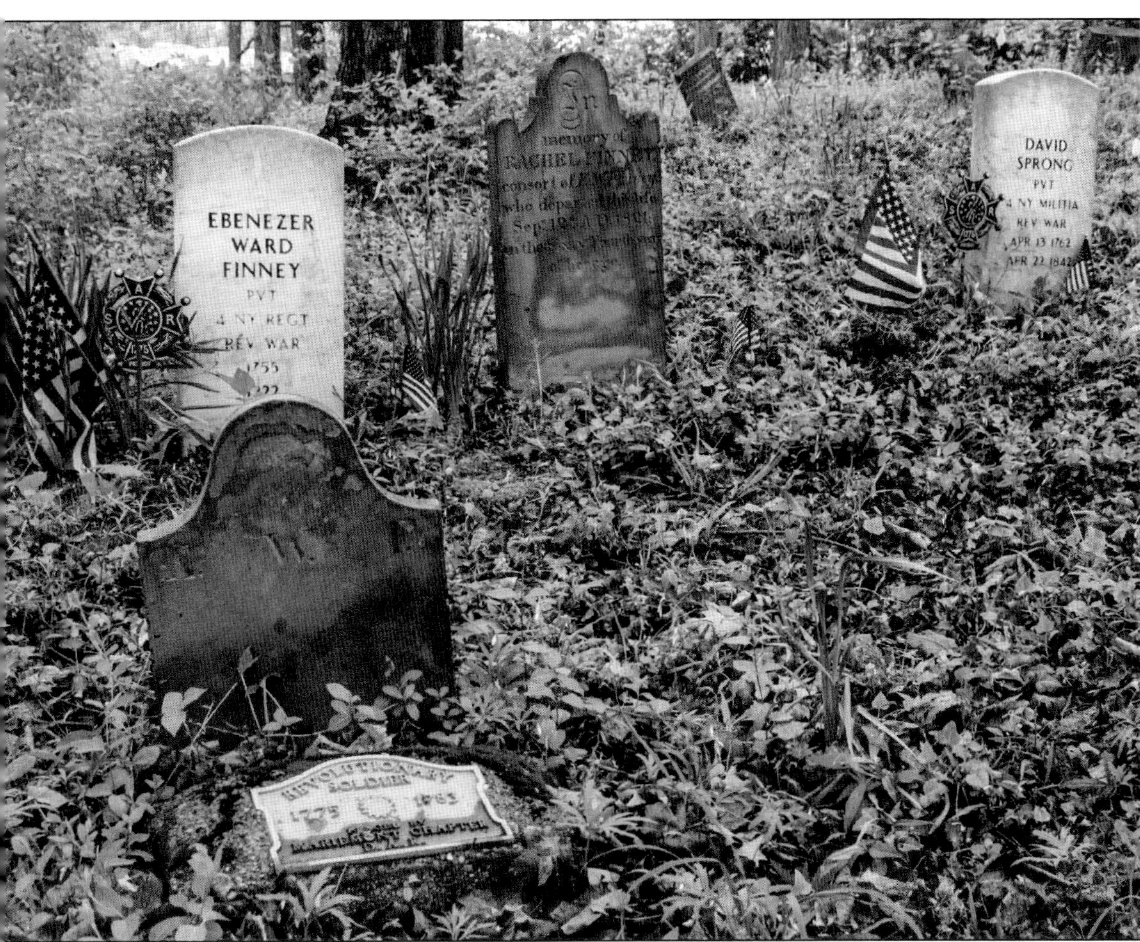

Ebenezer Finney (seen left) experienced firsthand the violent creation of a new nation as a private in the Revolutionary War. He served in the 4th Regiment of Westchester County, New York, which was situated in between encampments of British and Patriot troops. After settling in Springfield Township, Finney designated a half-acre of his land as a cemetery on an ancient mound next to the settlers' new church. Most of Finneytown's original settlers are buried in Old Finneytown Cemetery, including veterans of the Revolutionary War and the War of 1812. Also called God's Half Acre and Old Wesleyan, this cemetery is on Winton Ridge Lane, south of Finneytown Local School District and within the Cincinnati city limits. Finney is buried next to his wife, Rachel. To their right are their daughter Lois and her husband David Sprong, also a Revolutionary War veteran. Today, the cemetery's upkeep depends upon civic groups. (Mark Evans.)

THE

KENTUCKY REVIVAL,

OR,

A SHORT HISTORY

Of the late extraordinary out-pouring of the Spirit of God, in the weſtern States of America, agreeably to Scripture-promiſes, and Prophecies concerning the Latter Day:

WITH A BRIEF ACCOUNT
OF THE ENTRANCE AND PROGRESS OF WHAT THE WORLD CALL

SHAKERISM,

AMONG THE SUBJECTS OF THE LATE REVIVAL IN OHIO AND KENTUCKY.

PRESENTED TO THE
TRUE ZION-TRAVELLER,
AS A MEMORIAL OF THE WILDERNESS JOURNEY.

By Richard M'Nemar.

"When ye ſee a cloud riſe out of the weſt, ſtraightway ye ſay, there "cometh a ſhower; and ſo it is: And when YE FEEL the ſouth wind "blow, ye ſay, there will be heat; and it cometh to paſs——Can ye "not diſcern the ſigns of the times.

CHRIST.

CINCINNATI:
FROM THE PRESS OF JOHN W. BROWNE,
OFFICE OF LIBERTY HALL.
1807.

The 1800s charismatic "New Light" Christian movement, also called "the Kentucky Revival," caught fire with the first Finneytown pioneers. Their church embraced the New Light doctrine, which is best remembered for the members' spontaneous physical movements during worship. New Light fervor spread from the Kentucky backwoods to southern Ohio. The New Light and Shaker movements in southern Ohio and Kentucky are detailed in this 1807 history (pictured). Finneytown's New Light Church continued into the mid-19th century. In his 1886 history of nearby College Hill, Samuel Cary described the Finneytown church: "The New Lights were numerous on and near Winton Road east of College Hill . . . the Snodgrasses, the Finneys, the Sprongs, and Jessups, good men and thrifty famers belonging to the sect. It was with this sect that the exercise known as the 'jerks' originated." The "jerks" was a spiritual expression involving twitching the head, arms, and shoulders. (Author's collection.)

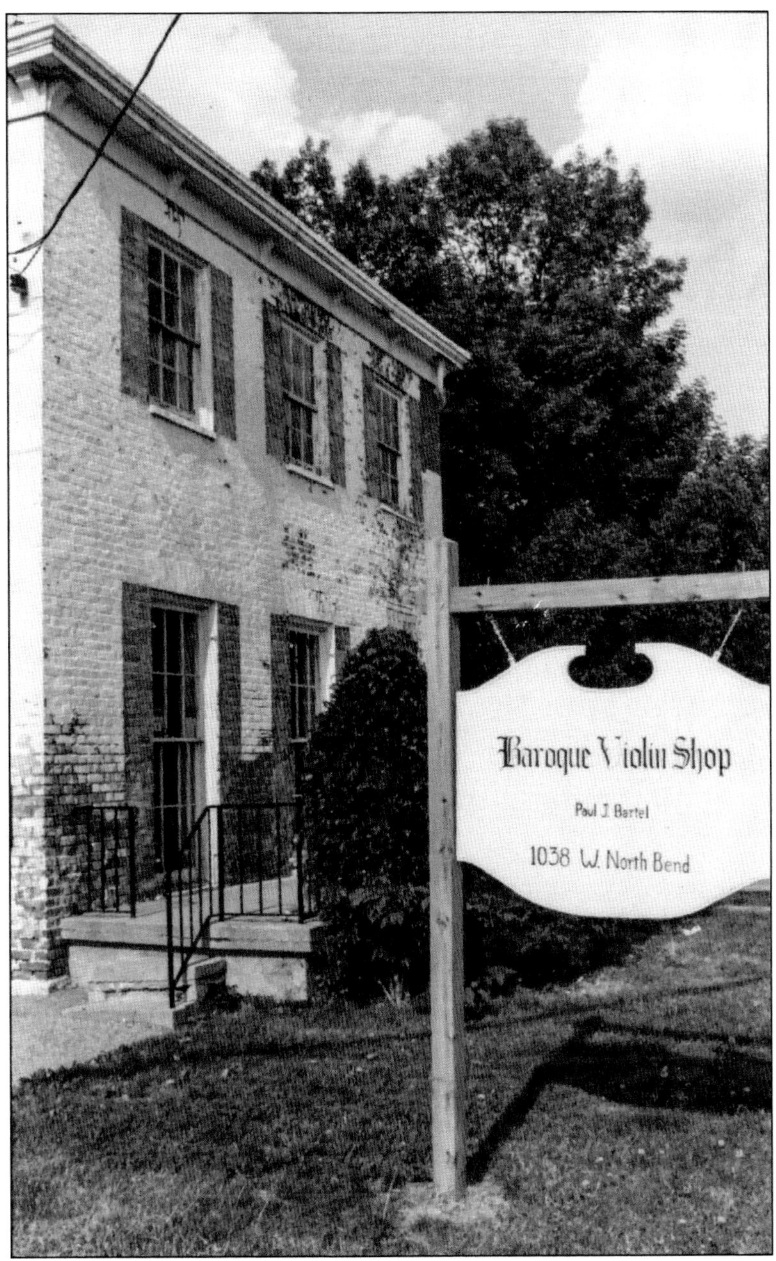

In the early 1980s, Paul Bartel (1952–2019), a violin restorer, musician, and educator, acquired the historic Brown-Jessup House for his Baroque Violin Shop. Through his efforts, it became the first Finneytown house placed in the National Register of Historic Places. Daniel Smith, a farmer from Maryland who moved to the area in 1812, built the Federal-Style brick house before 1825 along North Bend Road and walking distance from the Finneytown settlement. At the time, North Bend, among the county's oldest roads, was called "Cleves to Carthage Trace." The Jessup family, which farmed nearby, lived in the house from the 1830s to the 1860s. In the late 19th century, rooms were added to the rear of the house. Bartel, a former Finneytown High School music teacher, was restoring the house in the 1980s when this photograph was taken. The violin shop continues to operate in one of Finneytown's most historic structures. (Baroque Violin Shop.)

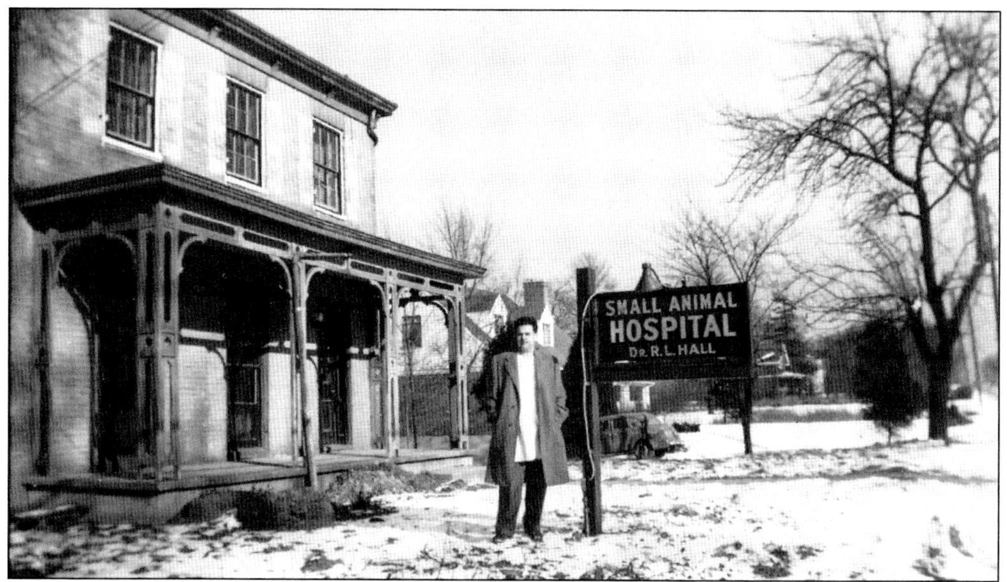

From the 1920s through 1945, German farmers Gustav and Elizabeth Strecker and their family lived in the Smith-Jessup House. One winter, Gustav raised a newborn calf in the house's dirt basement after its mother died. In 1946, veterinarian Russell Hall (pictured) converted the house into a small animal hospital. The house had a front porch at the time. (Baroque Violin Shop.)

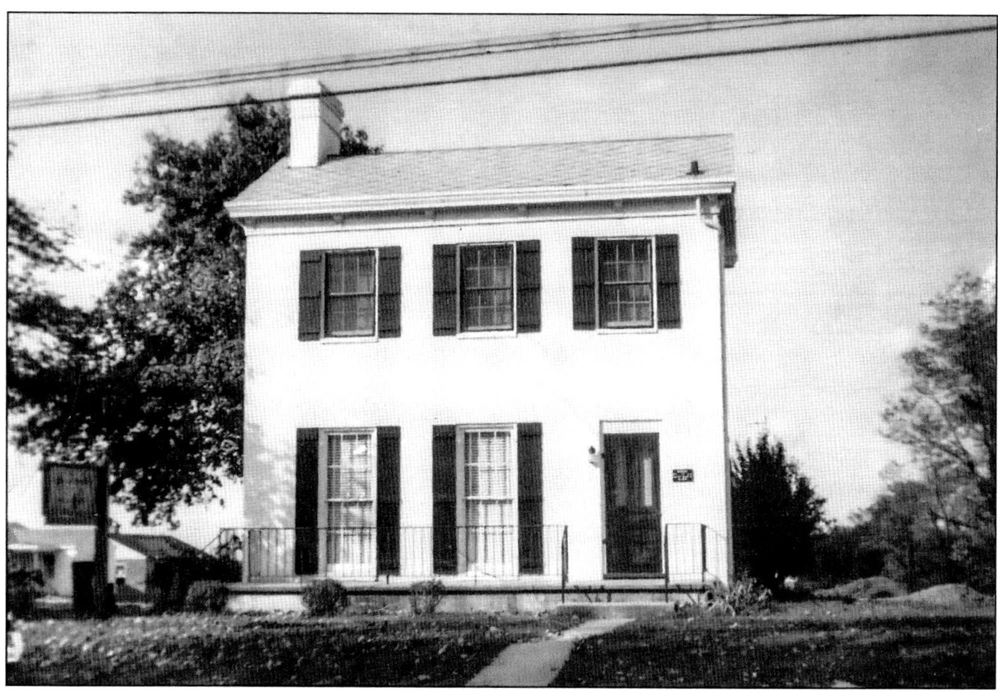

For decades, the house's brick had been painted white. When Paul Bartel purchased the house, the pioneer house had fallen into disrepair. His goal was to "bring back the grandeur of the house, which was built in a period of craftsmanship," he told the *Cincinnati Enquirer*. (Baroque Violin Shop.)

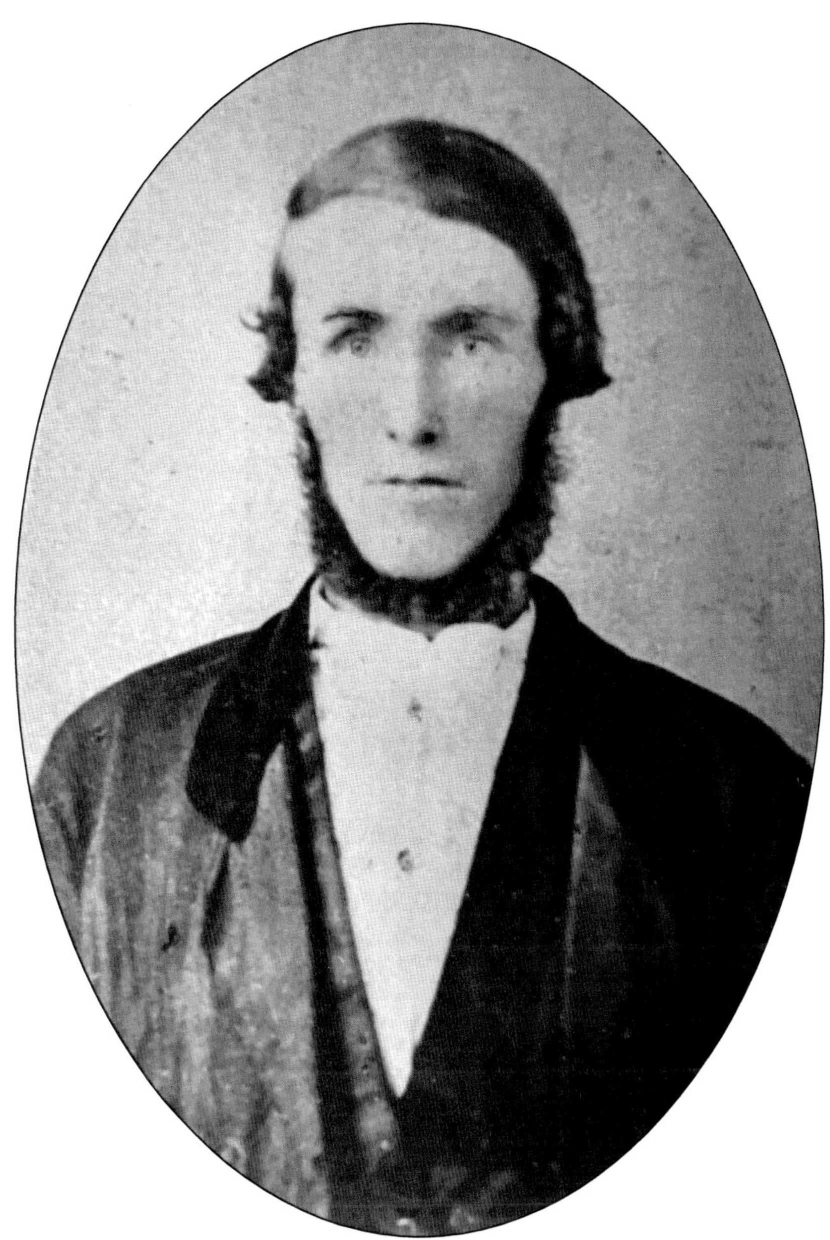

After the Civil War ended in 1865, James (pictured) and Letitia Wallace acquired farmland on both sides of unpaved Winton Road and a half-mile north of North Bend Road. On his land was the original Finneytown schoolhouse, built in 1860, located near today's Warder Nature Preserve. The couple raised six children on their Finneytown farm. Wallace had assumed a quieter life in Finneytown after serving in the infantry of the Ohio 82nd Regiment of the Union Army. He fought in several Civil War battles, including two against Confederate troops led by General Stonewall Jackson. Wallace was wounded at the bloody Battle of Chancellorsville. He was discharged as a second lieutenant. Natives of Ireland, James and Letitia Wallace immigrated to the United States in the 1850s. After Wallace died in 1896, a son, James Wallace Jr., managed the Finneytown farm. After he died in 1907, the property and farmhouse along Winton Road were sold to William Kuhlmann. (William Neidermeyer.)

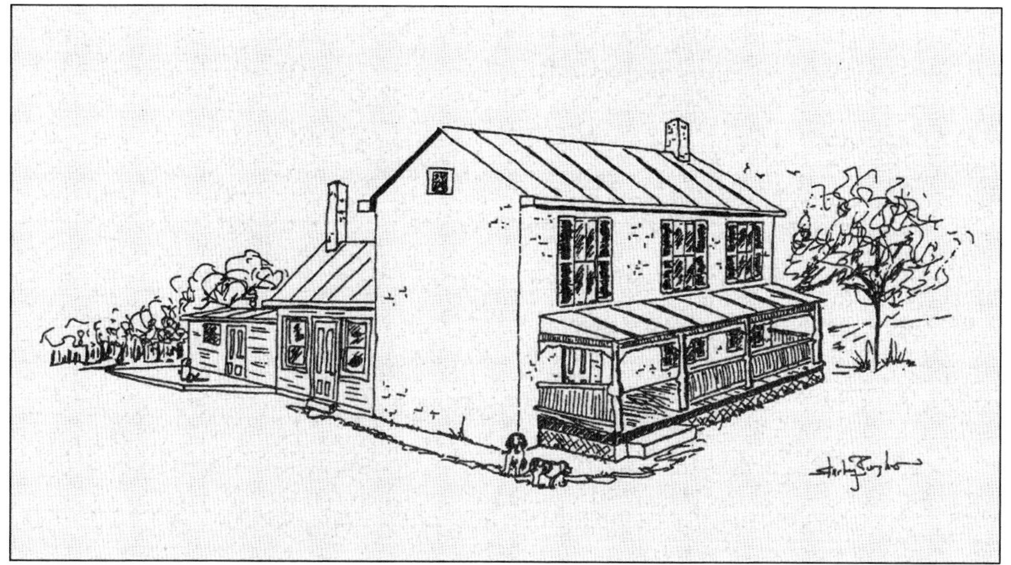

The pioneer VanZandt family arrived in Finneytown in 1804 and established a farm at the southeast corner of Winton and Galbraith Roads. In the mid-1800s, Reuben and Eliza VanZandt raised a large family at the homestead (pictured). Using an original photograph, the late artist Shirley Burgher created this rendering. In the 1950s, VanZandt Road, running east-west through Finneytown, became Galbraith Road. (Karen Kuhlmann.)

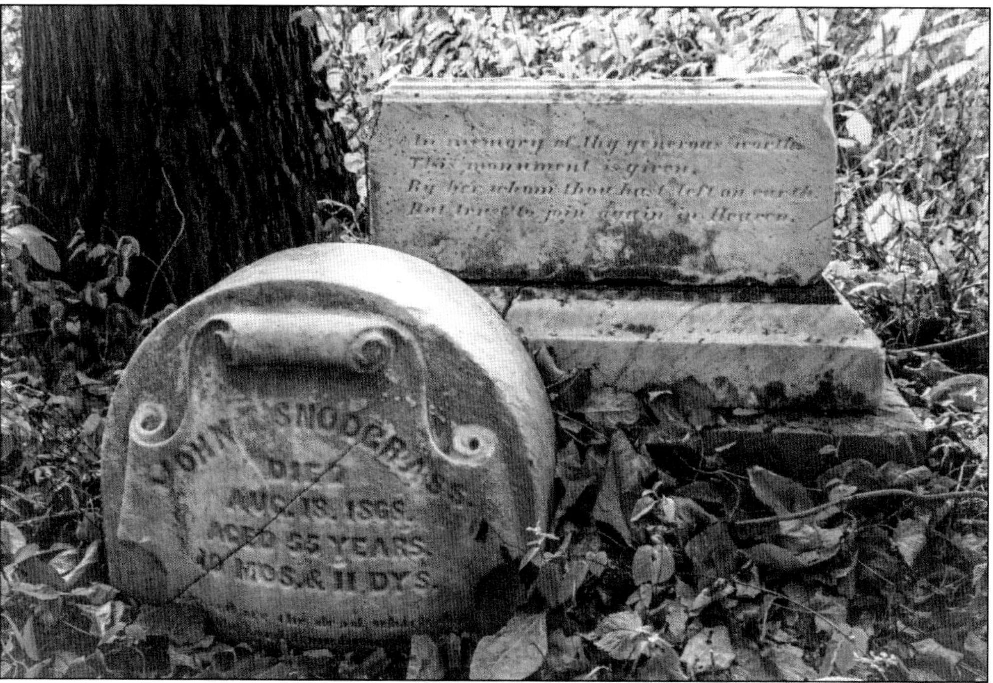

In 1897, Old Finneytown Cemetery attracted national attention after the body of John Snodgrass, buried in 1868 (pictured), was exhumed and reinterred in nearby Spring Grove Cemetery. After his coffin was raised, his body was found preserved as a "solid, stony substance" and "a remarkable instance of human petrification," reported the *Cincinnati Enquirer*. Soon, stories of a "Petrified Man" in Finneytown appeared in newspapers nationwide. (Author's collection.)

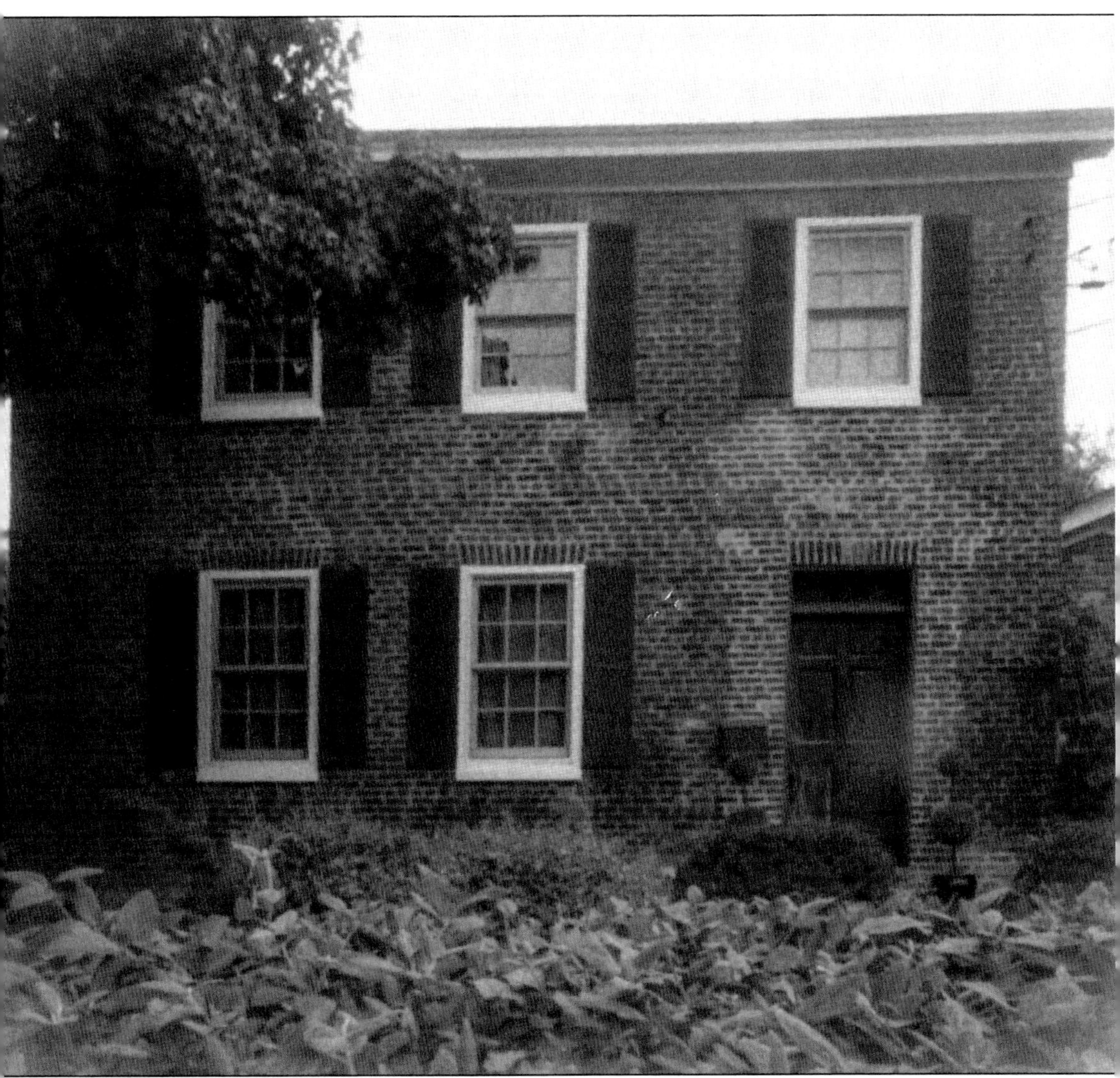

Around 1908, Verona Emminger acquired this 1840s brick farmhouse on the east side of Winton Road and south of Compton Road. She arrived from downtown Cincinnati with quite a reputation. In 1904, police suspected Verona of fatally poisoning her husband, Albert Emminger. While Verona attracted scandalous headlines, police lacked conclusive evidence to arrest her. "No one can ever take his place with me," she told the *Cincinnati Post*. However, three months after her husband died, she married Theodore Heckle, and they moved to the Finneytown house. In 1910, the *Cincinnati Enquirer* reported on Theodore's claim that Verona had chased him with a gun. Verona said her husband "falsely connected her with one Albert Seifert." Two months after they divorced, Verona married Seifert, and he claimed she assaulted him and "threw his clothes out of the house." Eventually, Verona left town and stayed out of the newspapers. (Mark Evans.)

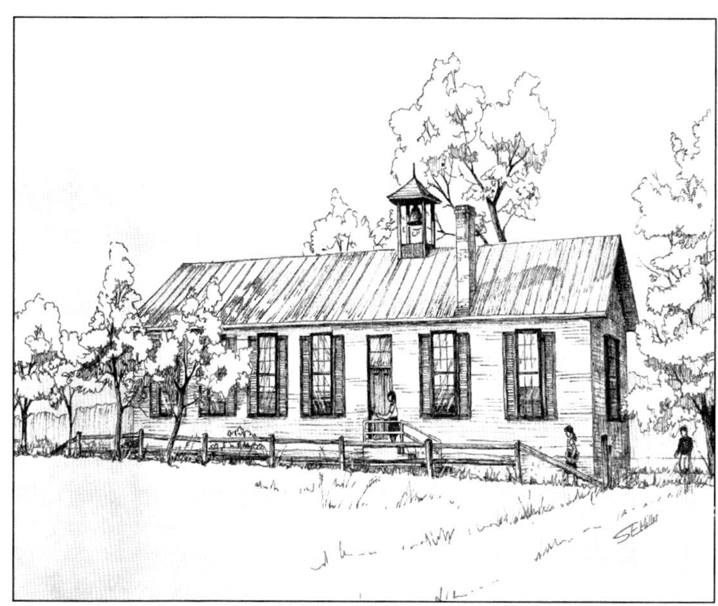

For 162 years, Finneytown elementary school children were educated at the site of this schoolhouse (pictured) on Winton Road and across from Timber Trail. This two-room structure, built in the 1870s, replaced the original 1860 schoolhouse. Artist S.E. Miller, who operated a studio in Finneytown, created this illustration of the 19th-century schoolhouse using an original photograph. (Finneytown Local School District [FLSD].)

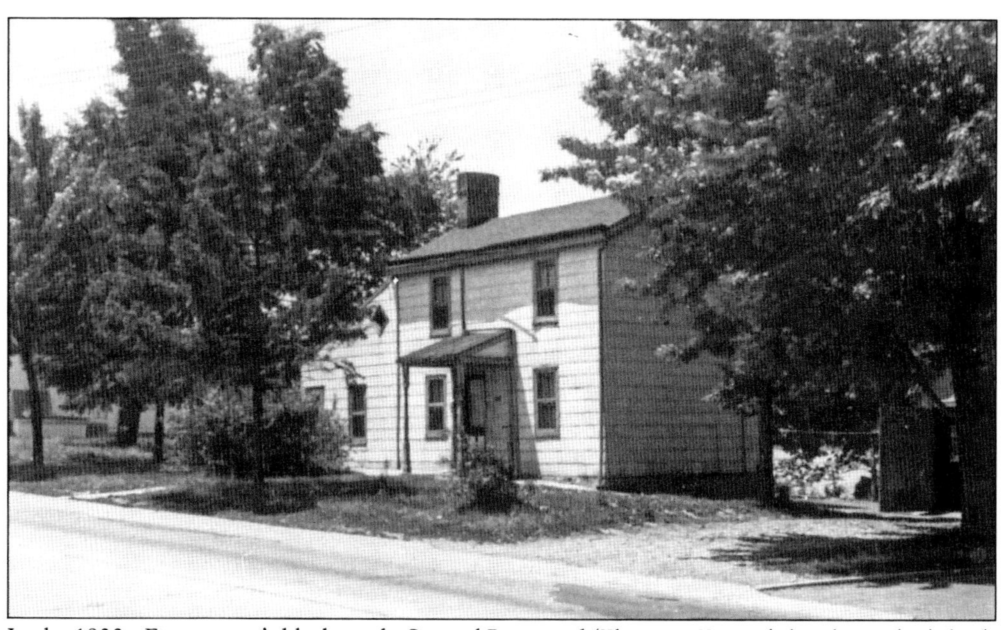

In the 1800s, Finneytown's blacksmith, Samuel Raymond (Ebenezer Finney's brother-in-law), built a log house on Winton Road near North Bend Road (next to today's Gold Star Chili). In 1953, his descendant Virginia Raymond Cummins photographed the house seen here, which, by then, was covered by a more modern exterior. In the cellar, she found the original log beams. It was demolished in 1970. (Christopher Riley.)

Two

Country Town

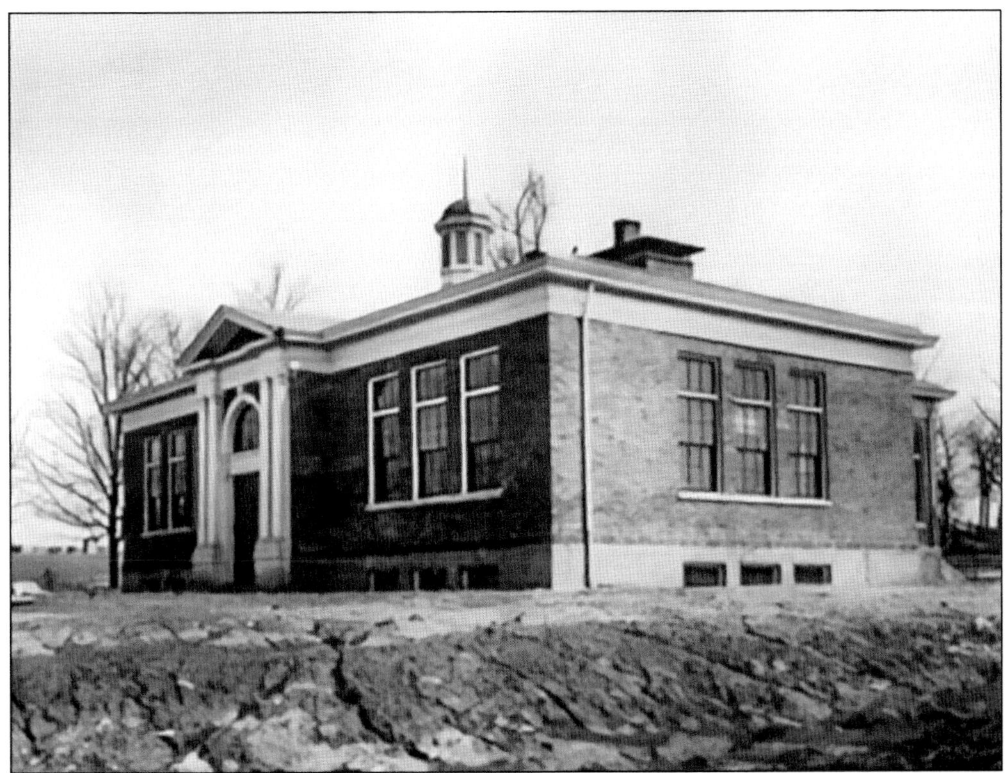

In 1915, the Finneytown Rural School District built this brick elementary school on Winton Road to replace the two-room schoolhouse. Designed by Samuel Hannaford & Sons, the school was built for 80 students, grades first through eighth. Over time, school expansions around the building obscured it from view. For decades, the 1915 building was part of Whitaker Elementary School, which was demolished in 2024. (Steve Battistone.)

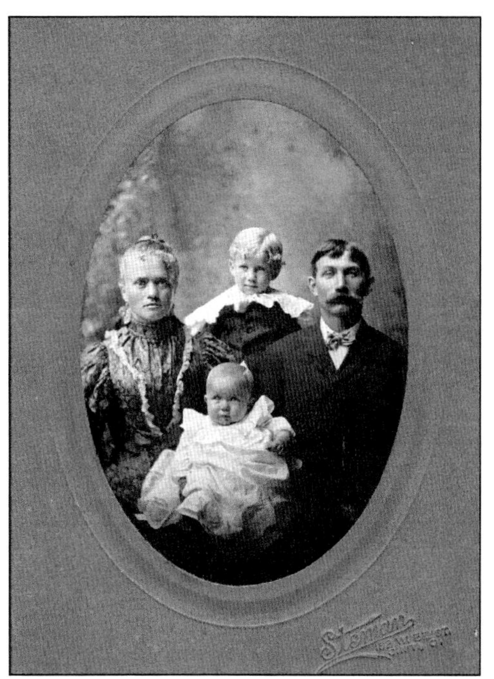

In the early 20th century, several commercial produce growers from nearby Winton Place moved to Finneytown. William and Elizabeth Kuhlmann (pictured) with their first children, William and Fred, established a large farm at the southeast corner of Winton and Galbraith Roads (site of today's Graeter's). They added a dairy business, which son William took over in 1930. It operated into the 1950s. (Gail Hafer Hauer.)

By World War I, the elder William and his wife, Elizabeth, had acquired more land further south along Winton Road and moved the family next to Finneytown School. They raised eight children. From left to right are (first row) Lydia, Minnie, Helen, and Anna; (second row) Harry, William, mother Elizabeth, father William, Edward, and Fred. (Gail Hafer Hauer.)

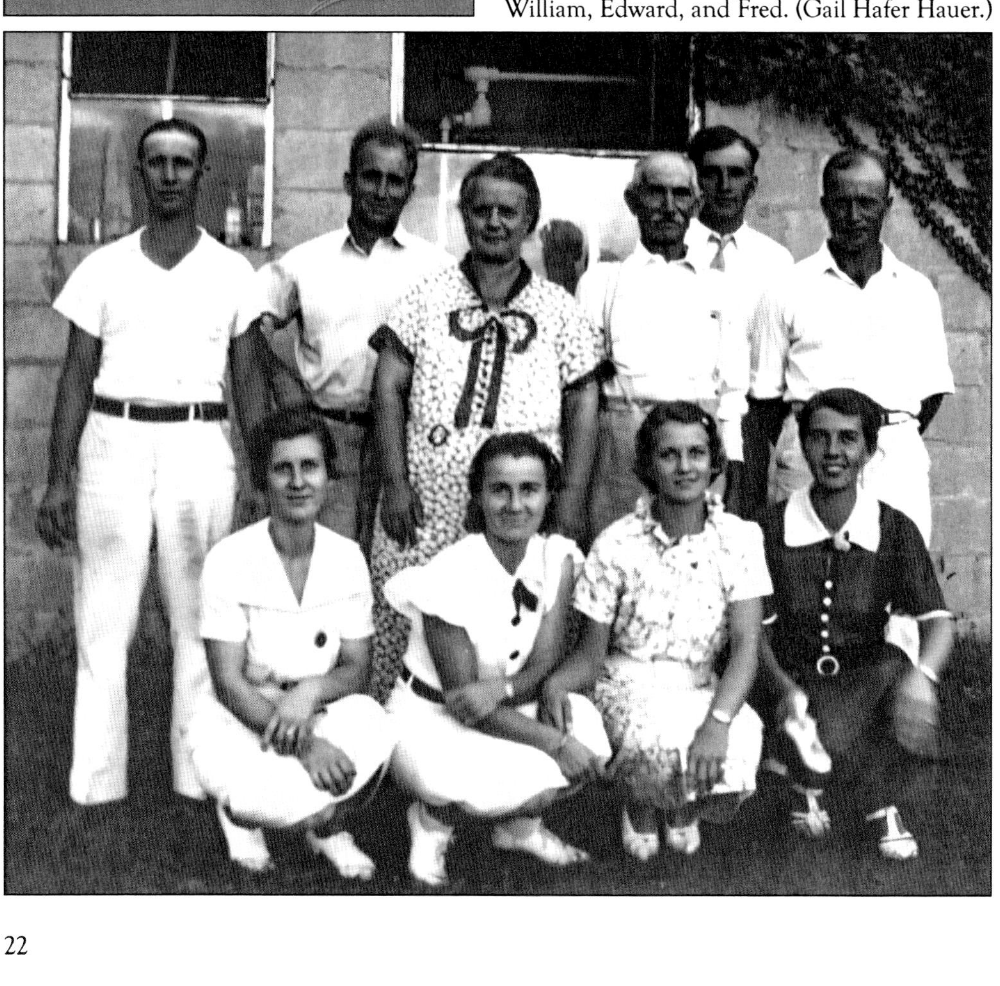

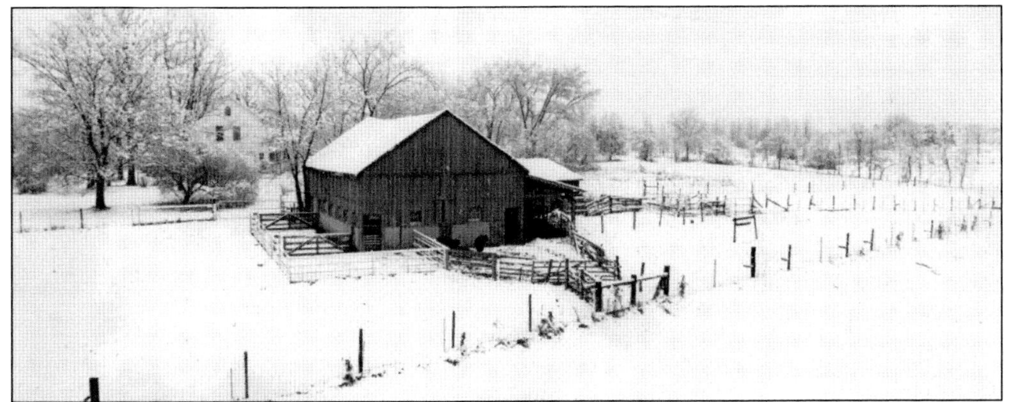

This vintage photograph of the Kuhlmann homestead on Winton Road near North Bend Road captures Finneytown's beauty and rich history. Largely unchanged today, the land is next to Warder Nature Preserve. In the 1800s, Jabez Bruen, a Revolutionary War veteran, farmed this land. When he died in 1814, his son Isaac Bruen, a War of 1812 veteran, took over the farm. (Gail Hafer Hauer.)

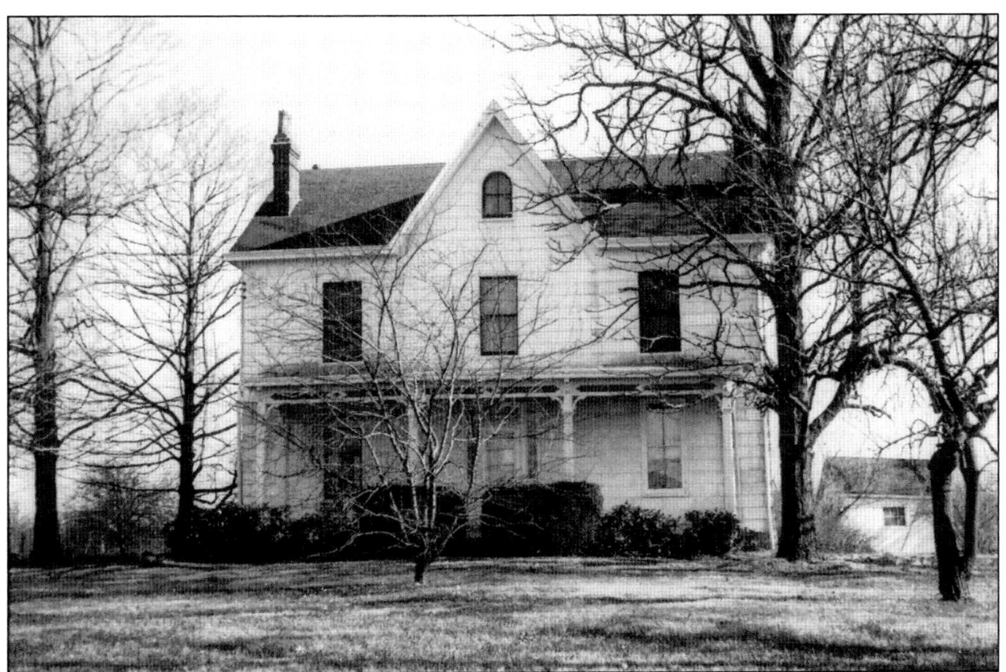

In 1866, Civil War veteran James Wallace and his family built this farmhouse next to Finneytown's first schoolhouse along Winton Road before the Kuhlmann family acquired the house and property. They provided boarding at the farmhouse to some of the neighboring schoolteachers. Kuhlmann descendants have owned the property and farmhouse ever since. (Gail Hafer Hauer.)

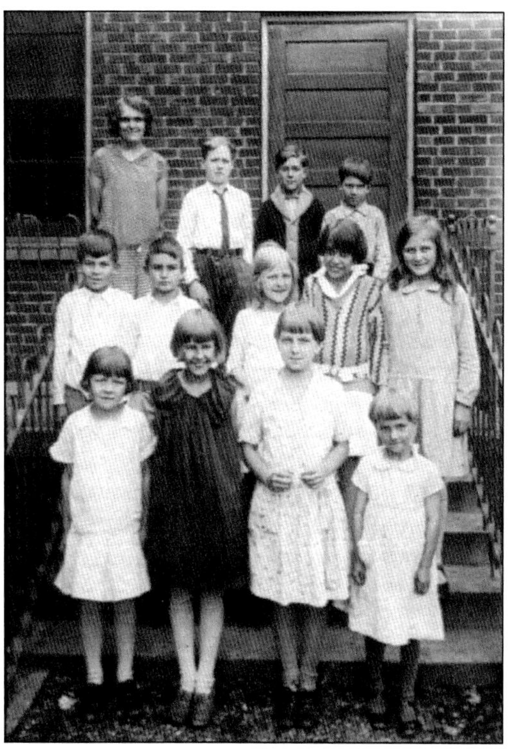

Finneytown School on Winton Road, seen here in about 1928, with grades first through fourth. From left to right are (first row) unidentified, Betty Knost, Myrtle Hoffmeier, and Ruth Louie; (second row) Vernon Louie, Robert Kempe, Miriam Ritchie, Ellen Strecker, and Naomi Ritchey; (third row) teacher Miss Denning, Dwight Miller, Dallas Brown, and Chester Brown. (Leslie Weisner.)

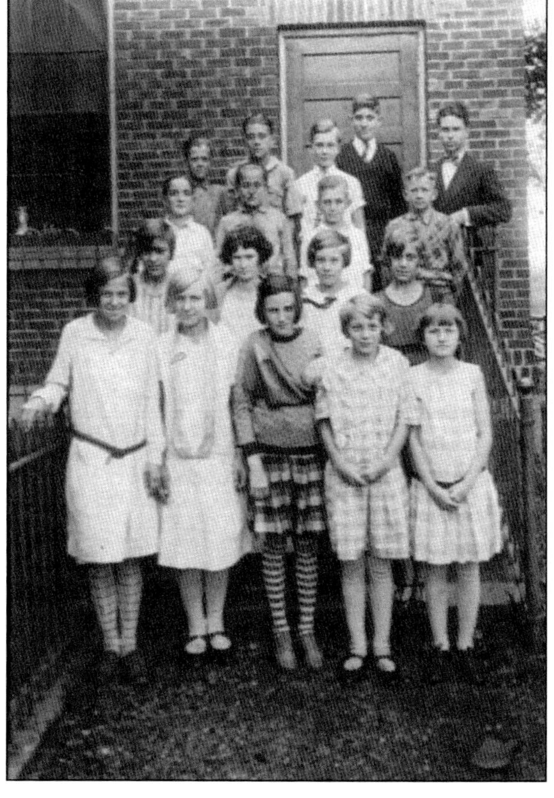

Finneytown School, pictured around 1928, with grades fifth through eighth. From left to right are (first row) Grace Hoffmeier, Rose Endress, Jean Hunnicutt, Louise Hackemeyer, and Lillian Hoffmeier; (second row) Olive Keifel, Florence Brown, Emily Bockelman, and Lillian Strecker; (third row) Tommy Hunnicutt, Raymond Crawley, Carl Endress, and Bill Hackemeyer; (fourth row) Blaine Keifel, David Crawley, Harry Bockelman, Bud Rennert, and teacher Mr. Prickett. (Leslie Weisner.)

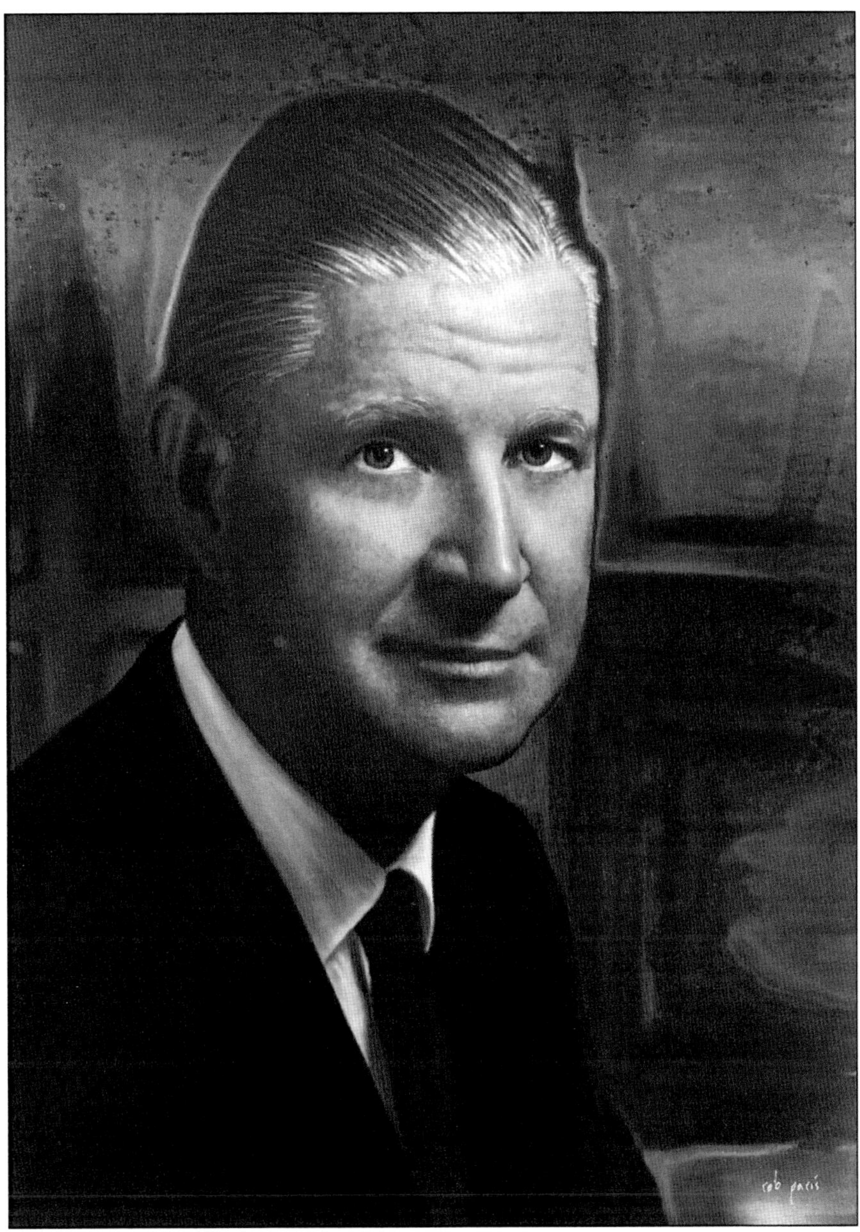

Telford Whitaker is a key figure in Finneytown history. In 1930, the 22-year-old University of Cincinnati graduate arrived at the 45-student school on Winton Road and assumed the roles of principal, teacher, and athletic director. In 1933, he helped to lead a campaign to finance the school's first indoor plumbing. A former college athlete, he coached the baseball and basketball teams to county prominence. In the 1930s, he also moonlighted as manager of a Cincinnati semi-pro baseball team. He left the Finneytown district in 1936 and then returned as school principal in 1945. In 1958, he became district superintendent when Finneytown High School and the secondary campus were constructed. In 1960, the elementary school on Winton Road was named Whitaker Elementary. By that time, the public school district had more than 2,200 students. Upon Whitaker's retirement in 1965, public school enrollment had surpassed 3,000. He died in 1993. (FLSD.)

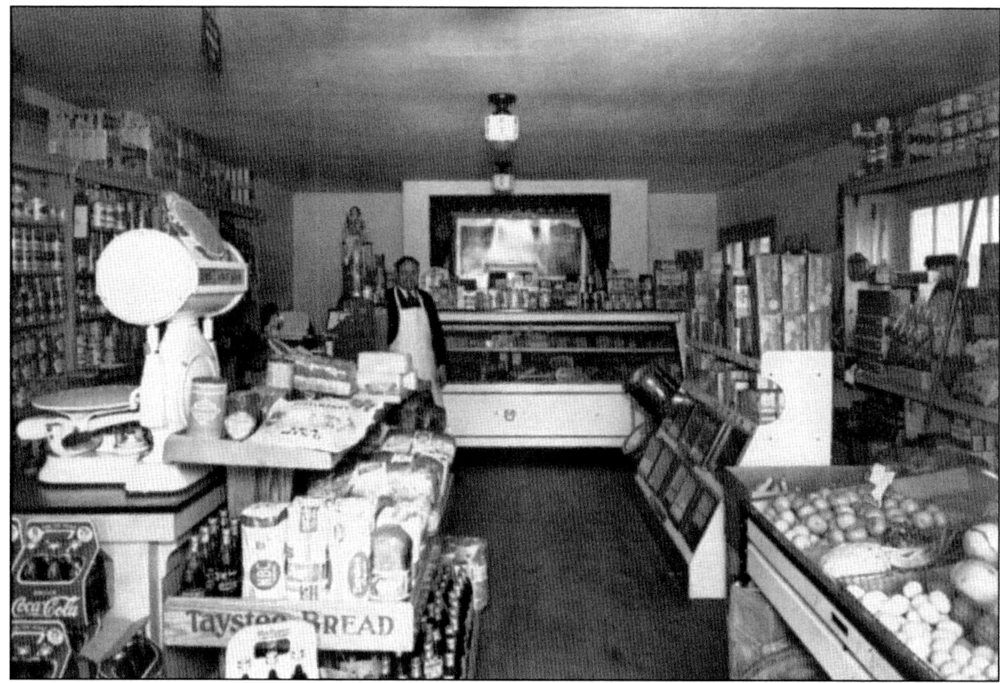

From the 1930s to 1952, Ernest G. Hanfbauer (pictured) ran the Hanfbauer Grocery Store on the northwest corner of Winton and North Bend Roads. He grew up in the produce industry. Early in the century, the Hanfbauers were among several German families to run large commercial produce operations down the hill from Finneytown in Winton Place. (Steve Battistone.)

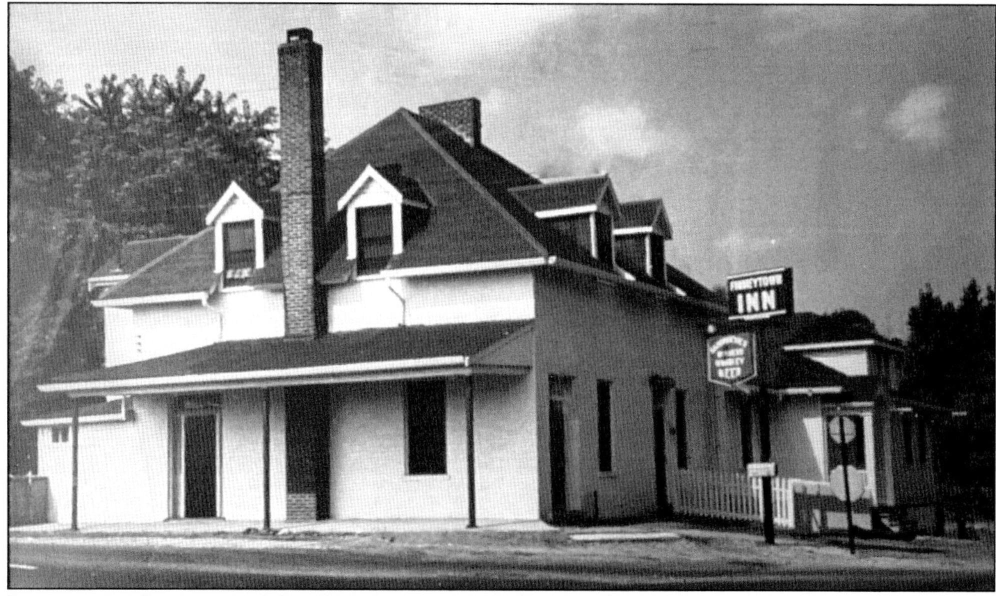

In an unpopular move with locals, Finneytown Inn (pictured) on North Bend Road was demolished in 1960 in order to expand and reconfigure Winton Road. The building was originally a mid-19th-century saloon and store. Christian Hoeweler had operated the popular spot since 1934. After the complex was demolished, a new Finneytown Inn opened nearby and operated until the early 1970s. (Hoeweler family.)

In 1919, Anthony and Mary Nieman, and their six children established a massive nursery and farm in Finneytown on both sides of Winton Road. The property bordered Winton, Galbraith, and Daly Roads. From the early 1930s through the early 1960s, several residential subdivisions, as well as St. Vivian Church, were created on land parceled off the Nieman Nursery. This brochure is from the 1940s. (Gail Hafer Hauer.)

NIEMAN
NURSERY

LANDSCAPE DESIGN
NATURAL PLANTINGS
FORMAL GARDENS
PRUNING SHRUBS AND TREES
GARDENING CONSULTATION

EVERGREENS
ORNAMENTAL TREES
SHRUBBERY
FRUIT AND SHADE TREES
RARE ROCK PLANTS
PERENNIALS

Visitors welcome to Gardens at any time . . . for appointment 'phone Jackson 7182

WINTON ROAD—Half mile north of North Bend Road at College Hill.

The Landscape for the Model Home at the Music Hall Exhibition and at Mariemont was designed by Nieman Nurseries.

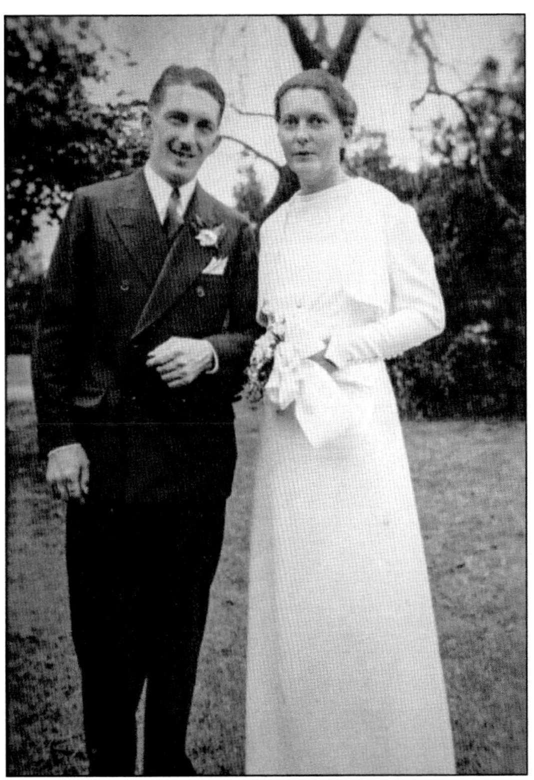

Marion Nieman (1906–1991), photographed at her 1937 wedding to John O'Rourke, was the daughter of Anthony and Mary Nieman. Active in the Finneytown nursery for years, Marion specialized in perennials. Eventually, she and her husband opened O'Rourke Hardy Perennials. She stayed in the nursery business her entire life. (Judith O'Rourke.)

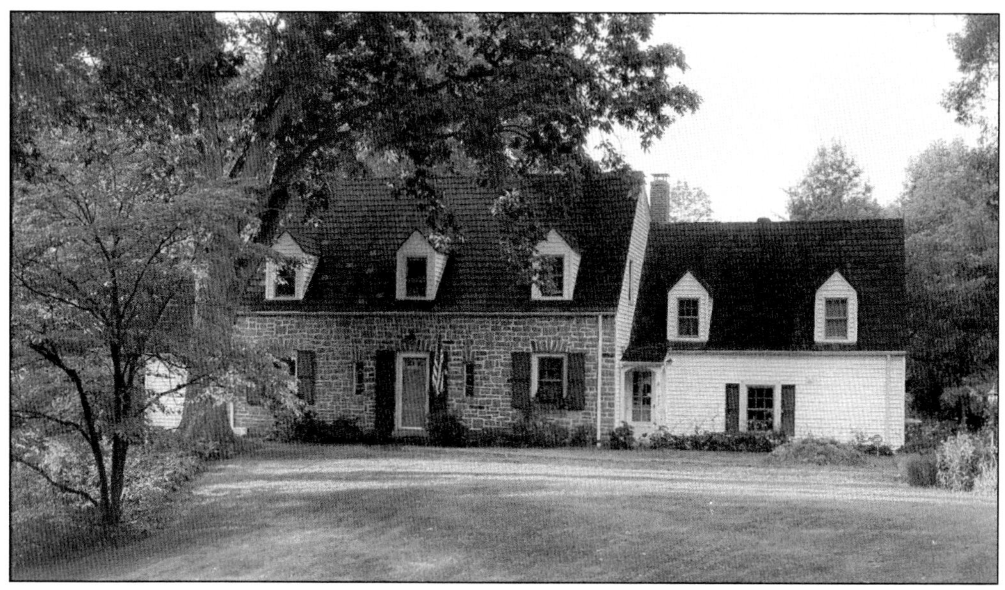

In surviving the 1930s Great Depression, the Niemans were resourceful. Before Prohibition ended in 1933, they raised acres of grapes, which John Nieman, son of Anthony and Mary, quietly delivered to nearby winemakers. At the same time, the family sold some of its land along Galbraith Road for the development of "country estates." Then, in the early 1940s, daughter Nettie Nieman, who ran the nursery for decades, sold additional nursery land to develop stately homes along North Hill Lane off Winton Road, including this grand house (pictured) with a fieldstone front exterior. Below is the original blueprint, on which the Nieman Nursery specified the trees and shrubbery. (Both, Jan Boling.)

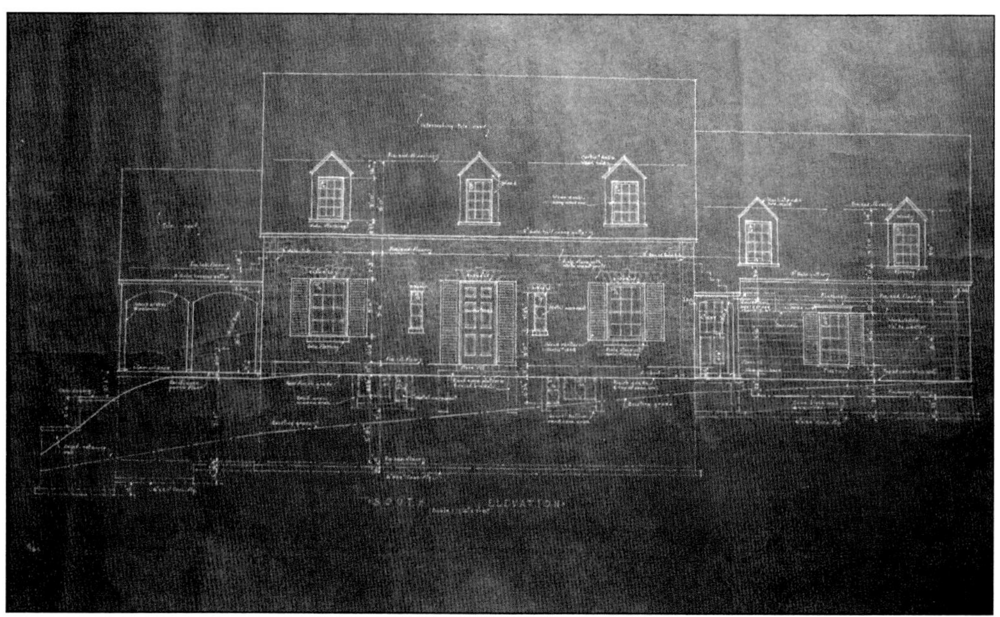

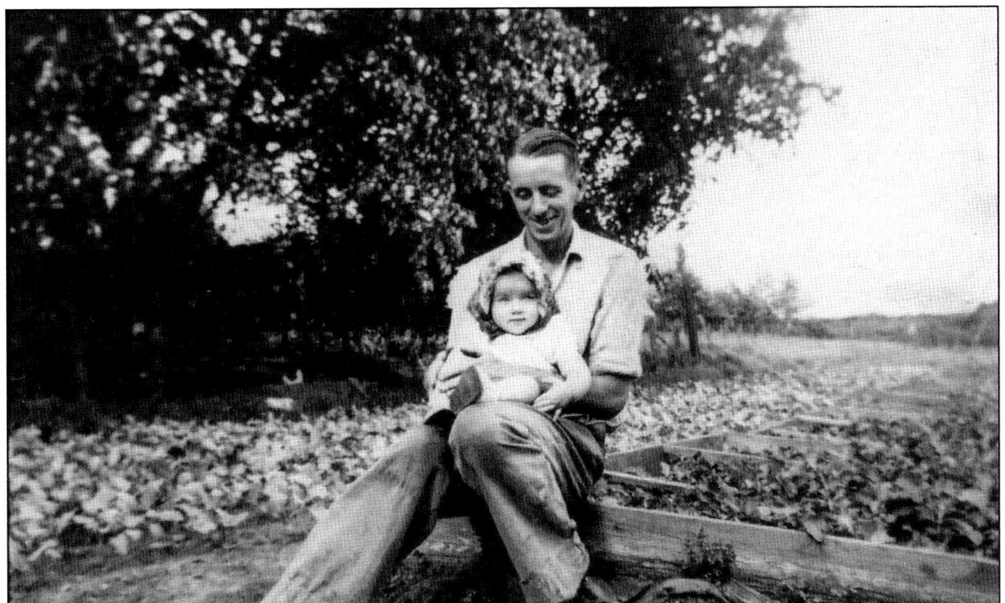

Howard Hafer is photographed with his daughter Gail (pictured) at the Kuhlmann farm on Winton Road in the 1940s. After Howard and Minnie Kuhlmann married, they lived with her parents at the homestead. Gail, who later married golf pro Bob Hauer, has lived there throughout her life. Her early memories include holding signs along Winton Road in successfully opposing Cincinnati's efforts to annex Finneytown. (Gail Hafer Hauer.)

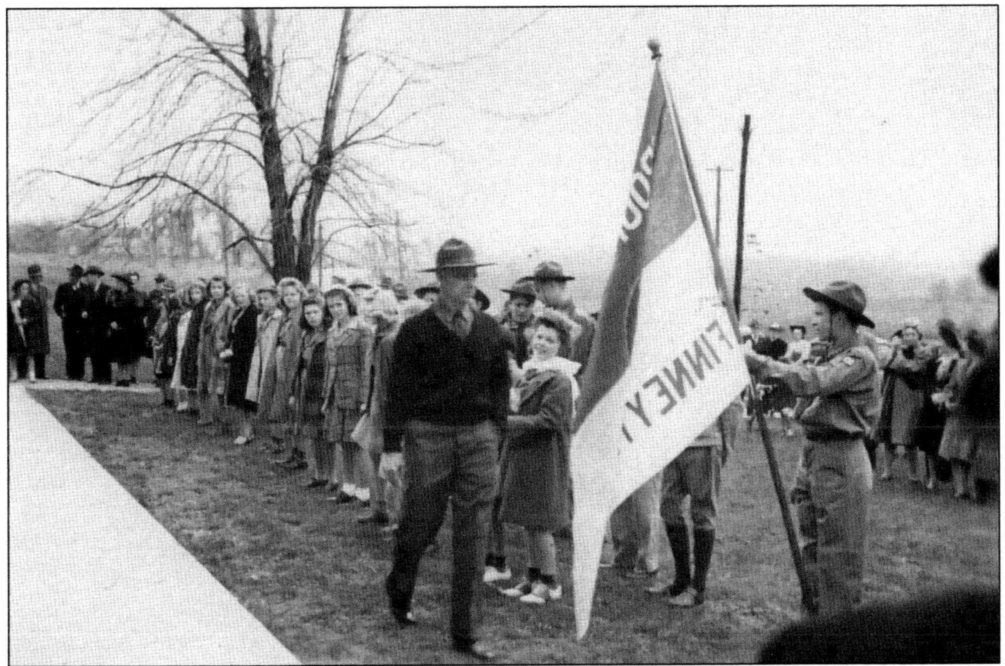

On the eve of World War II, Ernie Staubach founded Finneytown Boy Scout Troop 390. Photographed inspecting his Scouts during a 1946 ceremony at Finneytown School, Staubach was also part of a leadership team that founded the community's Faith Lutheran Church. Troop 390 played an important role in the lives of local boys for decades. (Leslie Weisner.)

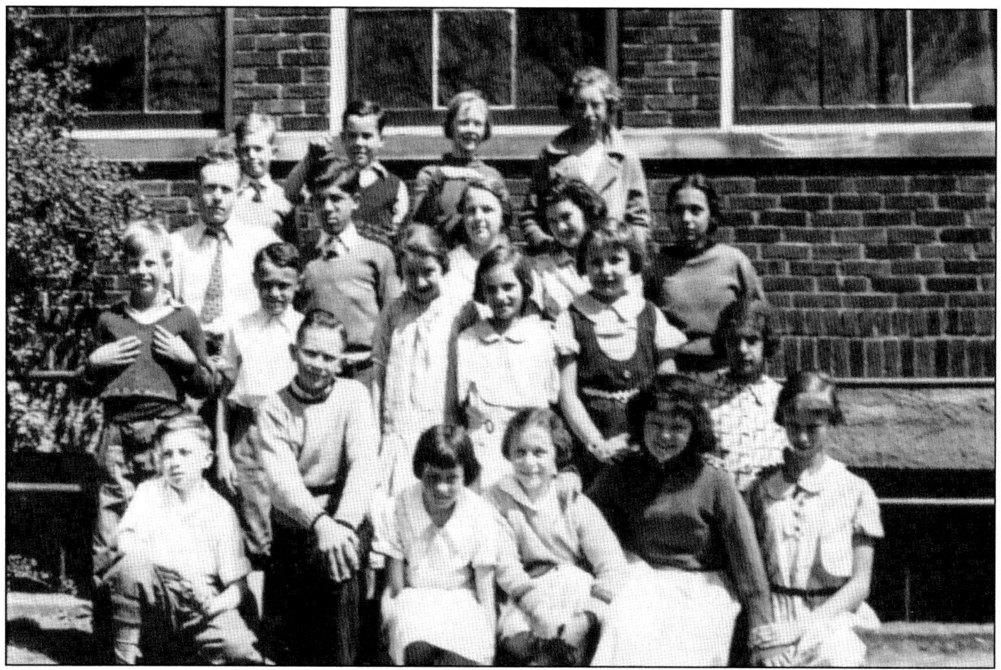

Future World War II prisoner of war Charles E. Bennett is photographed here in 1936, fourth row and second from left, as a Finneytown School eighth grader. While a radio operator on a distressed US B-24 over Germany in 1944, he had to bail out. He was captured and endured more than a year in a German Stalag-17 prison camp. In 2011, he died in Arizona at age 88. (Leslie Weisner.)

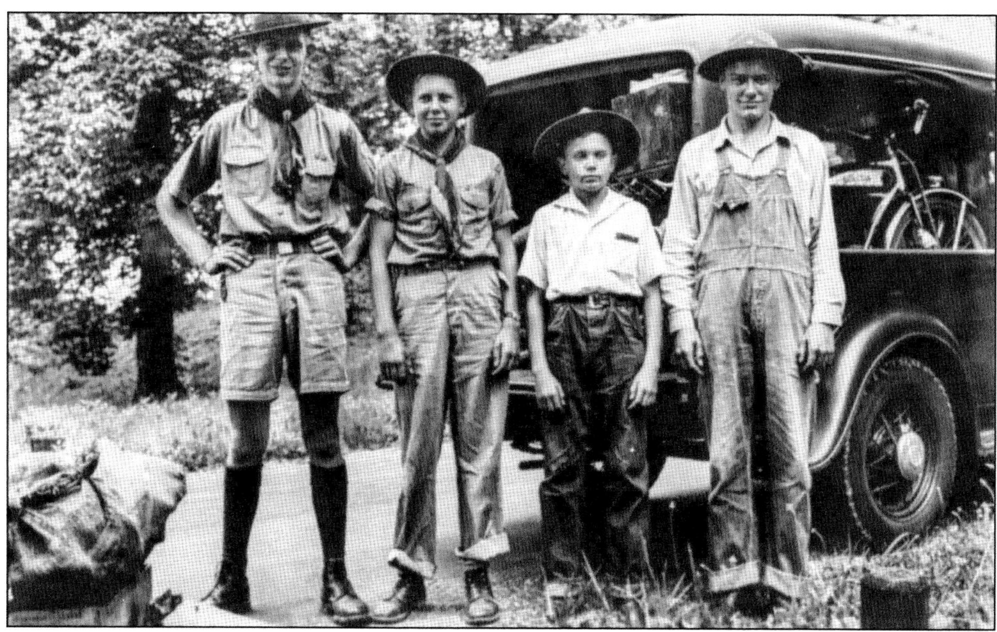

In the late 1930s, four members of Finneytown Boy Scout Troop 390 prepare for a camping event. Left to right: Fred and Dave Erhardt, Edward and Henry Strecker. Years later, members of Troop 390 credited their experiences with the Finneytown Boy Scouts in preparing them for the rigor of military service in World War II. (Leslie Weisner.)

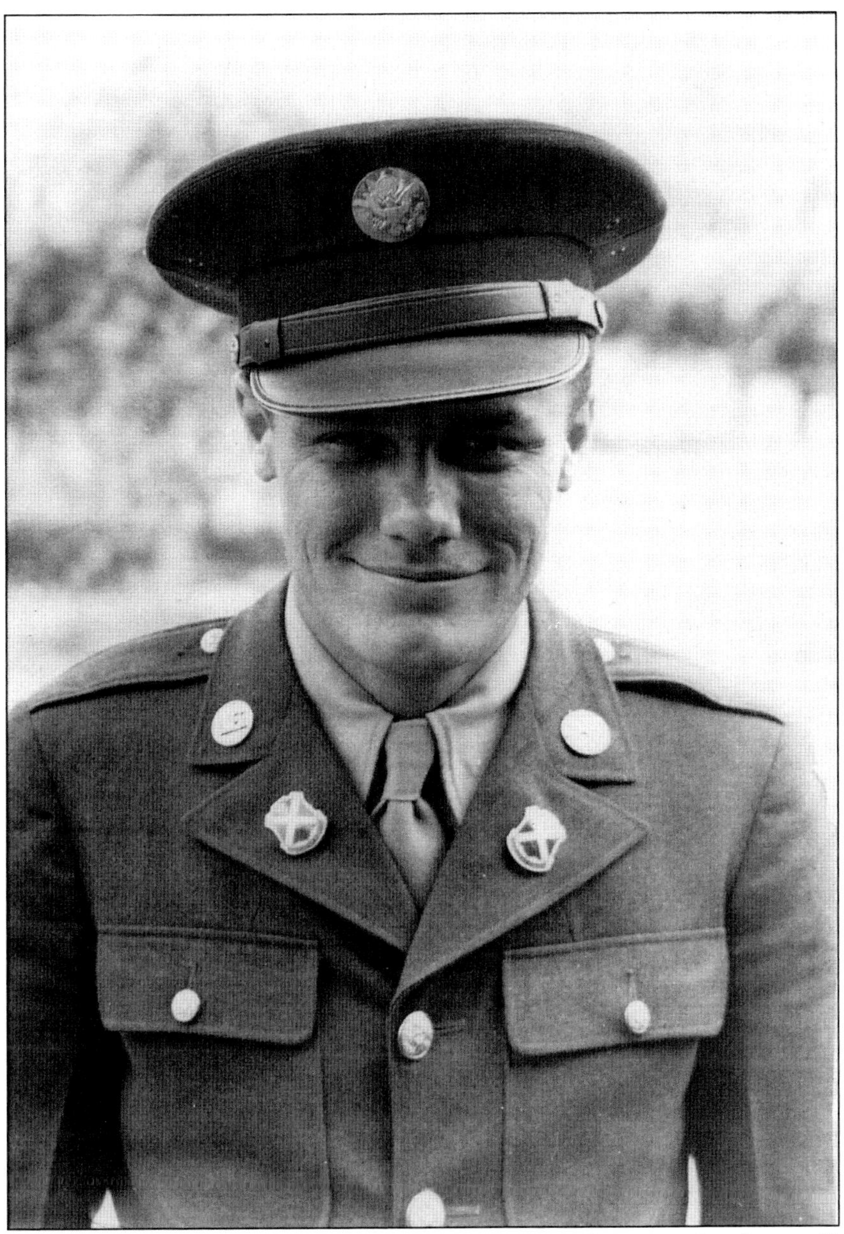

As a kid playing in Finneytown's fields and camping in its woods, Henry Strecker couldn't have imagined the horrors he would soon face. He grew up with his family in a frontier farmhouse (today's Baroque Violin Shop) and attended Finneytown School and Mt. Healthy High School. Then World War II arrived. During 20 months of frontline fighting with an Army rifle company, Strecker engaged in several bloody battles in Europe. He earned a Purple Heart, Bronze Star, and Silver Star. His Bronze Star citation detailed his "holding a strategic position" while outmanned and barraged by enemy fire. He witnessed the liberation of Paris as one of the few survivors of his original infantry company. "He never thought he would make it home alive," said his daughter Leslie Weisner. But he did. In late 1945, Strecker's remarkable war record landed him the role of spokesperson for the Cincinnati campaign promoting US victory bonds. He lived in the area until his death in 2010. (Leslie Weisner.)

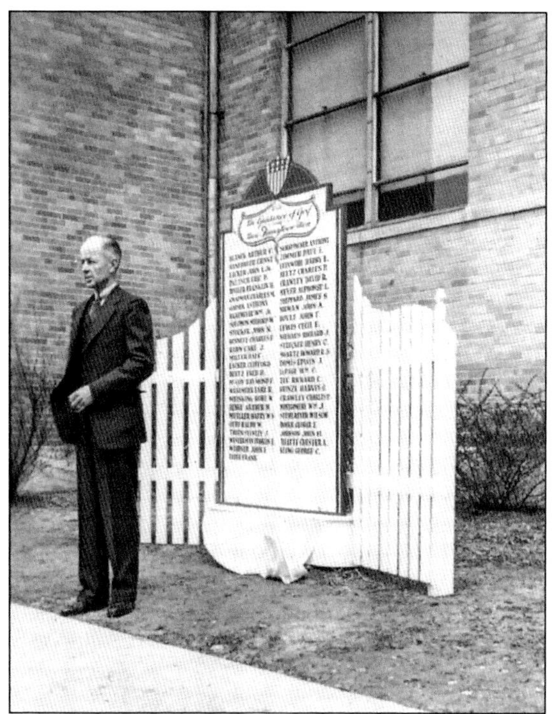

At a ceremony in 1946, Finneytown Civic Club president R. Dale Shannon stood at the plaque honoring Finneytown veterans in front of the school. During the 1930s, Finneytown School only graduated a dozen or so boys each year from the eighth grade. However, more than 40 of these boys served during World War II. (Leslie Weisner.)

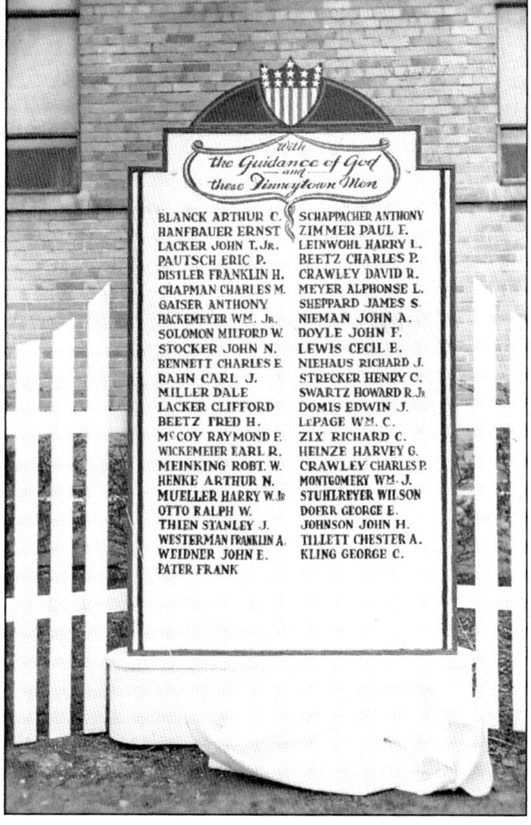

For several years, this Honor Roll was posted in front of Finneytown School to recognize the former students who served in World War II. Like veterans Charles Bennett and Henry Strecker, many of these young men had been members of Ernie Staubach's Finneytown Boy Scout Troop 390, which explored the serene woods of this country town. (Leslie Weisner.)

In 1870, Sisters of the Good Shepherd in downtown Cincinnati acquired rural property on North Bend Road overlooking Mill Creek Valley (across from today's St. Xavier High School) and established Our Lady of the Woods Training School for girls in troubled circumstances. The school expanded with classrooms, dormitories, a convent, and a chapel. It was named Girls Town in the 1940s. (St. Xavier High School.)

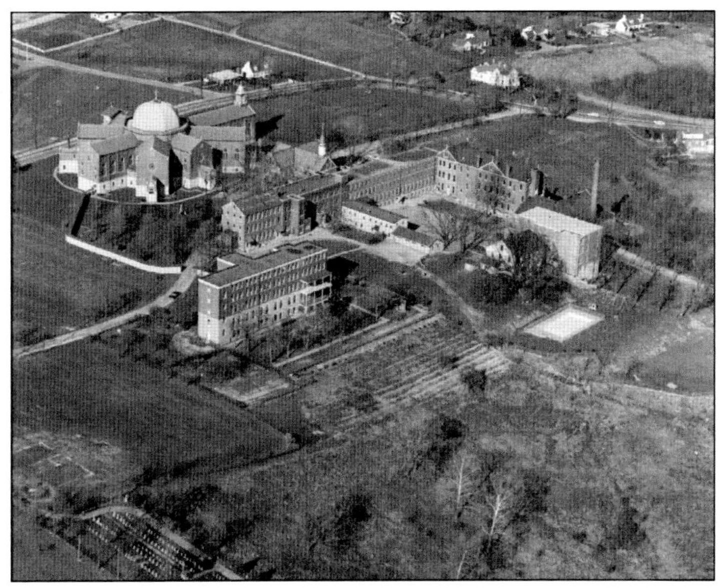

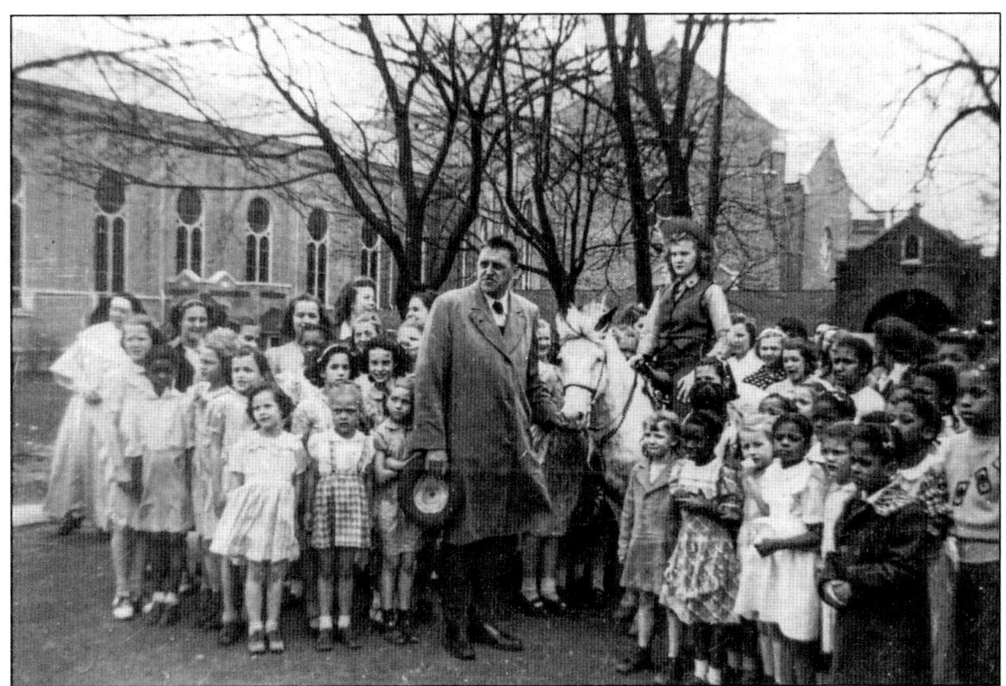

This pre-1945 photograph of African American girls at the Convent reflects the progressive nature of this educational institution. The Sisters welcomed girls of different races and religious backgrounds. After moving to North Bend Road, the Sisters dismantled a homestead in downtown Cincinnati and rebuilt it at the Convent to house African-American girls. By 1896, these girls resided in a brick dormitory. (St. Xavier High School.)

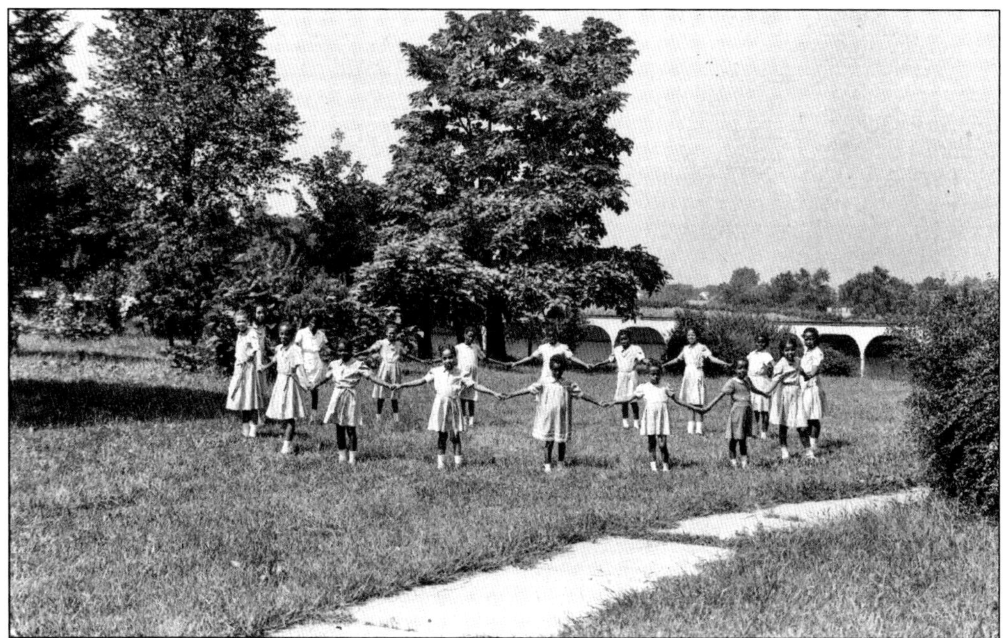

This vintage photograph at Girls Town further highlights its student diversity. Outside of Girls Town, few African Americans lived in early-20th-century Finneytown. The school curriculum focused on business and secretarial skills, as well as cooking and sewing. The girls also worked on the property's farm and raised money. (St. Xavier High School.)

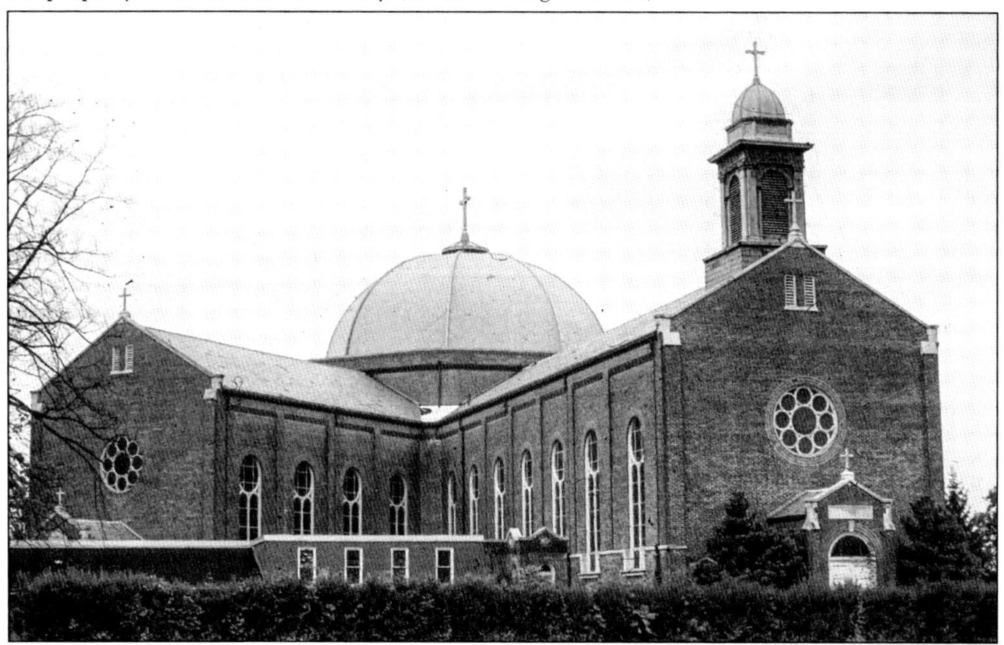

In 1912, about 3,000 people watched Archbishop Henry Moeller place the cornerstone for the domed chapel at Girls Town. The octagon-shaped chapel enclosed seven separate chapels that converged into a large sanctuary and altar. By the time the Girls Town campus closed in 1971, the Sisters had educated thousands of girls. St. Xavier High School later acquired the property. (St. Xavier High School.)

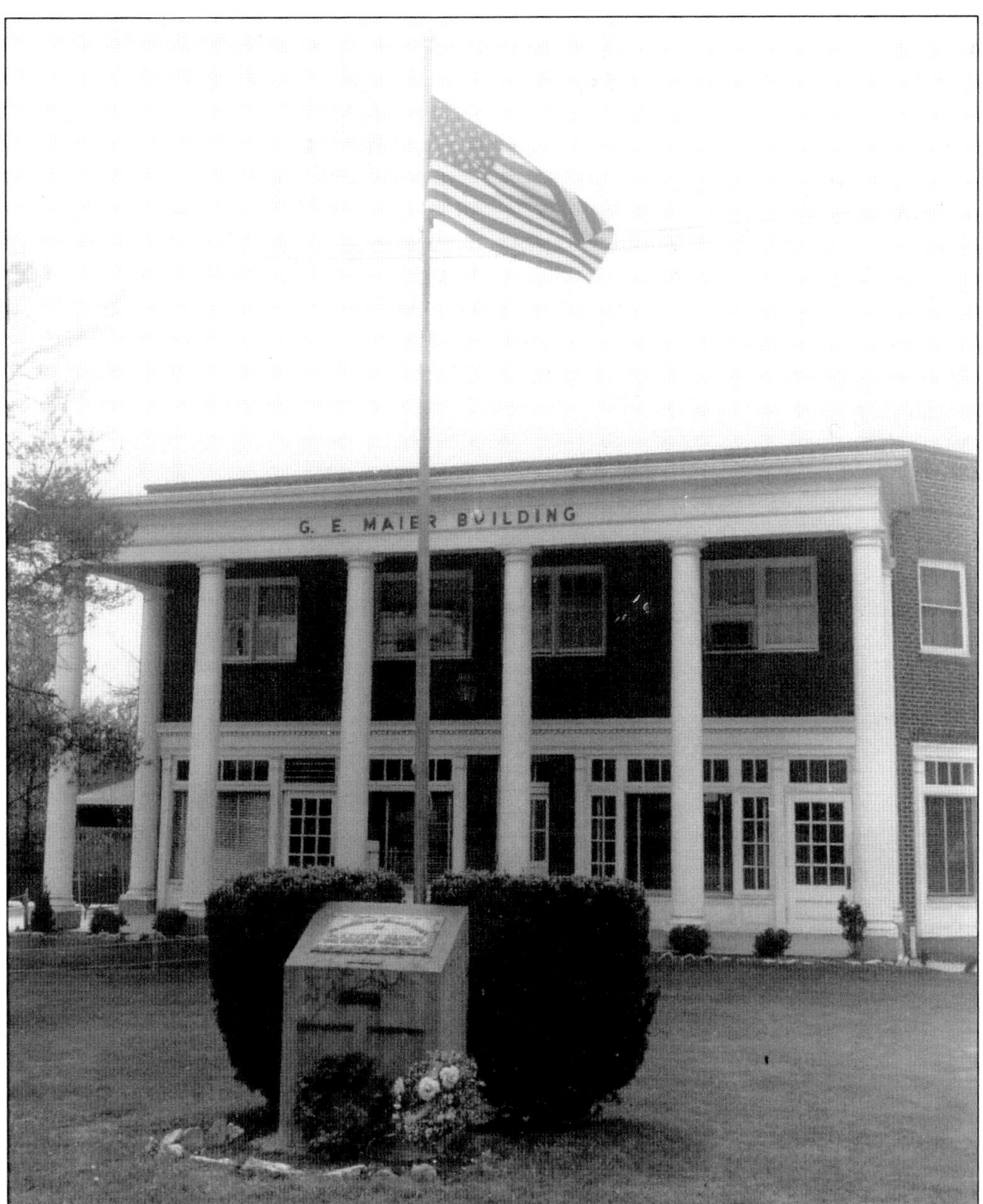

As the intimate enclave of Parkview Heights, Finneytown's first subdivision, developed in the late 1930s, the community needed a retail center. In 1941, a commercial building was built at North Bend Road and Northern Parkway for stores and apartments. John Zanitsch Grocery and Shafer General Store were early tenants. Zanitsch, a Parkview Heights leader, operated the grocery for years. From 1943 through 1946, the building's owners, Louis and Margaret Richter, encouraged a fast-growing Catholic congregation to hold masses in the basement. As a result of the couple's generosity, the congregation named their new church after the couple's daughter, Vivian. In 1946, St. Vivian Church purchased Nieman property on Winton Road for a church and school. In 1947, Parkview Civic Club built a memorial and flagpole in front of the Parkview building to honor its World War II veterans. When this 1960s photograph was taken, the property had become the G.E. Maier Building and housed Gregory E. Maier's school equipment distributorship. (Rob Leininger.)

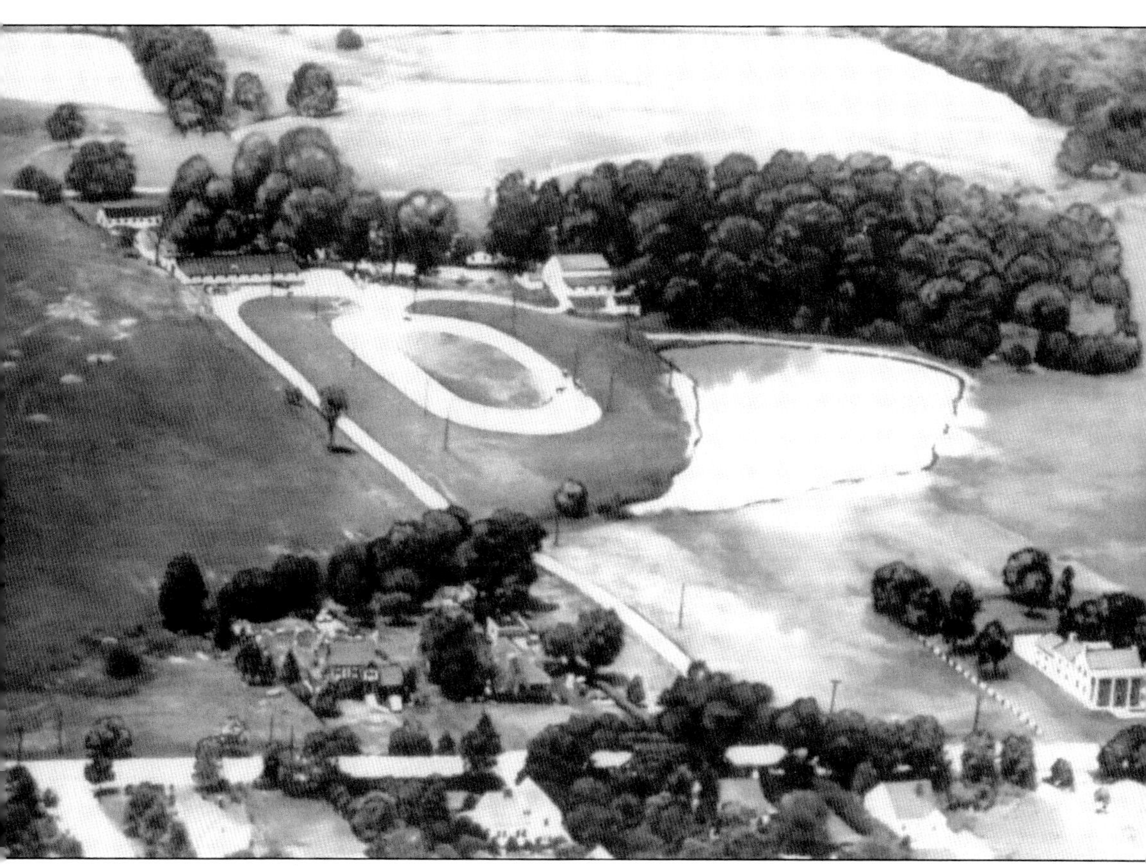

This 1940s aerial image captures a serene landscape in the heart of Finneytown, which is unrecognizable today. Two-lane Winton Road runs along the bottom. The circular track in the center was part of Clearview Riding Stables, which operated at the site of today's Brentwood Shopping Plaza. Owned by horse exhibitor and breeder William Hafer, Clearview provided stables, offered riding lessons, and hosted horse shows and contests. Clearview Stables events were in the local papers on a weekly basis. The pond next to the track was available for public fishing. Today, a Kroger store is at the site of the pond. After Hafer acquired a military surplus tent in the mid-1950s, Clearview hosted the Cincinnati Summer Playhouse to large crowds for several years. Across Winton Road from the riding stables was Clearview Tavern, a popular and notorious roadhouse run by area rockabilly star Rusty York. (Steve Battistone.)

Three

A Serene Nursery

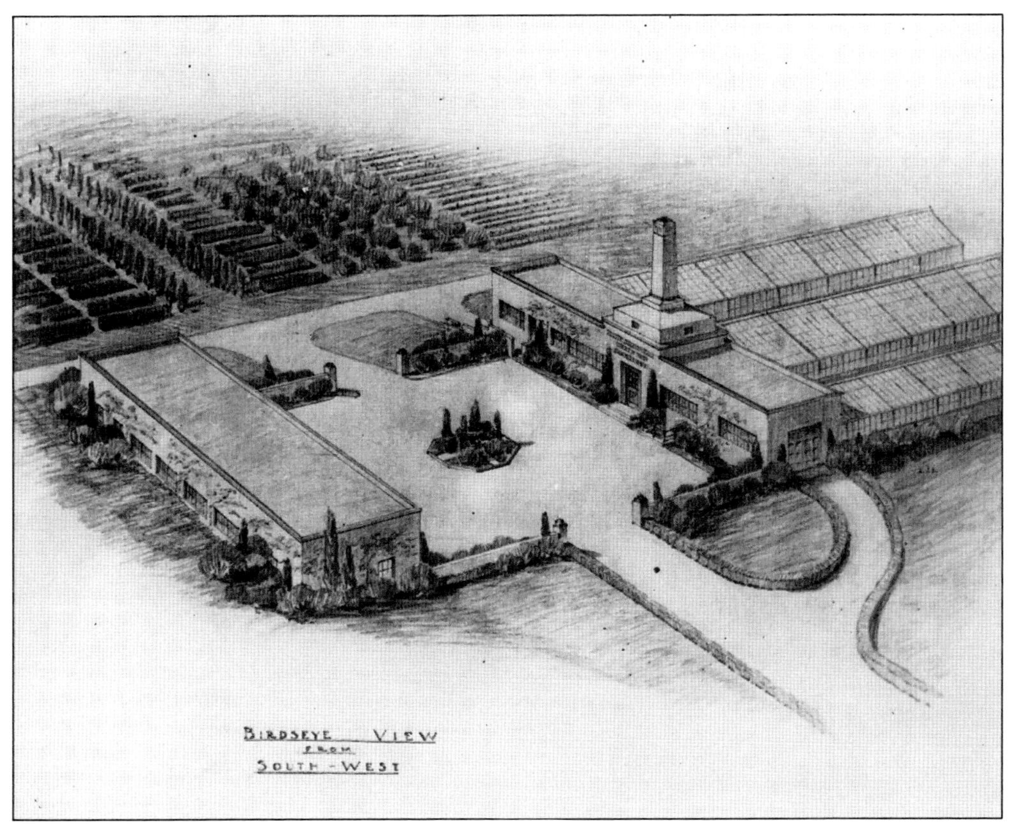

In 1930, the Cincinnati Park Board (CPB) established Warder Nursery on 50 acres of Finneytown farmland near North Bend Road and east of Winton Road. For decades, the nursery raised trees, shrubs, and flowers for Cincinnati parks, special displays, and roadways. The nursery was named after Reuben H. Warder, former Cincinnati Parks superintendent and son of John Warder, founder of the American Forestry Association. (CPB.)

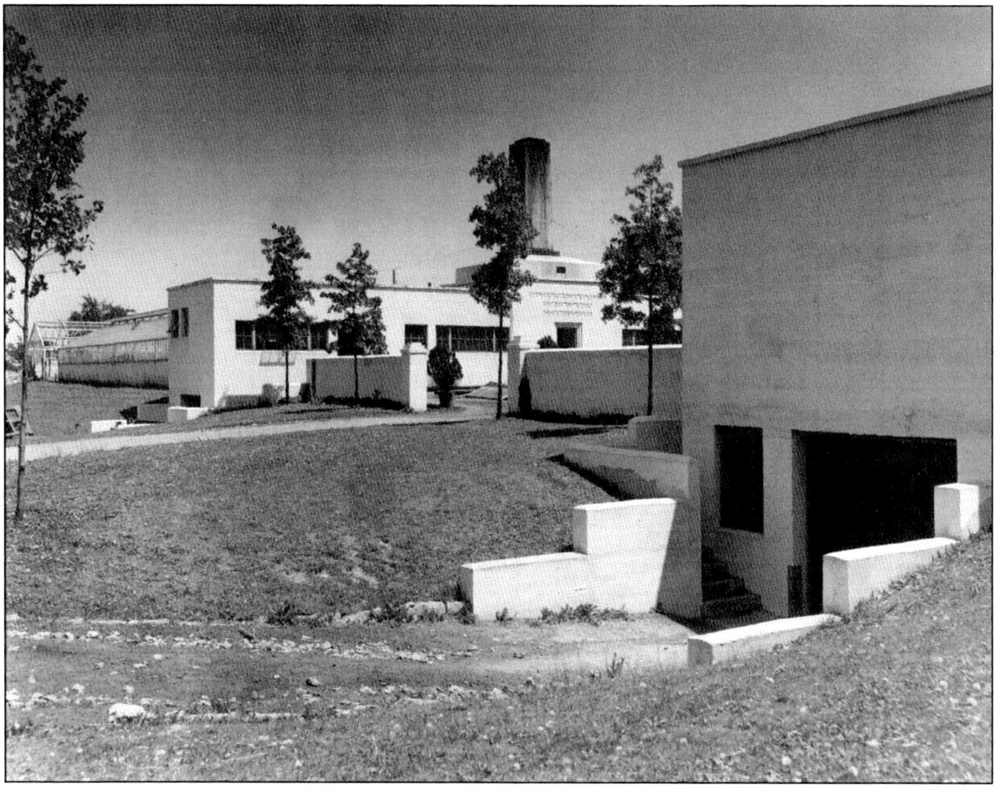

In 1931, the CPB constructed large greenhouses and service buildings at Warder Nursery and transferred its flower propagation activities from Eden Park to Warder. In 1933, Warder began its long tradition of supplying flowers for events at the new Krohn Conservatory (originally called Eden Park Conservatory). The US government's Depression-era Works Progress Administration (WPA) built a large barn on the grounds. In 1936, the CPB described Warder plants as "the finest and largest collection of blooming plants the park board has ever produced." That same year, the Finneytown Garden Club was formed and brought community attention to Warder Nursery. (Both, CPB.)

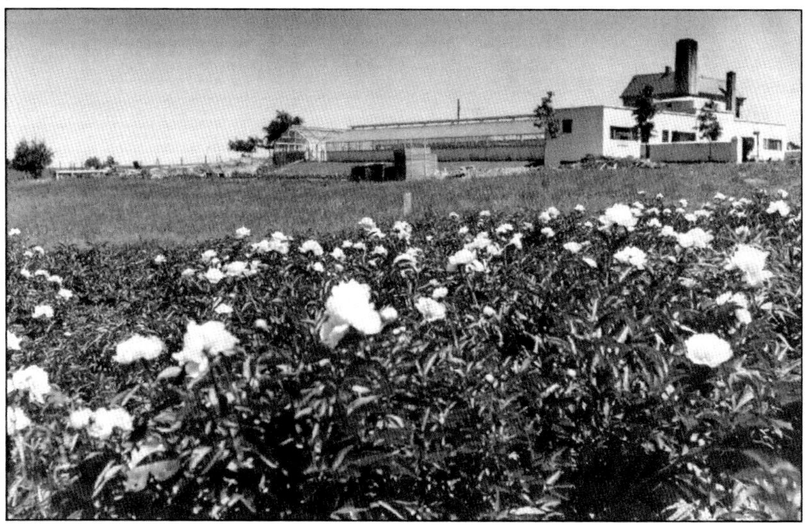

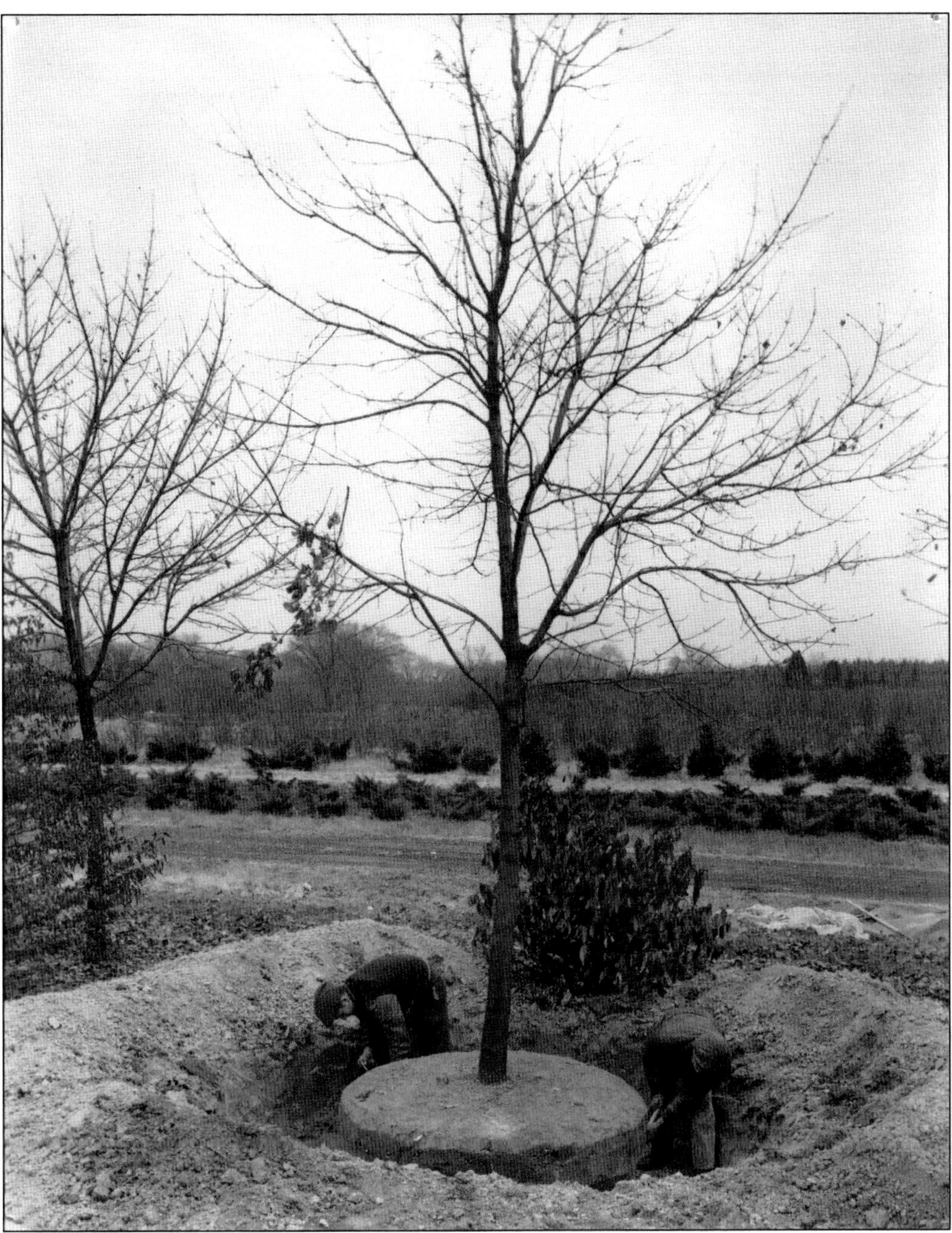

In the 1930s, Warder Nursery began growing trees for Cincinnati parks and roadways. After young trees grew to a suitable size, crews dug them out of the ground and transplanted them across the city, as seen in this 1950s photograph. Warder produced more than 160,000 trees and shrubs in its first decade of operation. In 1948, Warder received seeds from rare metasequoia trees in China, which were thought to have been extinct for millions of years. After Chinese scientists were stunned to find a living grove of metasequoia trees, they sent seeds to US horticulturists. Because of Warder's reputation, the nursery received some of the metasequoia seeds to grow. There were no instructions on how to raise the plants because only fossil remains were known to have existed. By 1954, several of Warder's metasequoia trees reached 12 feet tall. (CPB.)

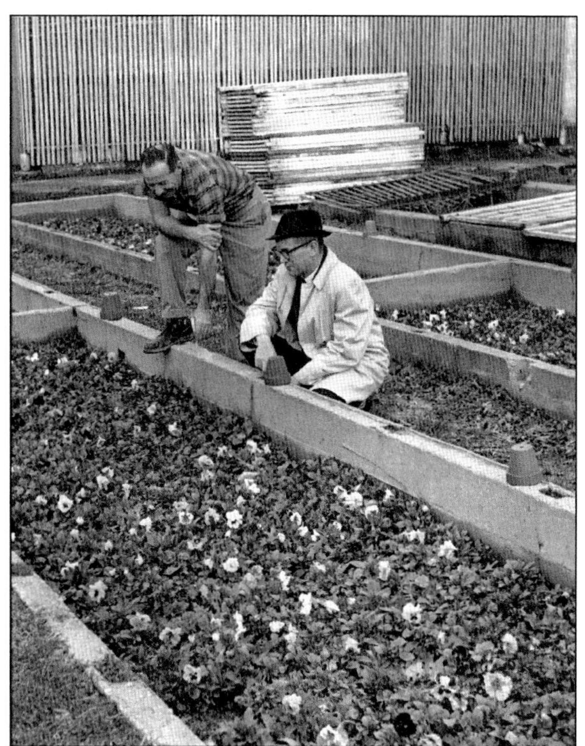

For decades, Warder Nursery was a darling of the local media. News stories often featured staffers preparing flowers for holiday floral displays. In this 1963 photograph, a smiling Warder supervisor, Harvey Burck (left), and CPB landscape architect Dalton Battin pose for the *Cincinnati Enquirer* as they inspect flowers in the nursery's ground boxes. (CPB.)

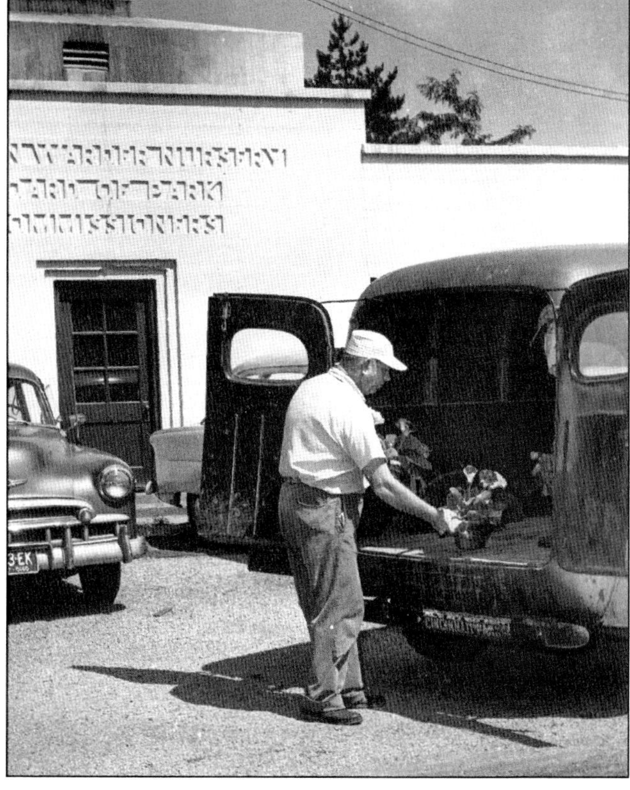

In 1957, longtime Warder employee Ray Bross loaded a truck with potted flowers on their way to Krohn Conservatory in Eden Park. For several decades, Bross and his two brothers worked at Warder Nursery. To this day, the tradition continues, as Warder still raises flowers, particularly poinsettias, for holiday Krohn displays. (CPB.)

Warder typically operated with a dozen or so full-time employees. While doing various tasks around the nursery and grounds, staffers also developed specialties. In the 1950s, Joe Reckle was Warder's "tree starter," and he oversaw thousands of tree seedlings. During winter months, he was a night watchman and stoked the greenhouse boilers. (CPB.)

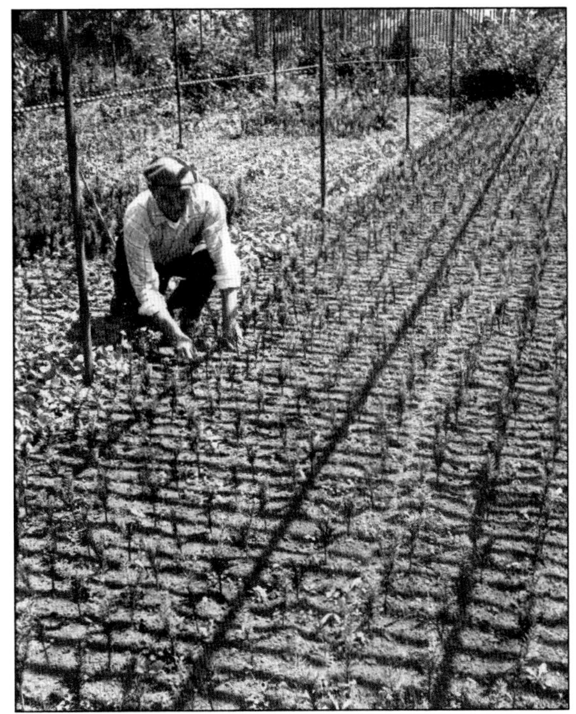

In this 1950s photograph, two Warder employees tended to hundreds of bushes growing in pots. For many years, Warder also received help in tending to the grounds from inmates on loan from the Hamilton County jail. Meanwhile, the Cincinnati Zoo unloaded tons of manure at Warder used as fertilizer. (CPB.)

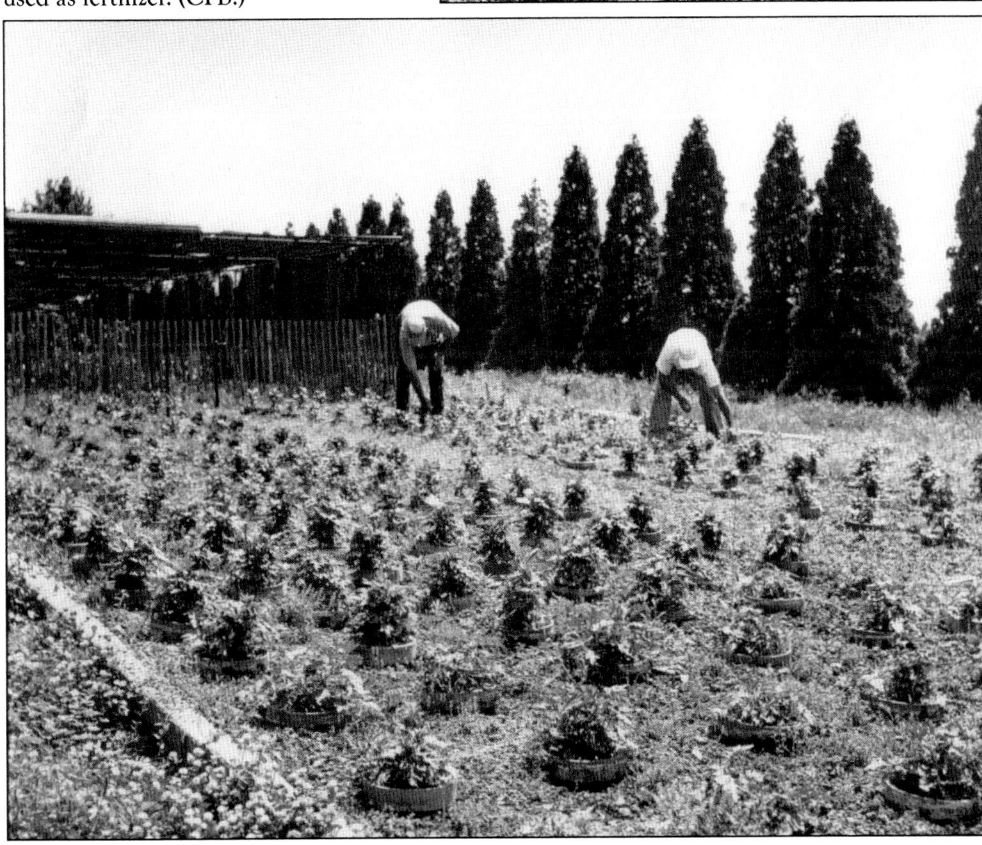

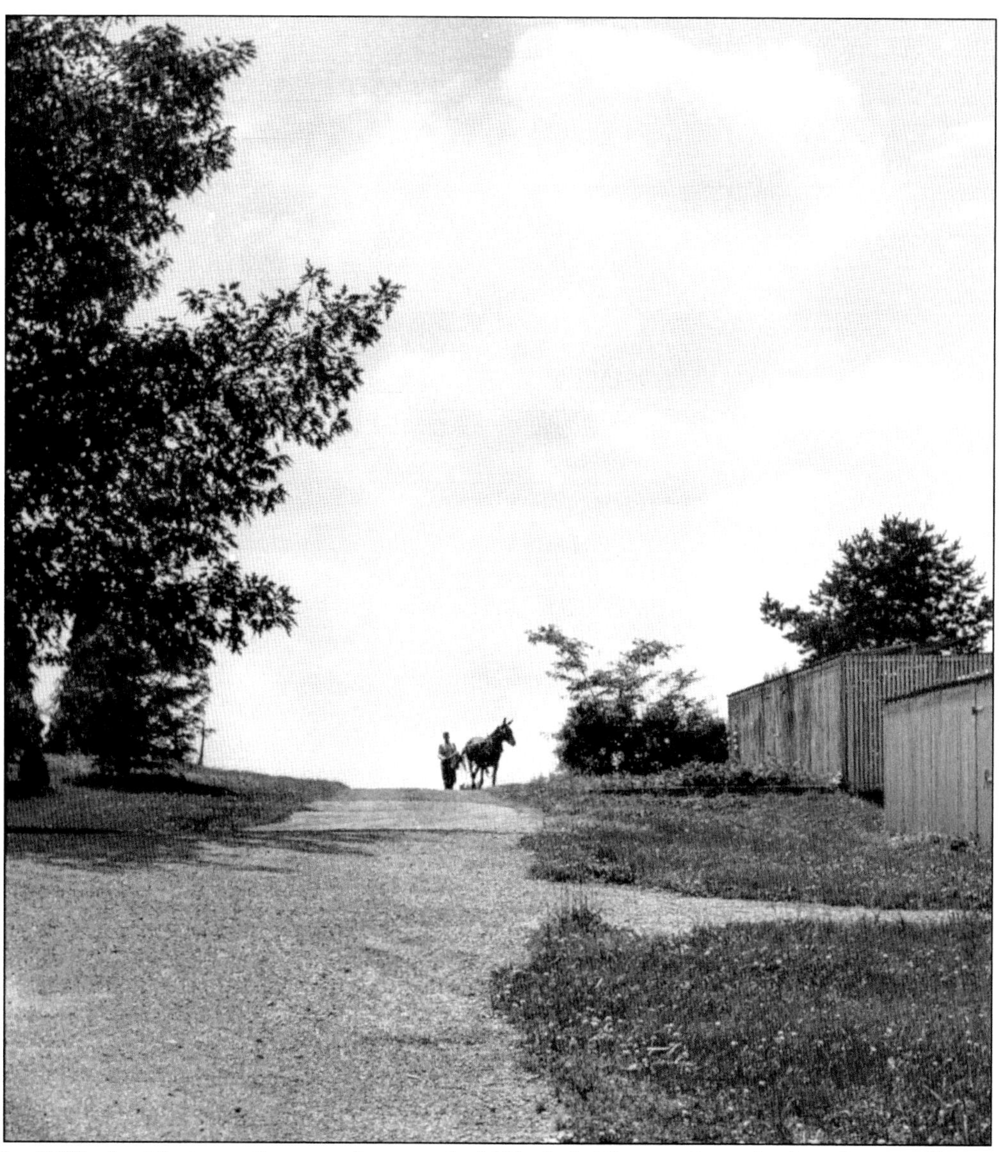

In 1957, the *Cincinnati Enquirer* photographed Warder's Thomas Bross leading "Big Red" past the lath house for a long day of plowing. There was no need for tractors when "Big Red" and "Jake," two mules at Warder in the 1950s, capably pulled plows on the grounds. Warder kept the mules in stalls inside the WPA building. The nursery also provided the mules with pastureland. In 1949, Warder attracted local media attention when the CPB posted a job opening for a "mule skinner." Ultimately, 56 men applied for the lone position, though several didn't know what a mule skinner actually did. One applicant arrived for his interview with a large knife, thinking a "mule skinner" was a butcher. During Finneytown's 1950s residential and commercial boom, Warder Nursery and the nearby Nieman Nursery helped the community maintain some of its original rural atmosphere. (CPB.)

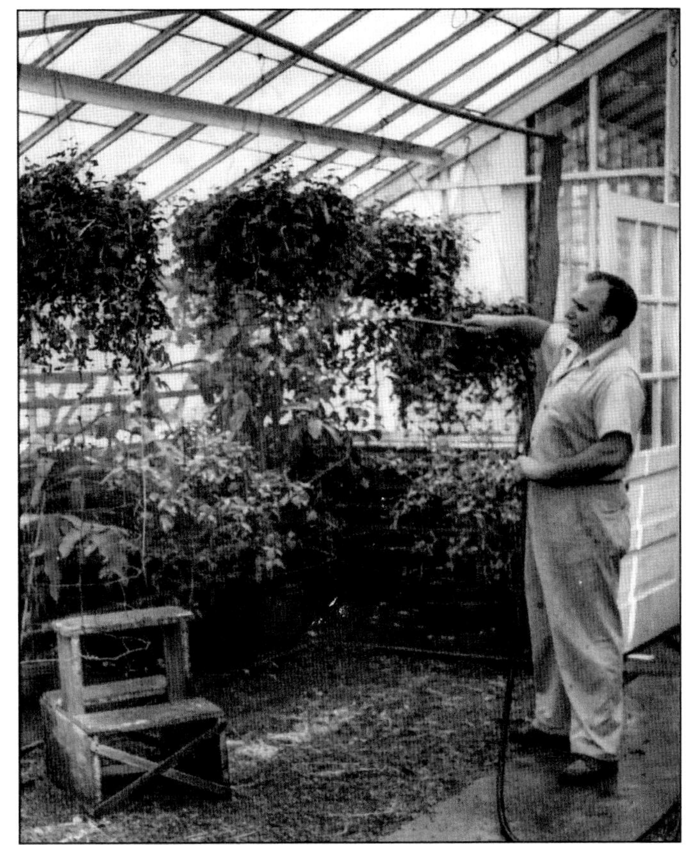

In this 1950s photograph, longtime employee Joseph Bonaventura tends to hundreds of hanging plants. Warder Nursery delivered hanging plants for facilities across the city, including General Hospital, Hamilton County Courthouse, and city firehouses. The greenhouses also maintained flower boxes throughout the year, which were taken to special events at Krohn Conservatory. (CPB.)

The Warder staff supervisor and family were provided living quarters on the grounds in a rustic 19th-century farmhouse next to the greenhouses. When the house was torn down in 2004, twelve bricks were saved and presented to each of the 12 children of the late Warder supervisor Harvey Burck. (CPB.)

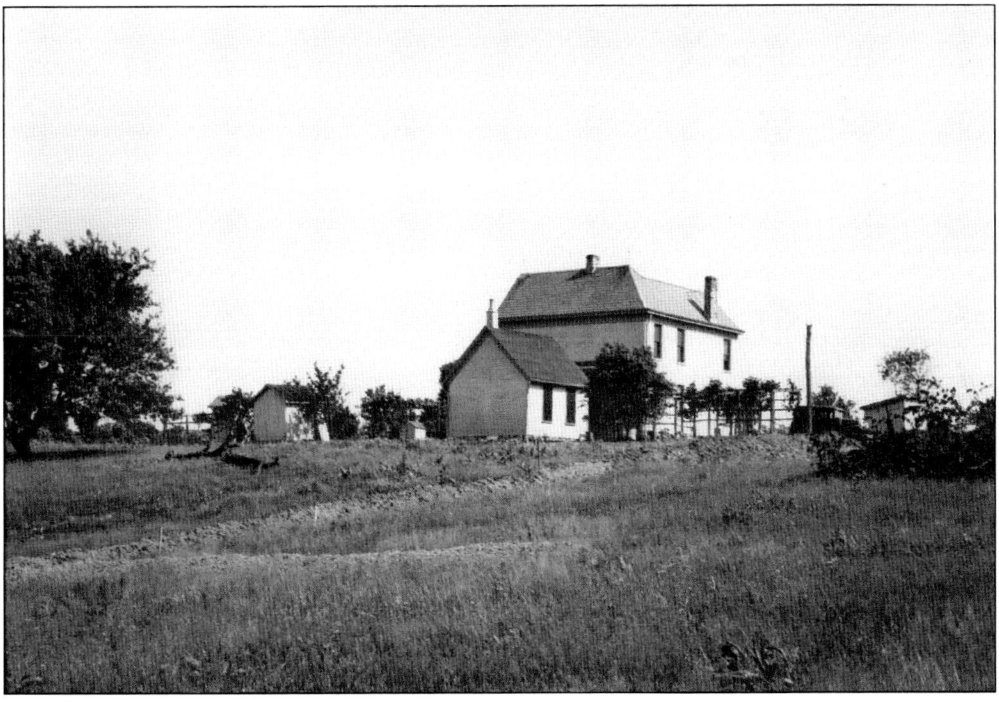

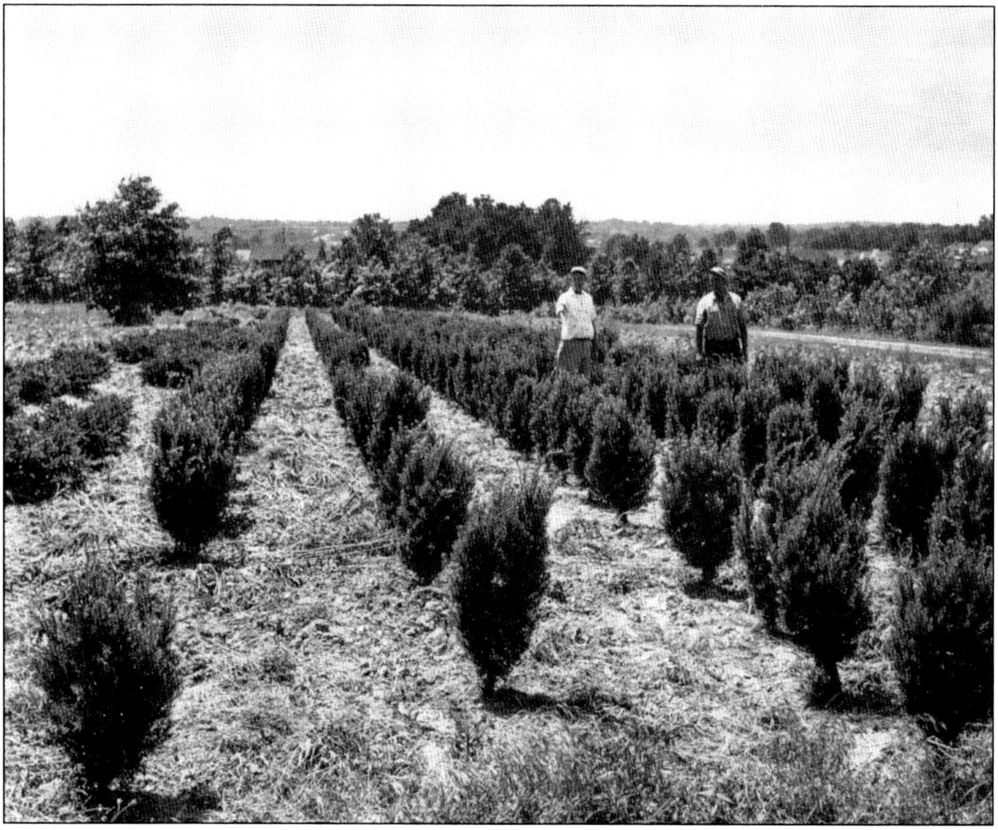

Warder often had up to 18,000 trees and shrubs growing at any given time. In this 1950s photograph, Harvey Burck (left) and Oscar Bross (right) inspect young evergreens. By the 1970s, the CPB had found it more economical to purchase trees from suppliers. As Warder operations shrank, Springfield Township, in 1998, purchased 40 acres of the nursery. (CPB.)

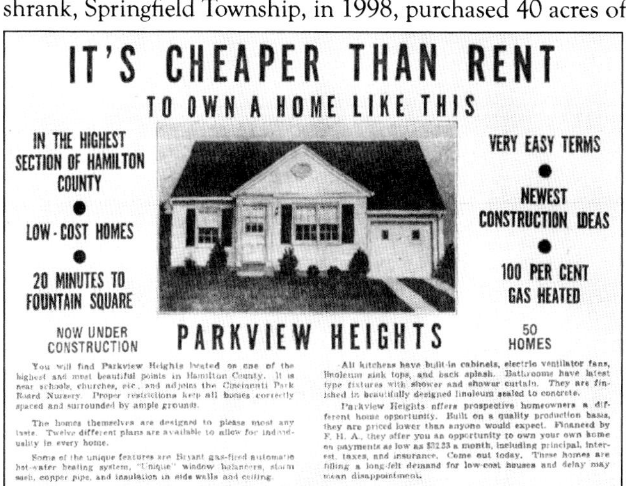

In 1937, developers seized land next to Warder Nursery and created Parkview Heights, Finneytown's first full-blown, residential subdivision. By 1940, five small streets with 40 small homes were constructed. The next year, a retail building was added. A key selling point: Parkview Heights was situated next to Warder at one of the highest points in Hamilton County. (Author's collection.)

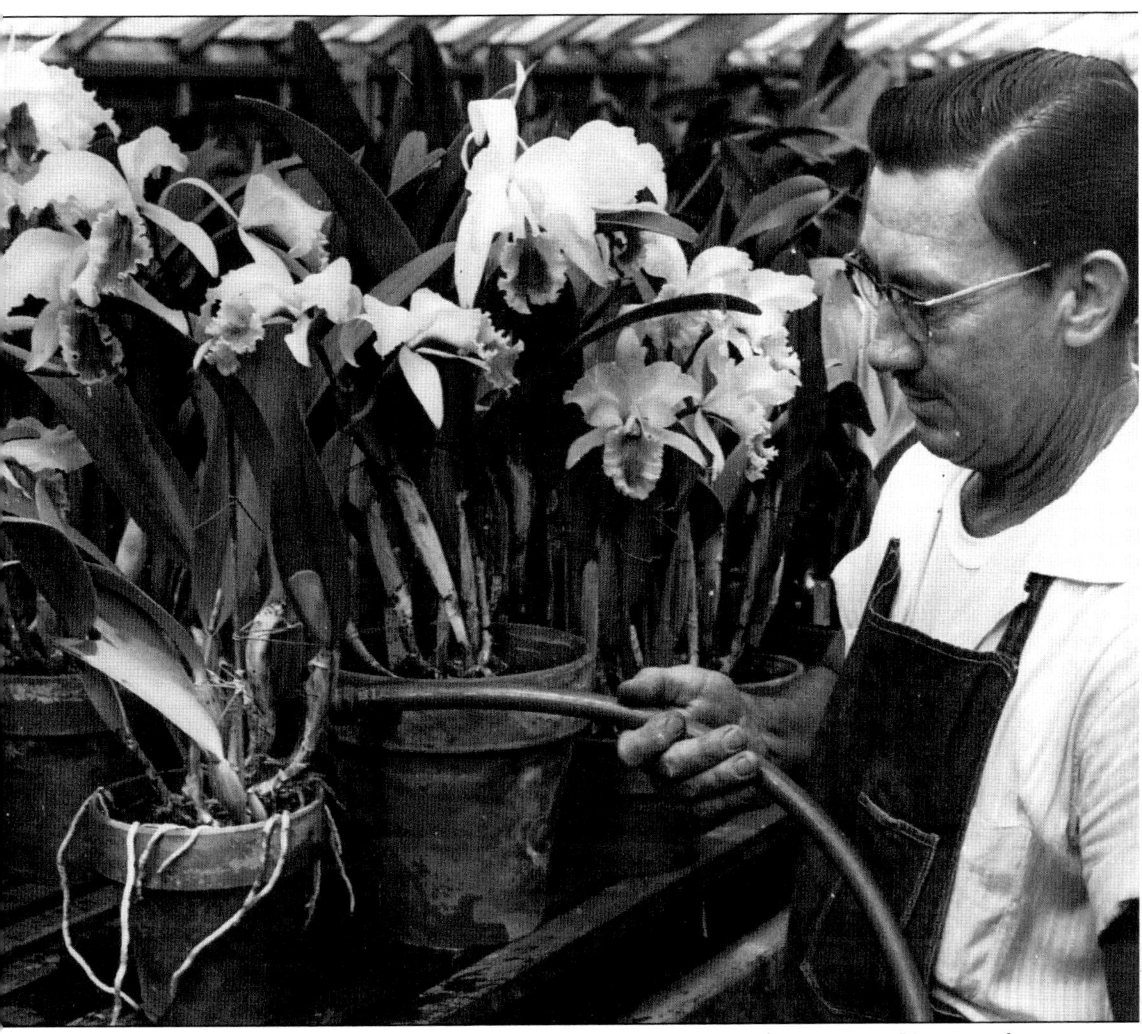

His birth name was Colonel Riley, in honor of a Civil War officer in his ancestry. However, for decades, he was also known as simply "Mr. Orchid." In the 1950s and early 1960s, he oversaw more than 3,000 orchids at Warder. Typical of nursery employees, Riley was self-taught. In 1926, he started as a park tree trimmer and gravitated to flowers. In 1933, when the Eden Park greenhouse activities moved to Warder, Riley spent the rest of his career in Finneytown. He kept files on each orchid. After 37 years with the CPB, Riley retired in 1962. Over the next 20 years, the nursery slowly declined. No longer used to grow trees and shrubs by the 1980s, the Warder was neglected. However, better days were ahead. In 2023, Springfield Township opened Warder Nature Preserve on the grounds. Also, the CPB still operates Warder's historic greenhouses, which provide flowers for Krohn Conservatory—as it did almost a century ago. (CPB.)

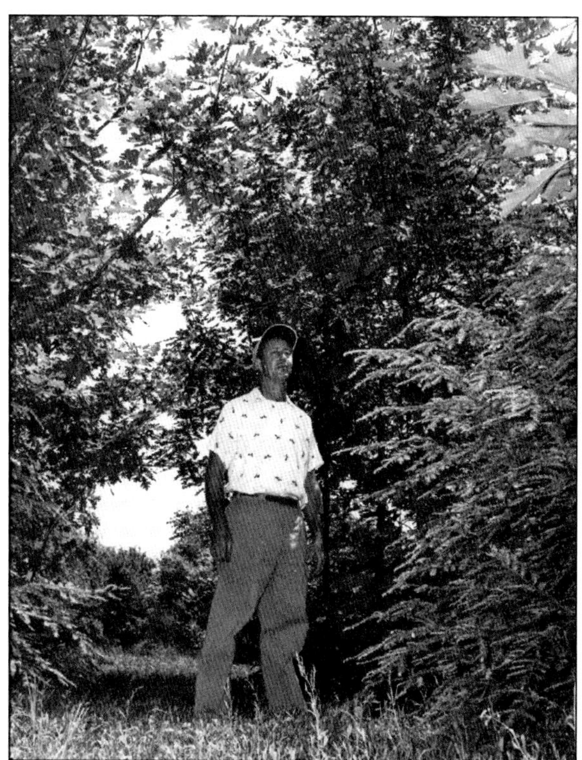

In establishing Warder Nature Preserve and walking trail for the general public, Springfield Township trustees fittingly named the restored pond after Harvey Burck. A Warder employee from 1946 to 1983, he started as a laborer, moved up to florist, and then nursery supervisor in 1956. With that promotion, he and his wife, Mary, and seven children moved into Warder's farmhouse. During their three decades of residence, the family grew to 12 children. "For us kids, growing up in the nursery was magical," said son Donald, pictured below in 1957 with his father holding a pot of begonias. "Dad was so good to the neighborhood kids. He let them wander the woods and fish in the pond. When the township named the pond after him, that was a beautiful day for our family and for Finneytown." (Both, Donald Burck.)

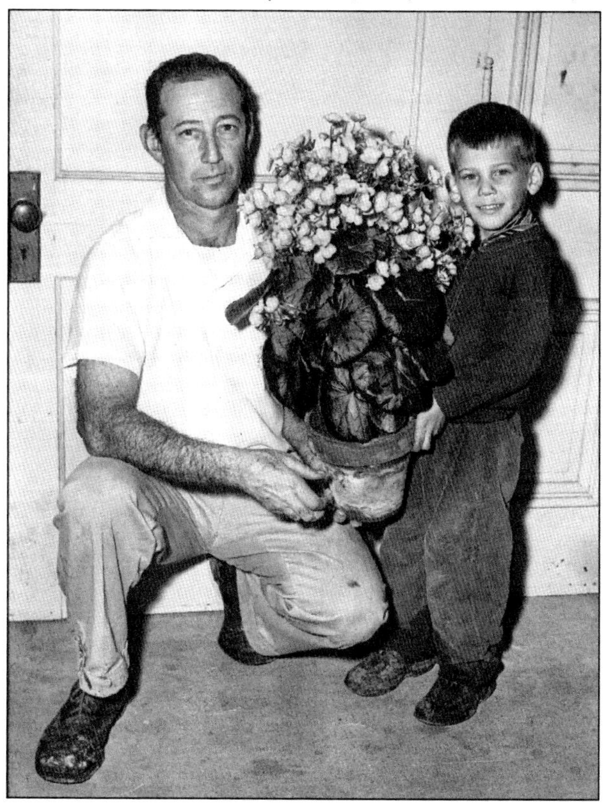

Four

BOOMTOWN USA

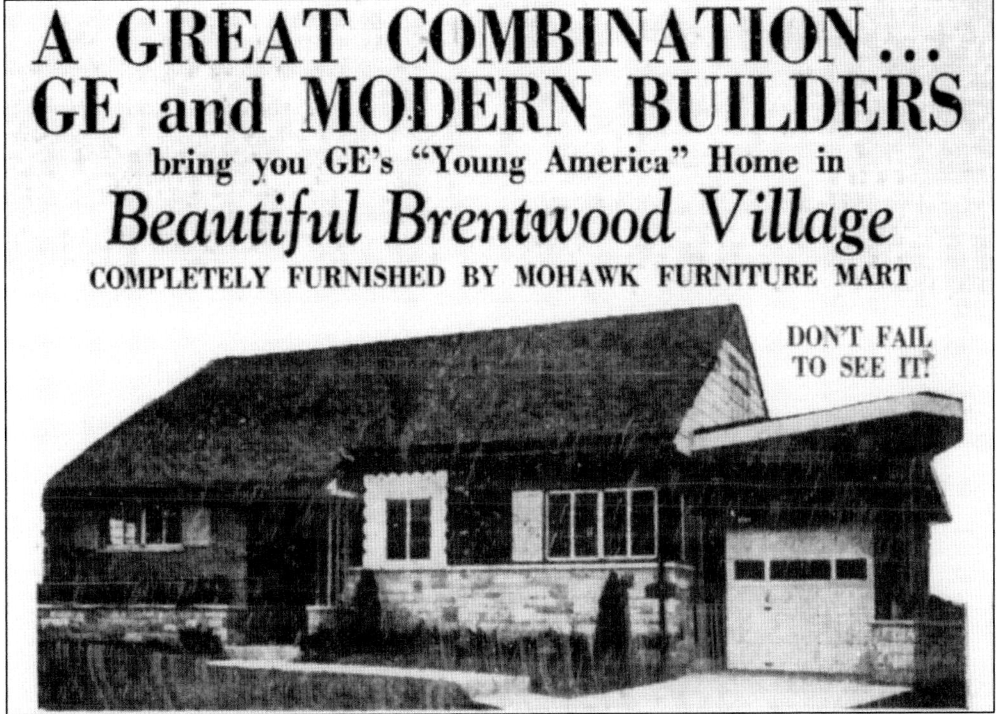
A GREAT COMBINATION...
GE and MODERN BUILDERS
bring you GE's "Young America" Home in
Beautiful Brentwood Village
COMPLETELY FURNISHED BY MOHAWK FURNITURE MART
DON'T FAIL TO SEE IT!

Finneytown transformed during the post–World War II boom. In the early 1950s, developer Modern Builders Inc. aggressively built tract homes in a subdivision named Brentwood Village, which was clustered around Hempstead Avenue. Modern Builders owned 1,440 acres in Brentwood Village. The small homes with GE appliances sold quickly to young couples. Brentwood was one of several subdivisions sprouting up on Finneytown farmland during this time. (Author's collection.)

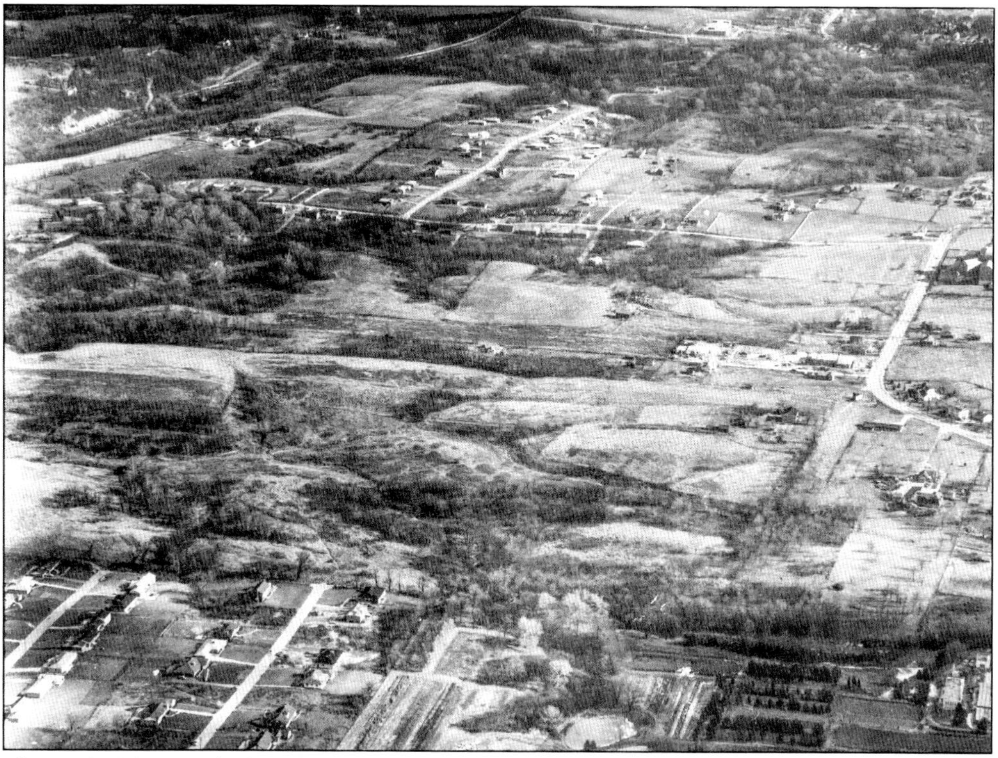

This mid-1950s aerial of southeast Finneytown captures two early subdivisions: Parkview Heights (lower left) and View Place (near the top). Overlooking Millcreek Valley, View Place was also called Jill's Hill. It became a haven for unique residential architecture. By the 1960s, View Place's growth accelerated with the construction of St. Xavier High School. (Author's collection.)

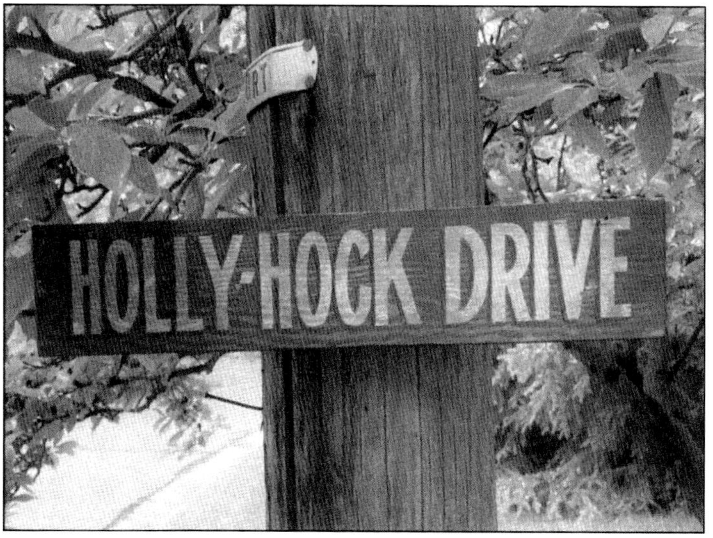

Finneytown subdivisions featured homes that sold at a wide range of prices, creating economic diversity. As tract homes popped up in Brentwood Village, Hollyhock Farms Inc. in 1949 constructed higher-priced homes off Compton Road near the Wyoming community. Hollyhock Drive, spelled Holly-hock on this early street sign, was the first entry point into a neighborhood of stately homes. (Clay Mizelle.)

In the mid-1950s, Cincinnati builder O.O. Thompson & Son presented this brochure to potential homebuyers in Thompson Acres, a subdivision on Kirkland Drive and Burgundy Lane. Built to an efficient design influenced by renowned architect Don Scholz, Thompson Acres homes were made of shingle, brick, stone, and wood siding. They featured overhanging rooflines and a small terrace, both classic treatments in affordable 1950s designs. Another attraction with Thompson Acres homes was the Carrier-brand Weathermaker central air conditioning system. At the time, this system provided an innovative lifestyle comfort at an affordable price. These Thompson Acres homes have weathered well over many decades. In recent years, several houses in the subdivision have been fully restored (below) as modern architecture experiences a revival. Thompson Acres is a 1950s timepiece of American suburban living. (Both, Jeff Kobberdahl.)

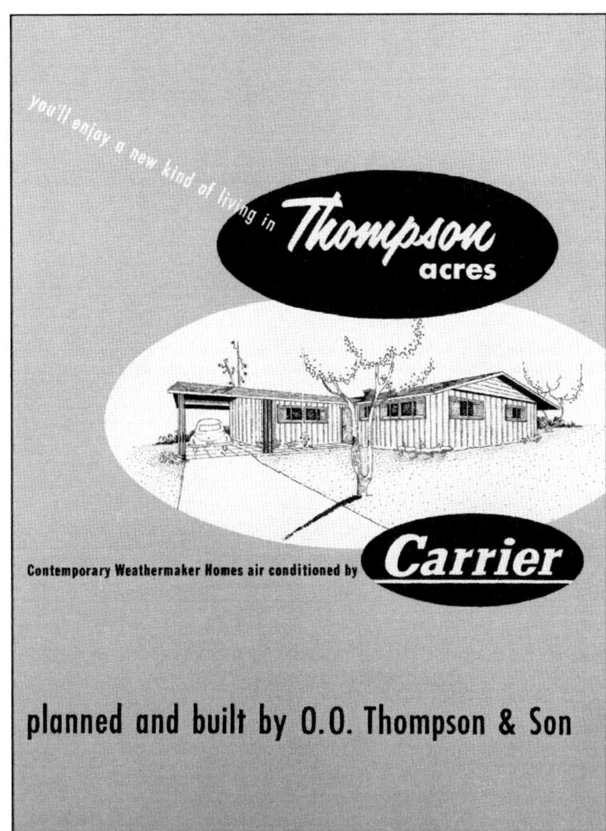

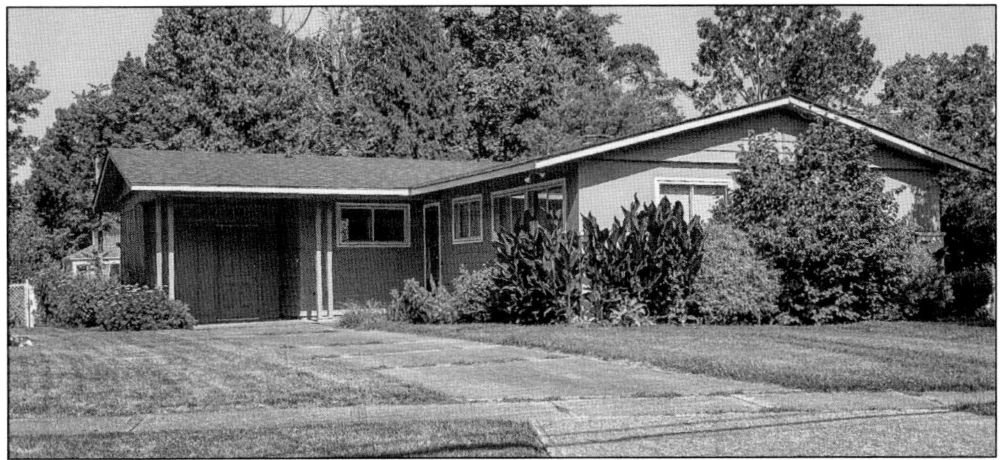

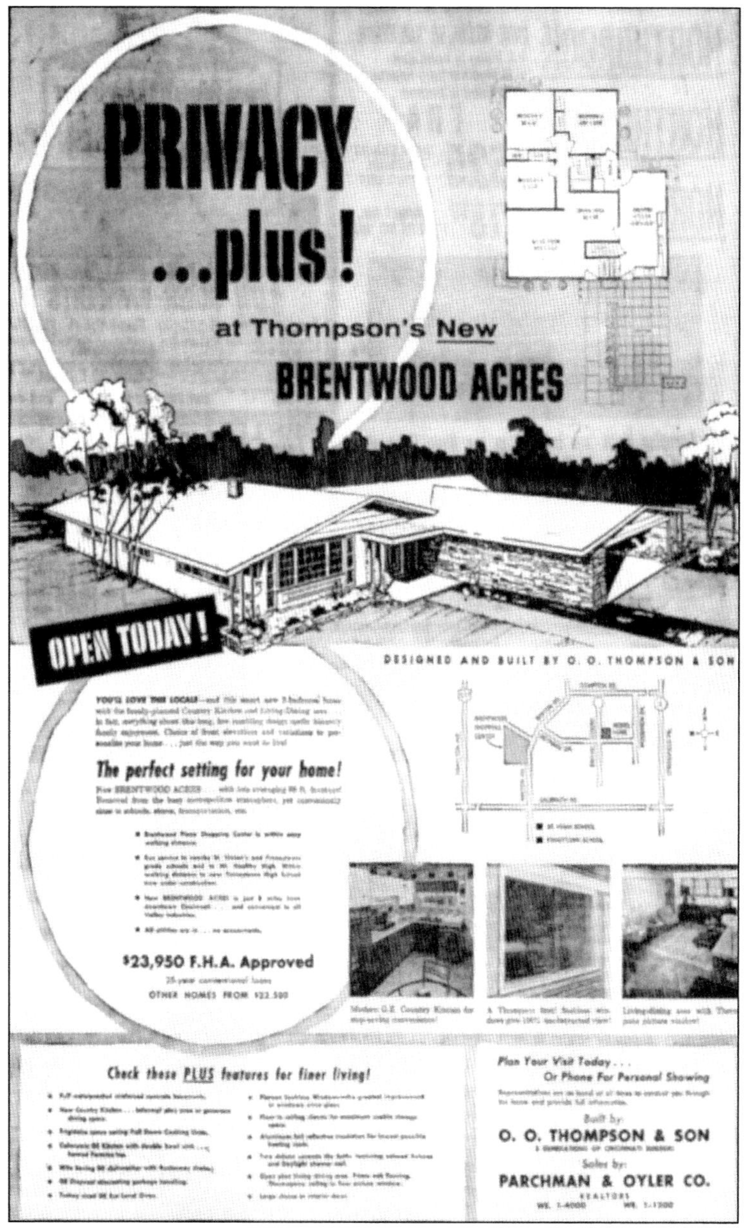

While Modern Builders aggressively expanded Brentwood Village west of Winton Road, O.O. Thompson & Son in 1957 planted a stake east of Winton Road at Reynard Avenue and Empire Court and named the subdivision Brentwood Acres. In addition to building traditional homes, Thompson built distinctive, single-story ranches with large front carports on Reynard, Empire, and Pringle Drive. The "model home" used to market Brentwood Acres, highlighted in this advertisement, is on the northeast corner of Reynard and Empire. These six-room homes were billed as "long, low rambling designs" with GE country kitchens and a "turkey sized" oven. Open-plan, living-dining room combinations with large picture windows were all the rage and an effective use of building space. Brentwood Acres was within walking distance from Brentwood Shopping Center, and the kids could take school buses to St. Vivian or Finneytown schools. (Author's collection.)

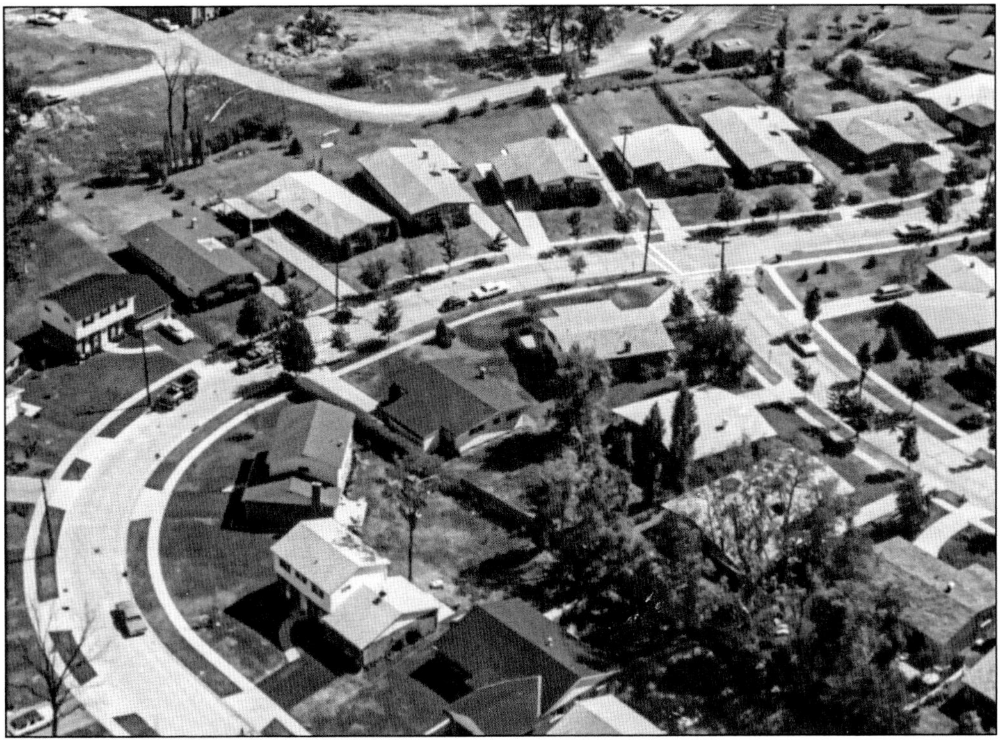

Modern Builders single-story homes near the top of this 1957 photograph of Fontainebleau Terrace strongly resemble "California suburban" homes of the same era. These low-level houses, with adjoining carports, give the neighborhood a distinct look, and they seem almost foreign to southern Ohio. These new homes attracted young employees of nearby P&G and GE. The houses were sold furnished. They were situated next to the new Finneytown High School. Also, they provided easy access to bus service to downtown Cincinnati. Unlike the home photographed below, many owners in later years modified and expanded the houses. However, many of these classic homes continue to be restored. (Both, Steve Battistone.)

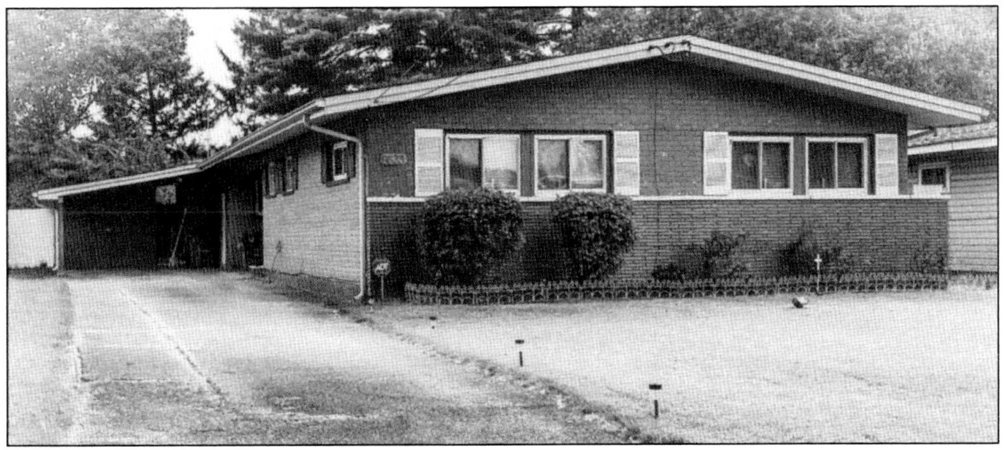

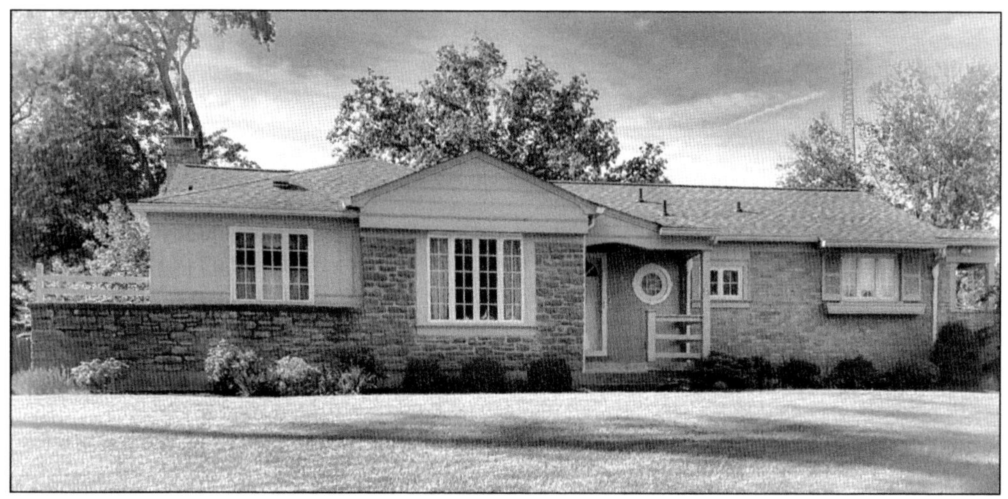

Beginning in the late 1940s, Lang Brothers construction firm developed the Greenfield Village subdivision west of Winton Road and north of North Bend Road. By the 1950s, the Lang designs became more upscale, and were advertised as offering "a lifetime of wonderful suburban living." As with this home on Springbrook Drive, exterior treatments of each Lang-built home used impressive designs and building materials. (Mark Evans.)

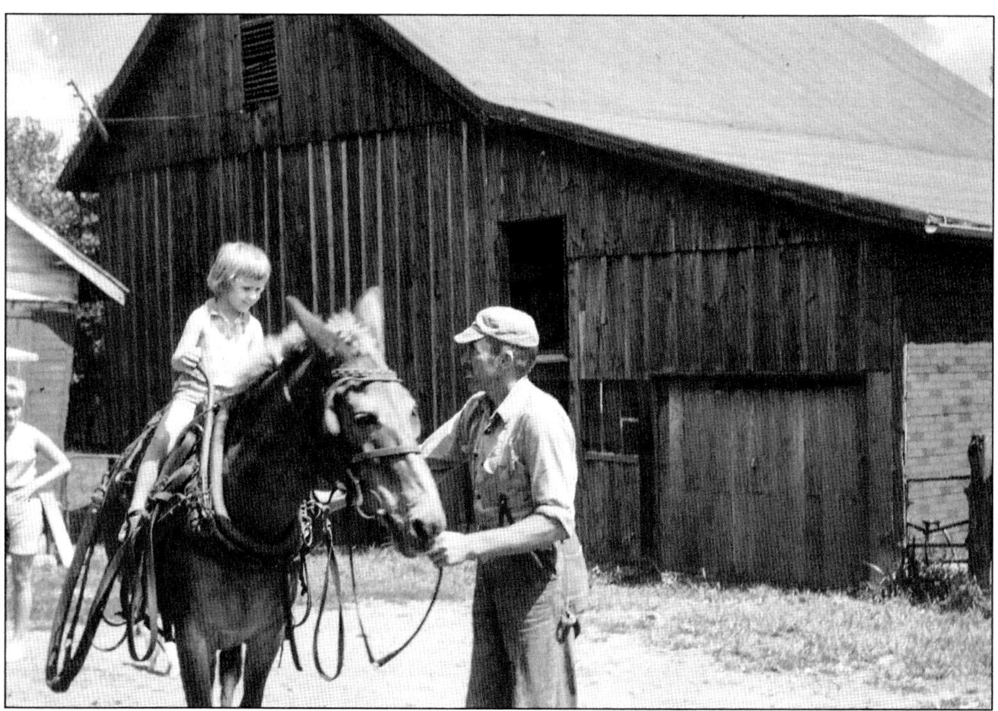

While Finneytown developed, a historic farm survived. In 1965, Lester Bahr put Lee Ann Stroffregen on his horse (pictured) at the Bahr family farm on North Bend Road. The family owned the farm from 1916 until 2021, when Dale and Carol Bahr donated it to Cardinal Land Conservancy to ensure its survival. The land has been farmed since 1804. The barn, built around 1809, survives. (Mark Besserman.)

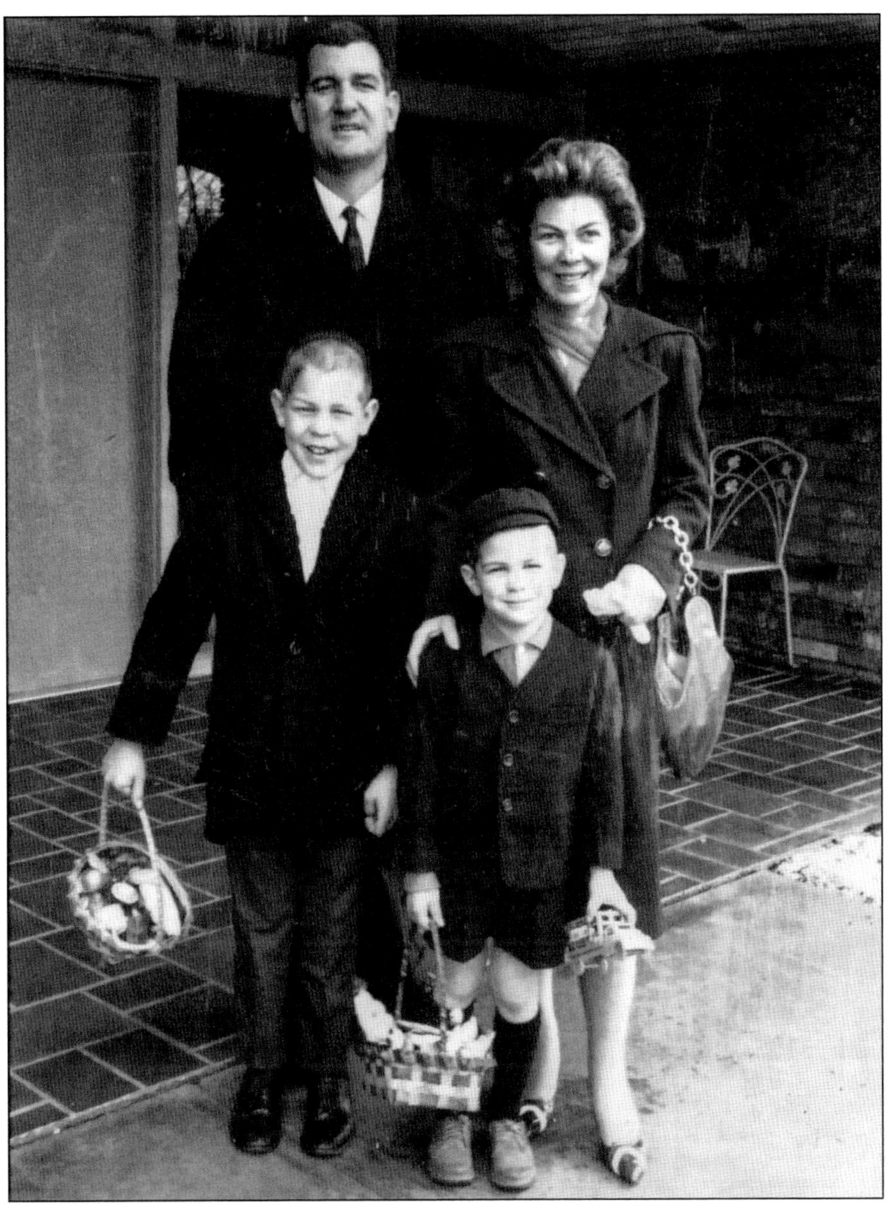

Don Lang, a significant real estate developer in Finneytown, is photographed at the family's Greenfarms Drive home during Easter in the early 1960s with his wife, Joan, and sons Steve (left) and Donny. He built a large mid-century modern home next door to prominent business leader Charles Keating Jr. and his family. The property had been part of Nieman Nursery. In the 1950s, Don was the homebuyer contact for Lang Brothers' Greenfield Village subdivision. In the early 1960s, he split from Lang Brothers (his father, Frank, was co-owner) and went on his own as a developer, forming partnerships with other builders, including Jack Wittekind. Working closely with Nettie Nieman, operator of Nieman Nursery, Don acquired nursery land and carved out streets while leaving the small trees. Various builders constructed custom homes in the neighborhood, which was called North Hill Estates. Some of Finneytown's most distinctive homes resulted from Don's vision for the new subdivision. He died in Palm Beach, Florida, in 2008. (Steve Lang.)

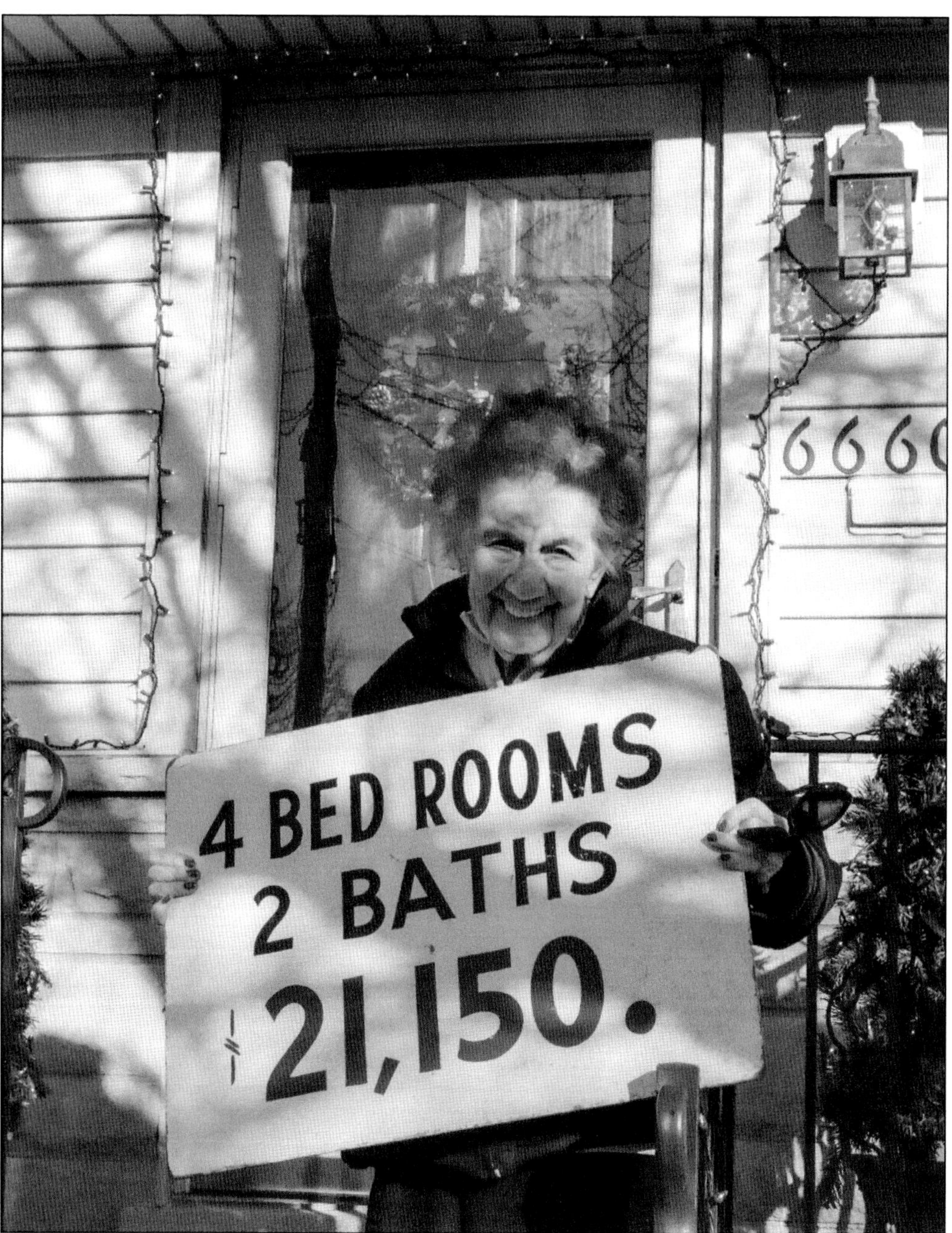

In 1958, when Bill and Merce Hershey read the yard sign at the Cape Cod house on Charann Lane, Merce wondered, "How can there be four bedrooms in that little house?" At the time, Paul Brothers Construction developed two subdivisions of smaller homes in southwest Finneytown, which included Charann Lane. Moving to Finneytown from Detroit, Bill and Merce raised five children in the house. After Bill passed away in 1981, Merce and the kids stayed there. At age 97, she posed in 2023 in front of her house of 65 years, holding the original sign that first caught her eye those many years ago. "It was like living out in the country back then," she said. "We could hear cows mooing on North Bend Road at night." Merce worked at Cottonwood Elementary School for 37 years. She retired at age 82 when the school was closed. (Mark Evans.)

In 1959, Henry's Hamburgers chain opened its first drive-in restaurant in the Cincinnati area (pictured) at Galbraith and Winton Roads (today's Wendy's). A hamburger was only 15¢. At the time, the Chicago-based Henry's was a larger hamburger chain than McDonald's. By the early 1960s, Henry's, the brainchild of Bresler's Ice Cream Company, had more than 200 drive-in restaurants across America, including several in Cincinnati. (Rob Leininger.)

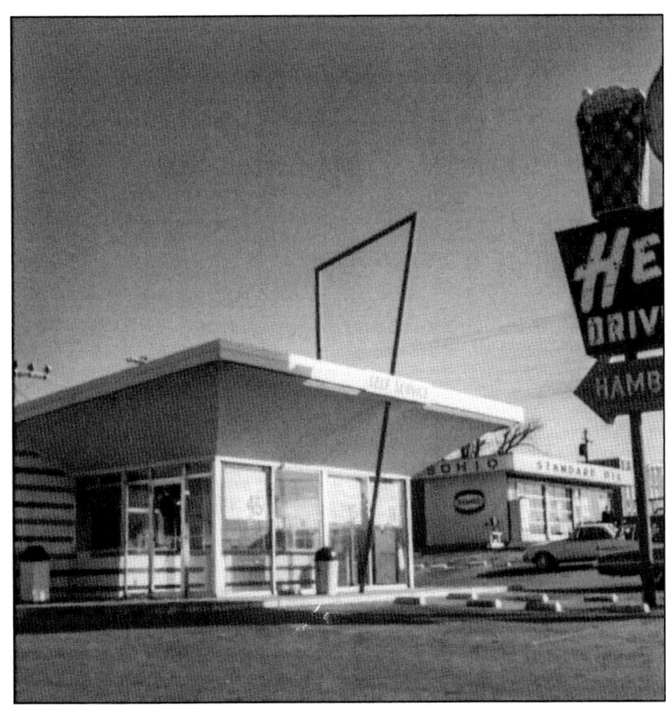

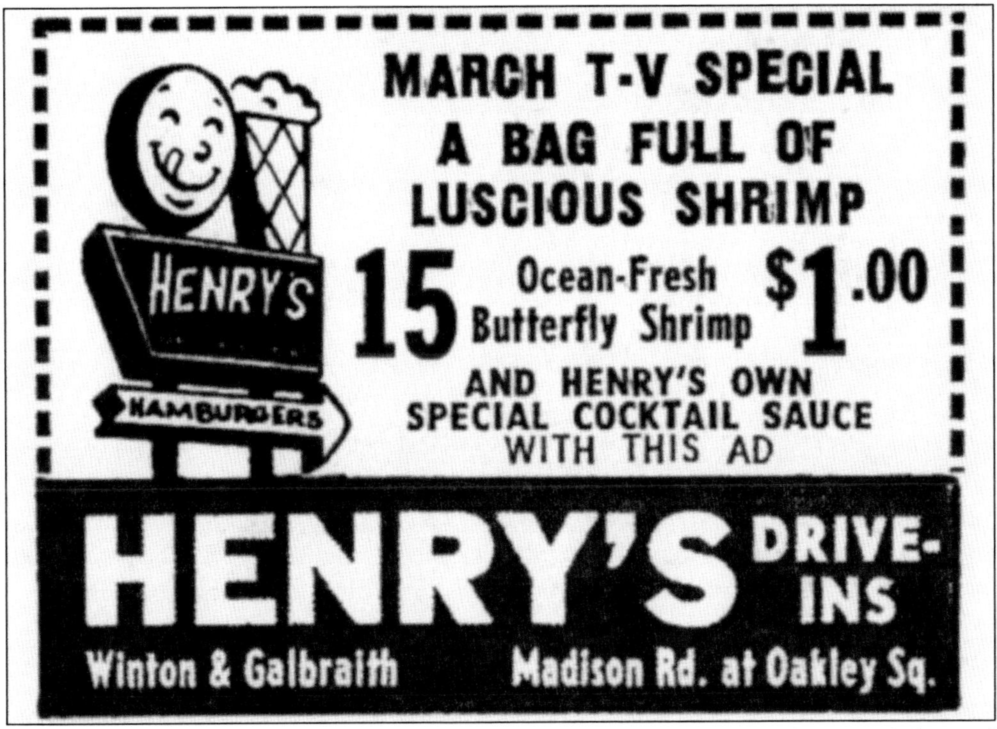

HENRY'S

HAMBURGERS

MARCH T-V SPECIAL

A BAG FULL OF LUSCIOUS SHRIMP

15 Ocean-Fresh Butterfly Shrimp $1.00

AND HENRY'S OWN SPECIAL COCKTAIL SAUCE WITH THIS AD

HENRY'S DRIVE-INS

Winton & Galbraith   Madison Rd. at Oakley Sq.

The Finneytown Henry's was highly visible, often holding promotions for its burgers, shakes, and "whale-of-a-fish" sandwiches. In 1960, civic leader Dolly Cohen fed 400 children from an area orphanage at the Finneytown drive-in. By the mid-1960s, the Finneytown drive-in offered the ultimate deal: 15 ocean-fresh shrimp for a dollar. (Author's collection.)

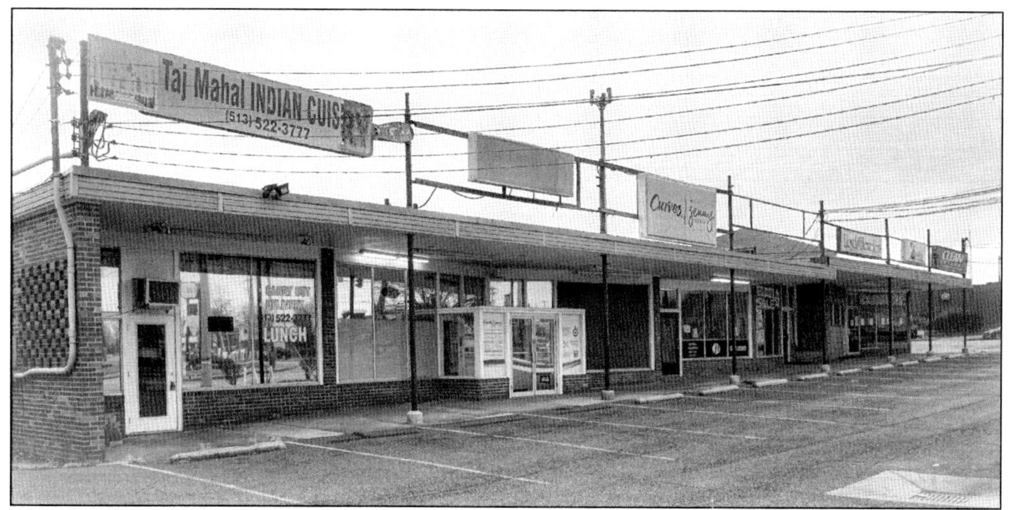

Photographed shortly before its demolition years ago, the strip mall on Winton Road across from Brentwood Shopping Plaza had been a retail fixture since 1960. Among the first tenants were Grote Bakery, Brentwood Beauty Saloon, Carter's Restaurant (with Colonel Sanders's "secret" chicken recipe), Jerry Mark's Pharmacy, and Wanda Lisa Lounge. Today, a Chick-fil-A restaurant occupies the site. (Mark Evans.)

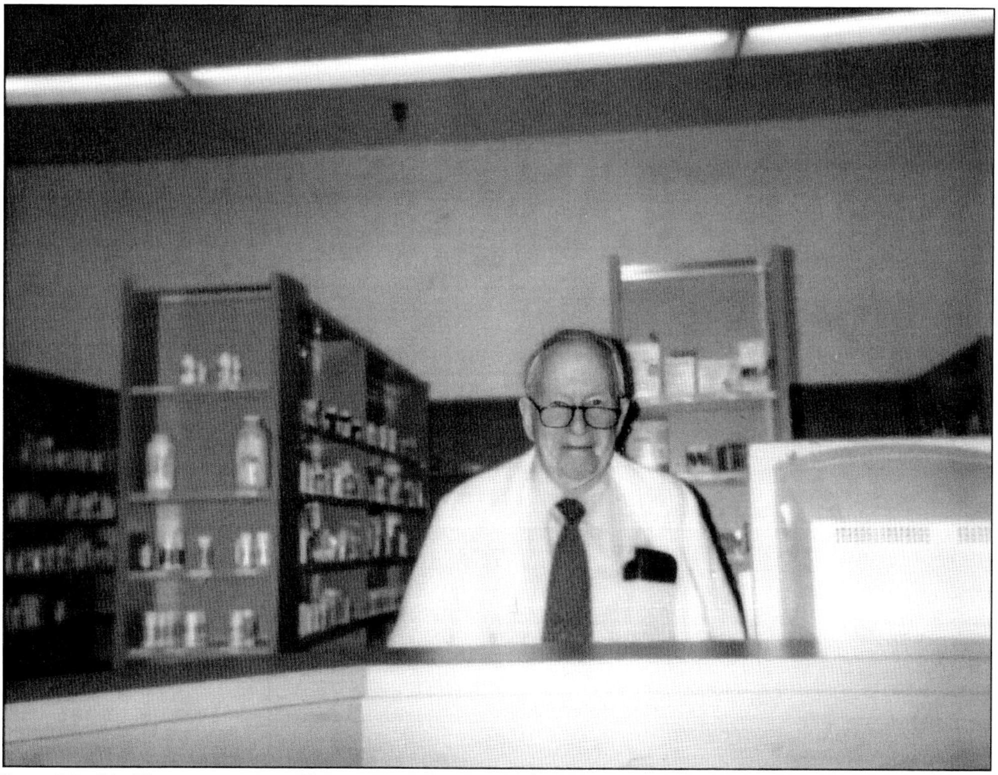

Jerry Mark's Pharmacy was a Finneytown business along Winton Road from 1960 to 1980. Jerry (pictured) and his wife, Bernice, were married for 72 years, and she worked with her husband in running his various pharmacies across the city. They raised their family in Finneytown. Jerry and Bernice both died within months of each other in 2021. (Stanley Mark.)

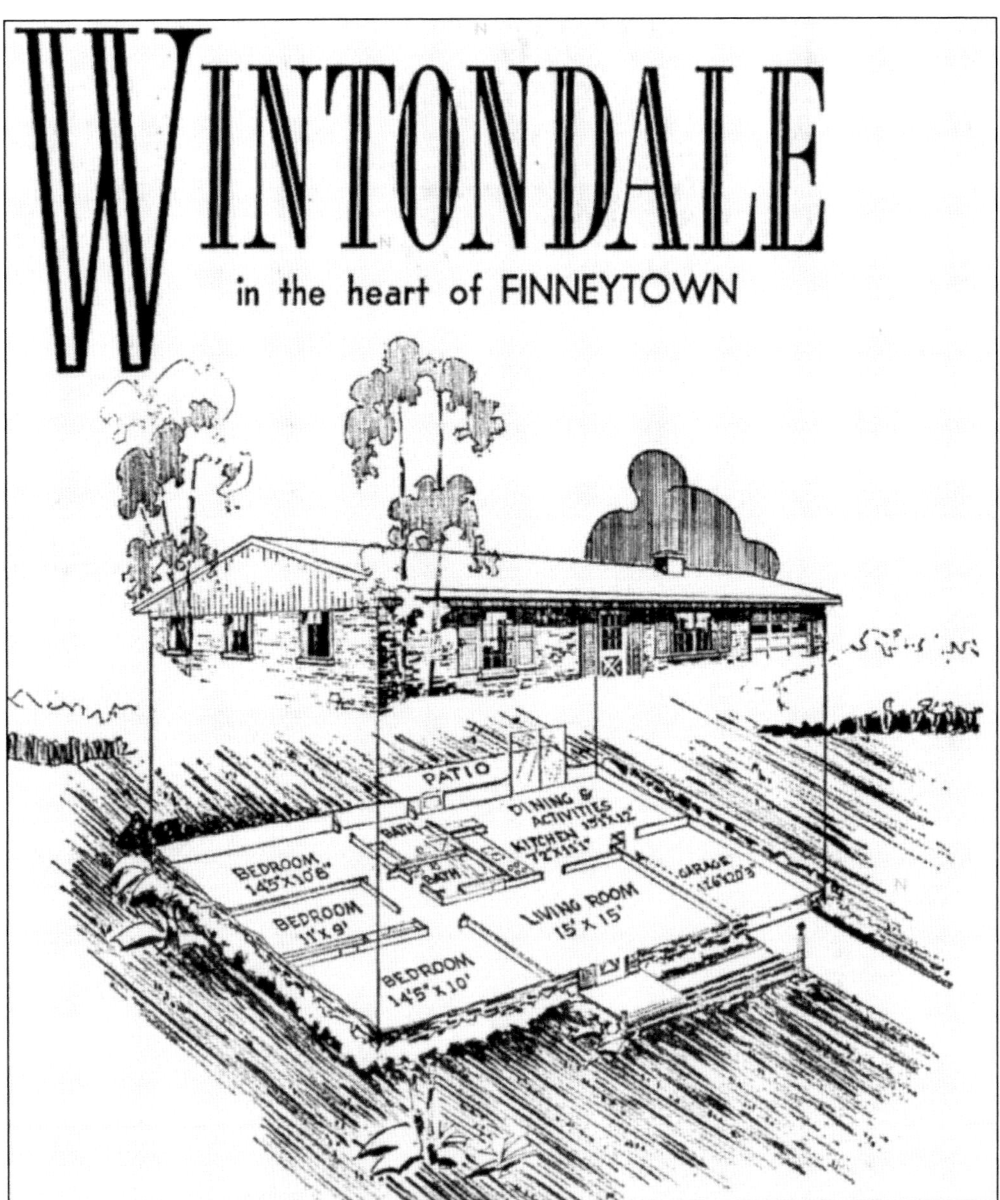

An interesting example of Finneytown's economic diversity is Wintondale. This 230-house subdivision was developed by LC Homes Inc. in 1960–1961 at the southeast corner of Winton Road and Galbraith Avenue. LC Homes built and sold tract homes on the former site of Kuhlmann Dairy for a $600 down payment (no down payment for military veterans) and a $90 monthly payment. Wintondale's main street off Winton Road was named North Hill Lane, which caused a stir with some residents across Winton Road. Their street was also called North Hill Lane, and their 1940s homes were much larger and stately. After residents from the original North Hill Lane complained, Hamilton County Commissioners in 1962 changed Wintondale's North Hill Lane to South Hill Lane, naturally causing a ruckus with Wintondale residents. Finally, commissioners relented and changed the street back to North Hill Lane. (Author's collection.)

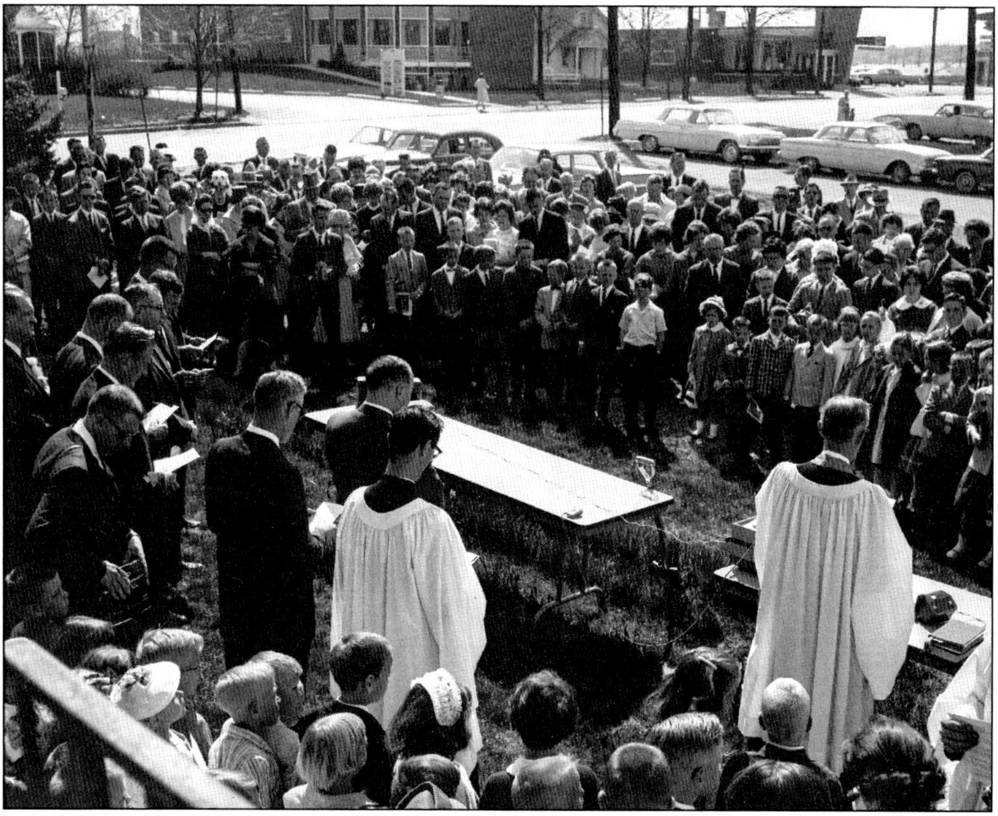

Faith Lutheran Church began in the mid-1940s as a mission church of Trinity Lutheran of Mt. Healthy. Members worshiped in Finneytown School before laying the cornerstone of a new church building in 1948 at the northwest corner of Winton and Galbraith Roads. As the congregation grew, members gathered outside in 1963 (pictured) for the ground breaking of a church expansion. (Faith Lutheran Church.)

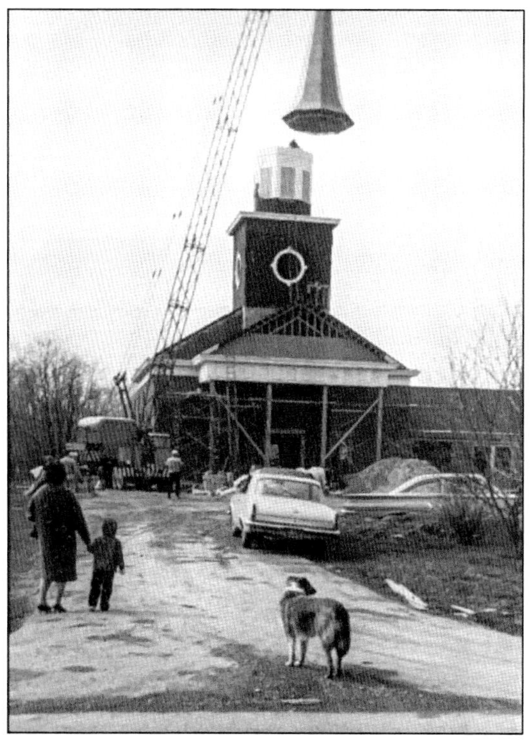

As the Finneytown population surged, Northminster Presbyterian Church (formed in 1944) outgrew its 1957 sanctuary along Winton Road. With a congregation of 1,300 members, the church in 1965 built a second and larger sanctuary, along with a fellowship hall and kitchen. The steeple is being added in this 1966 photograph. The first service in the new sanctuary was held on Christmas Eve of that year. (Northminster Church.)

From 1960 to 1974, Fr. Albin Ratermann pastored St. Vivian Church during an era of extraordinary growth. He oversaw construction projects for the church and elementary school. In 1962, school enrollment was 1,720 students. By the late 1960s, he pastored more than 1,400 families. A serious fan of the Cincinnati Reds (often mentioned in his sermons!), he died at age 85 in 1989 as pastor emeritus. (St. Vivian Church.)

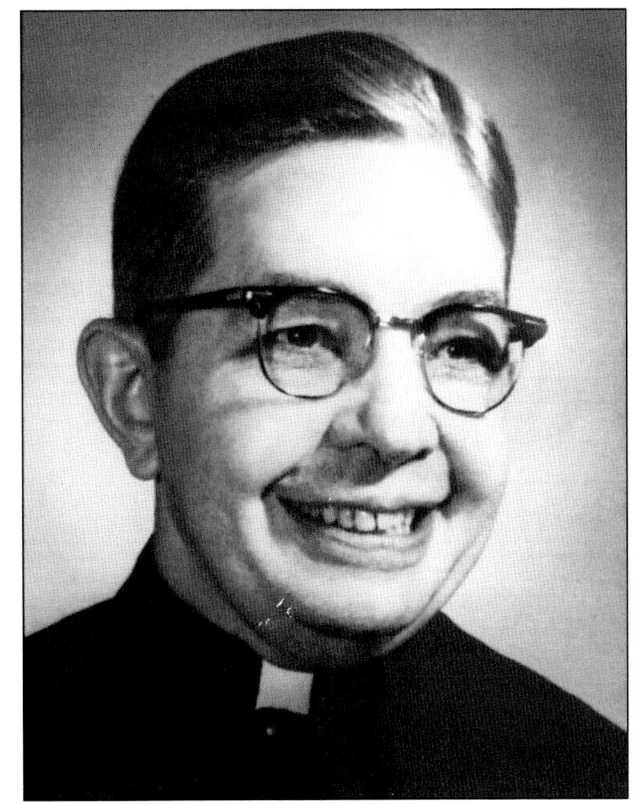

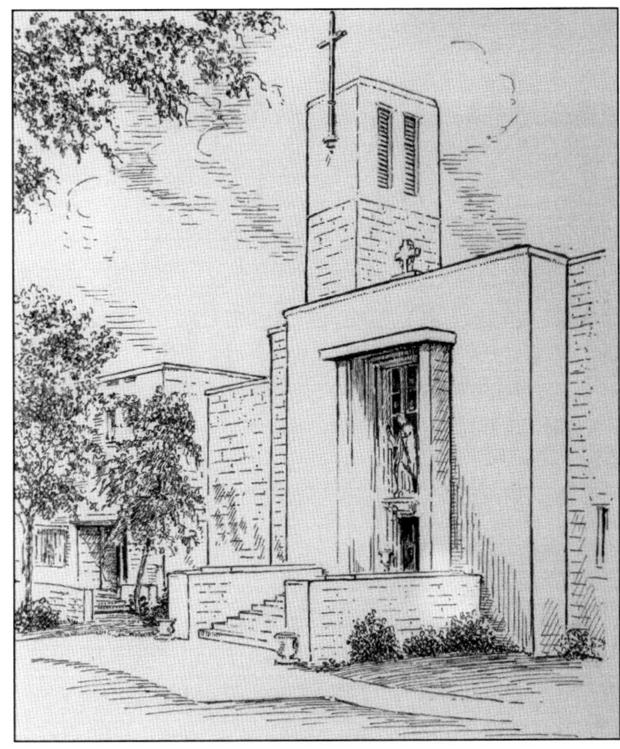

In 1962, Cincinnati's famed sketch artist Caroline Williams celebrated the fast-growing St. Vivian Church with this work. For five decades beginning in 1932, her popular "A Spot In Cincinnati" sketches appeared in Sunday's *Cincinnati Enquirer* editorial page. She highlighted Finneytown decades earlier with a 1933 sketch in the *Enquirer* of the Finneytown School on Winton Road. (St. Vivian Church.)

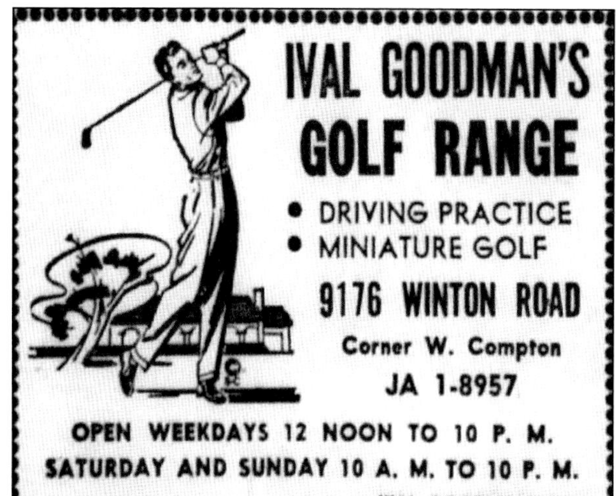

In 1956, retired Cincinnati Reds star outfielder Ival Goodman opened a golf driving range on rural land along Winton Road at the site of today's Springfield Township offices and firehouse and HighGrain Brewery. A two-time National League all-star and member of the Reds' 1940 World Series champions, Goodman operated the range and miniature golf course for four years. (Author's collection.)

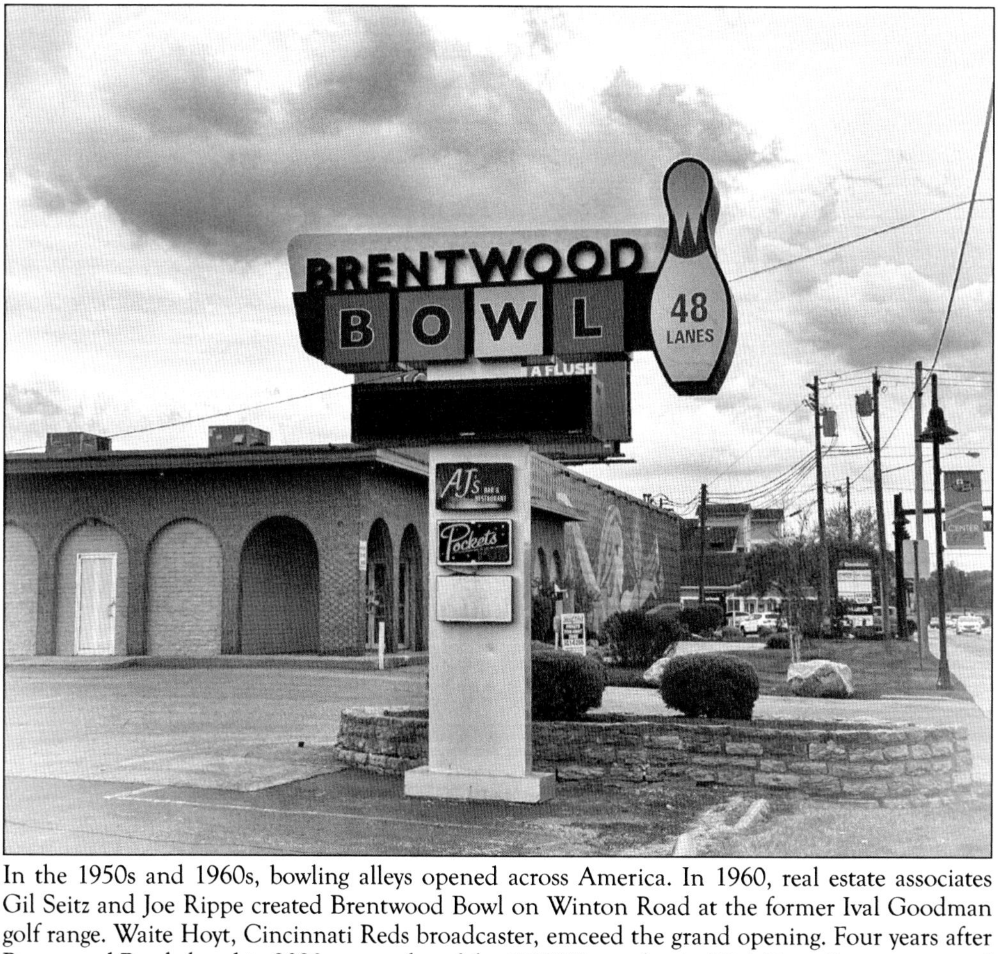

In the 1950s and 1960s, bowling alleys opened across America. In 1960, real estate associates Gil Seitz and Joe Rippe created Brentwood Bowl on Winton Road at the former Ival Goodman golf range. Waite Hoyt, Cincinnati Reds broadcaster, emceed the grand opening. Four years after Brentwood Bowl closed in 2020, a casualty of the COVID pandemic, HighGrain Brewery opened a restaurant and brewery in the restored complex. (Author's collection.)

From 1957 to 1968, Finneytown kids had a magical place in Tiny Town on West Galbraith Road. They could experience the 11 amusement rides for under $2. Horse enthusiast Dale Glardon, owner of a drywall company, first operated this sideline business with a horse track, where kids could take pony rides. Glardon also hosted rodeos. By 1958, the park added an assortment of rides. (Steve Battistone.)

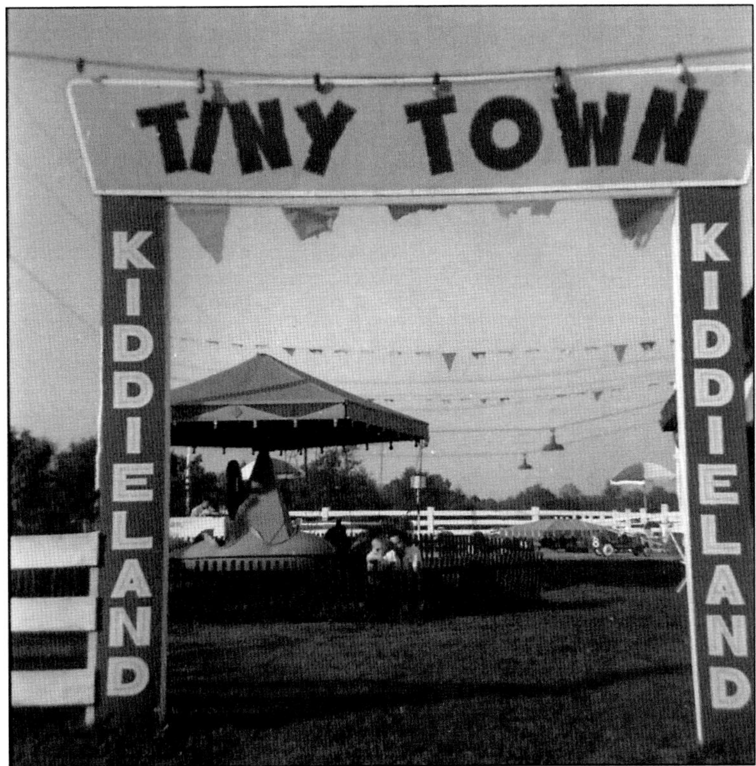

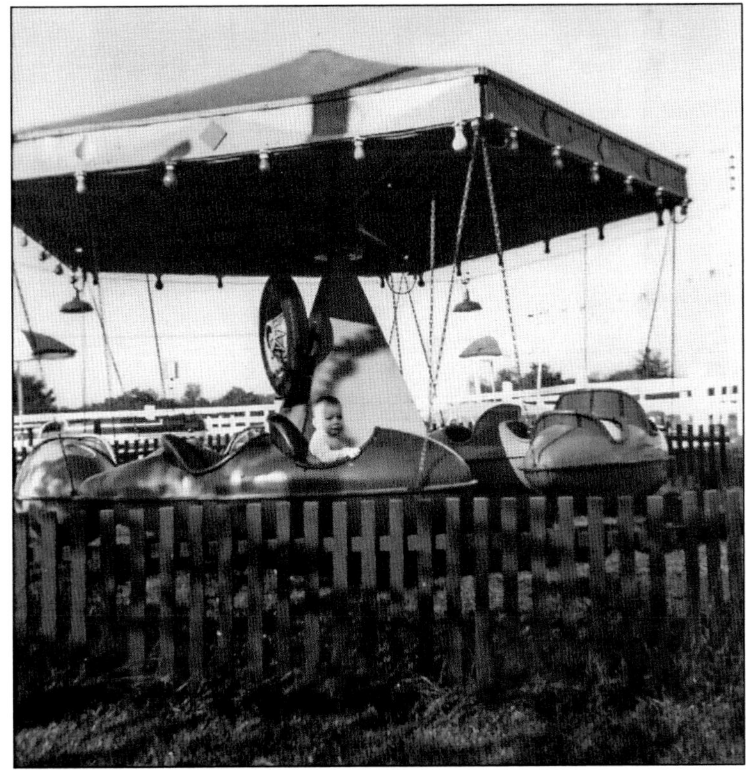

During America's "space race," what could be more exciting for a Finneytown boy than a ride on "the Rocket" at Tiny Town? In late 1968, Dale Glardon sold the park property to developers. The Prince Frederick apartment complex was built on the site. In 1969, Glardon placed an advertisement in the newspapers offering all of the Tiny Town rides for $3,100. (Steve Battistone.)

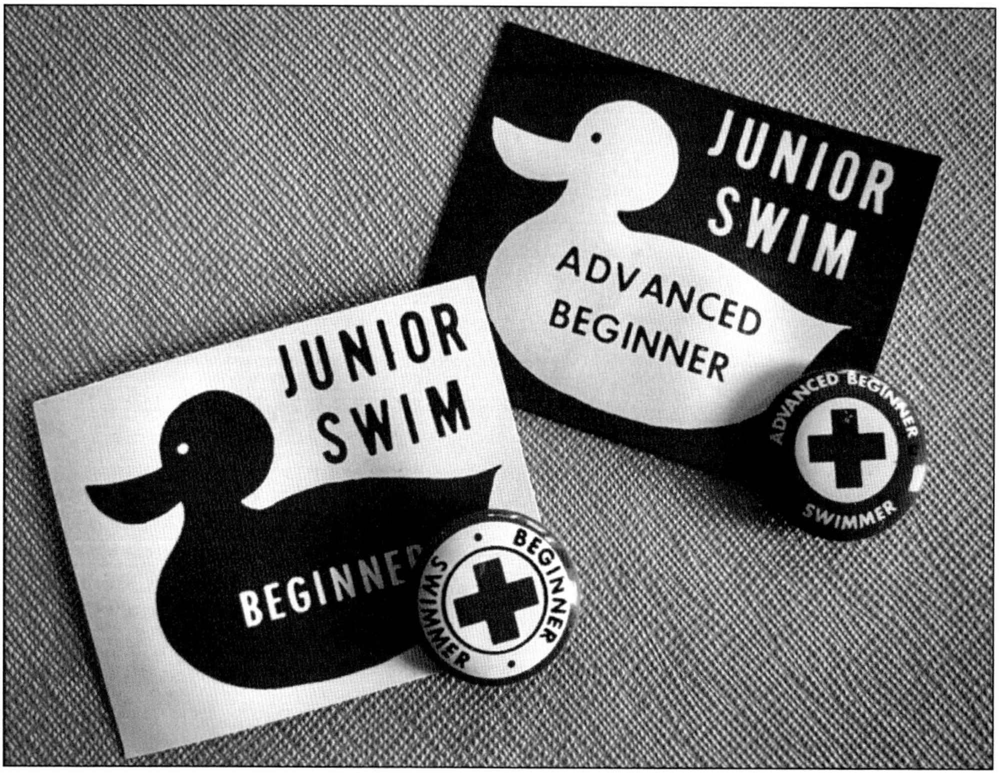

In the 1960s, at the popular Brentwood Swim Club behind Brentwood Shopping Plaza, kids eagerly earned duck patches (pictured), which they attached to their swimming suits. The different colored ducks represented levels of swimming proficiency. The coveted beginner's "red duck" was tantamount to a US passport, providing legal entry to the pool's deep end and diving boards. (Jean Lubker.)

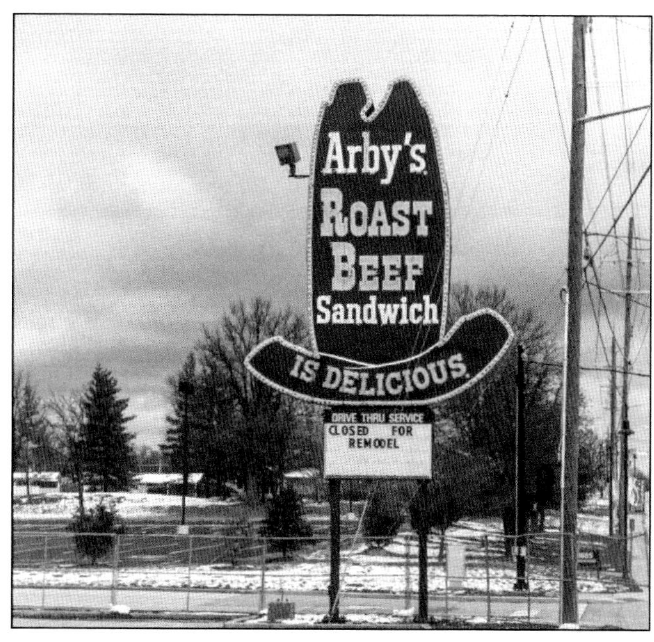

Paris has its Eiffel Tower. For 40 years, Finneytown had its majestic, 24-foot Arby's road sign. The local Arby's opened in 1968 as the sixth in the Cincinnati area. Lights around the brown western hat created a marvelous silhouette at night. Despite community pleas to save it, the sign was permanently removed during a 2013 renovation. It was donated to the American Sign Museum. (Chris Glass.)

Five

School Transformation

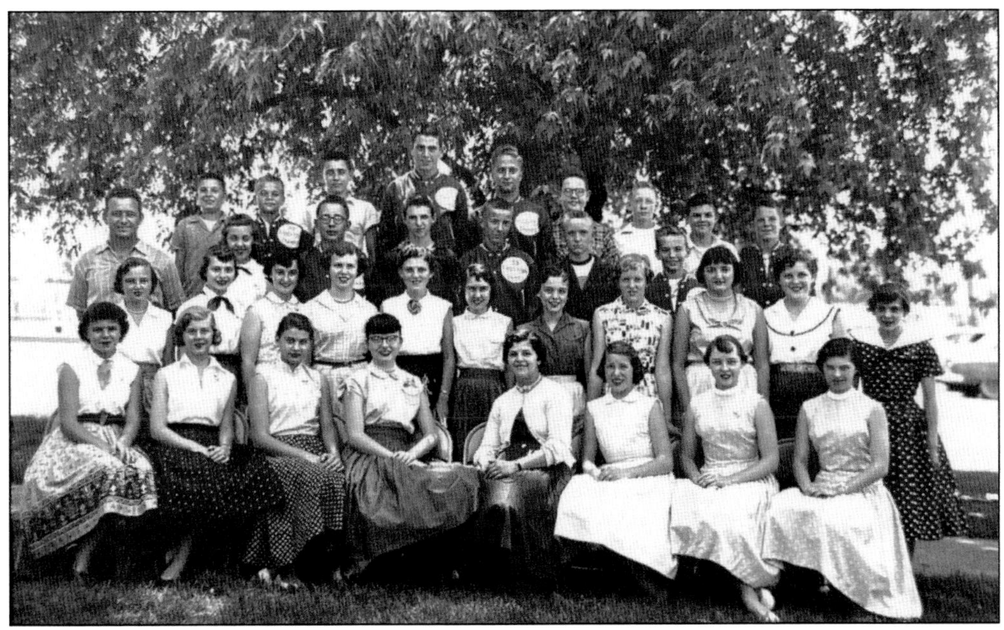

Charles "Mac" McNulty, far left, was a World War II naval officer who joined Finneytown School in 1947 as a teacher and coach. Big changes were coming to the district when he was photographed with 1955 eighth graders and faculty. When Finneytown High School was established three years later, he became its first athletic director. Today, the stadium is named after him. He died in 2012. (FLSD.)

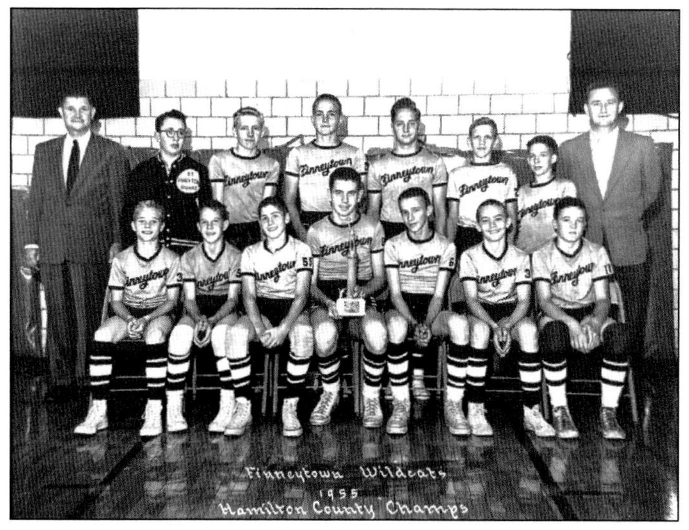

Coached by McNulty (top right) and assisted by principal Telford Whitaker (top left), Finneytown School's eighth-grade basketball teams in the 1950s were a powerhouse. This 1955 team won the county tournament led by Tom Whitaker, fifth from left. Four years earlier, his older brother, Billy Whitaker, led Finneytown School's undefeated team. Later, he played with Oscar Robertson at the University of Cincinnati. (FLSD.)

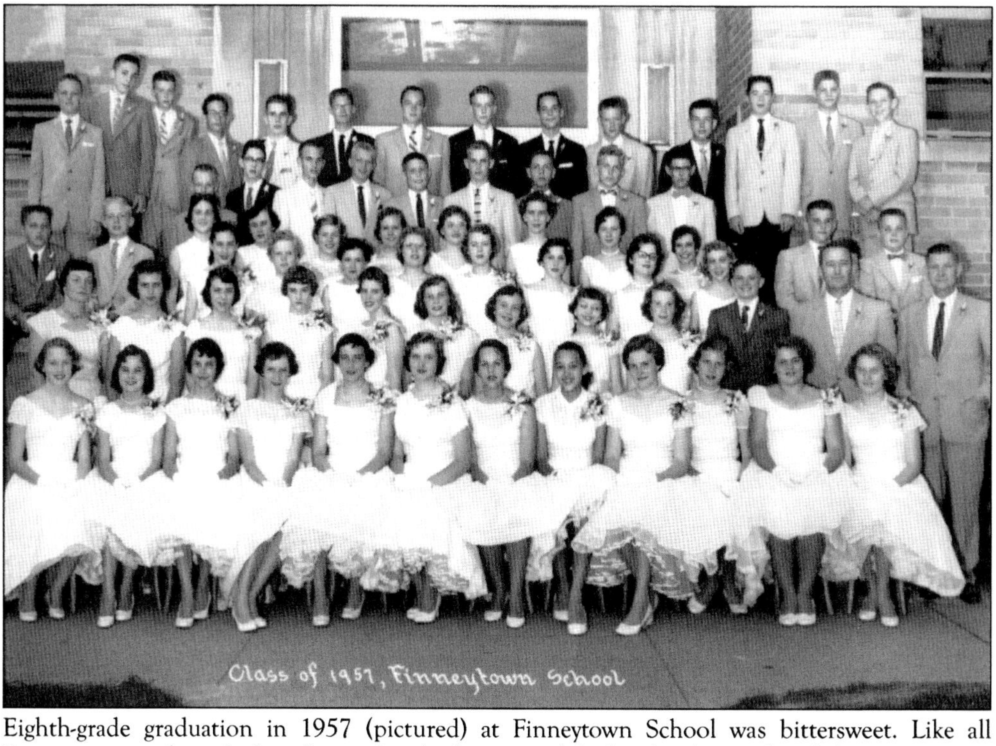

Class of 1957, Finneytown School

Eighth-grade graduation in 1957 (pictured) at Finneytown School was bittersweet. Like all Finneytown students before them, they had to attend high school outside of the community. However, soon after they graduated, construction began on the new Finneytown High School, which was built in stages. The 1957 eighth-grade class never attended Finneytown High School, while the succeeding class attended the new high school for all four years. (Gail Hafer Hauer.)

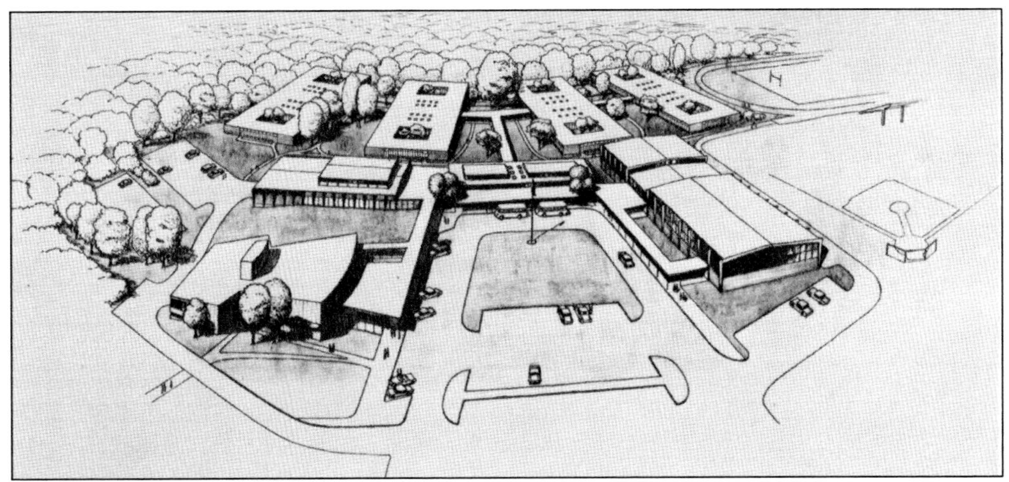

By 1955, Ohio law required public school districts to provide high school education or face a school merger. In 1956, Finneytown citizens voted to build and staff a new middle school and high school. The district hired Woodie Garber & Associates to design the new secondary campus. This ultra-modern look complemented the new homes of the Brentwood Village subdivision. (Holt & Reichard.)

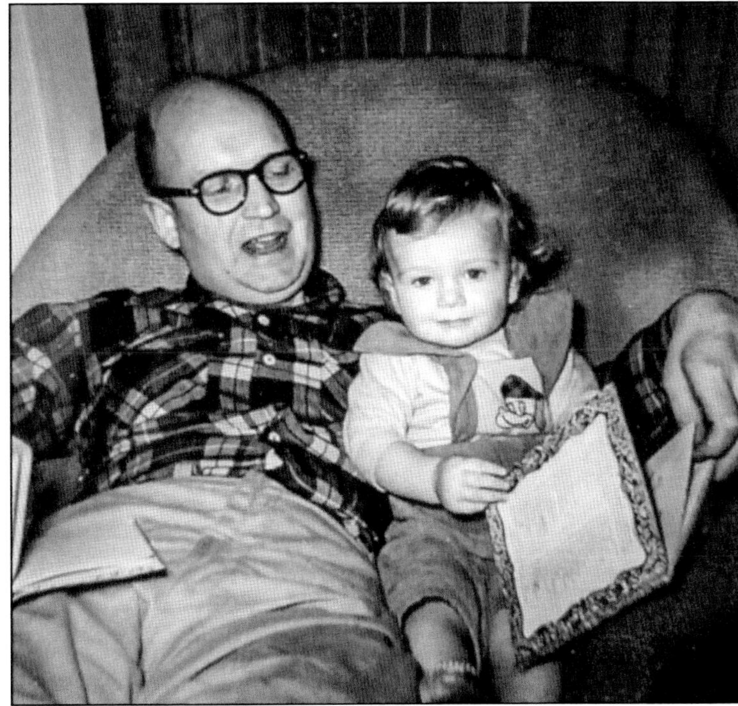

Woodie Garber of nearby Glendale, photographed in the 1950s with his daughter Elizabeth, was already recognized nationally for his modern architecture when his firm designed Finneytown's secondary campus. In 1953, *Time* and *Life* magazines featured his design of Cincinnati's downtown library. In 2018, Elizabeth Garber published *Implosion: Memoir of an Architect's Daughter*, which detailed Garber's architectural triumphs and personal tragedies. (Elizabeth Garber.)

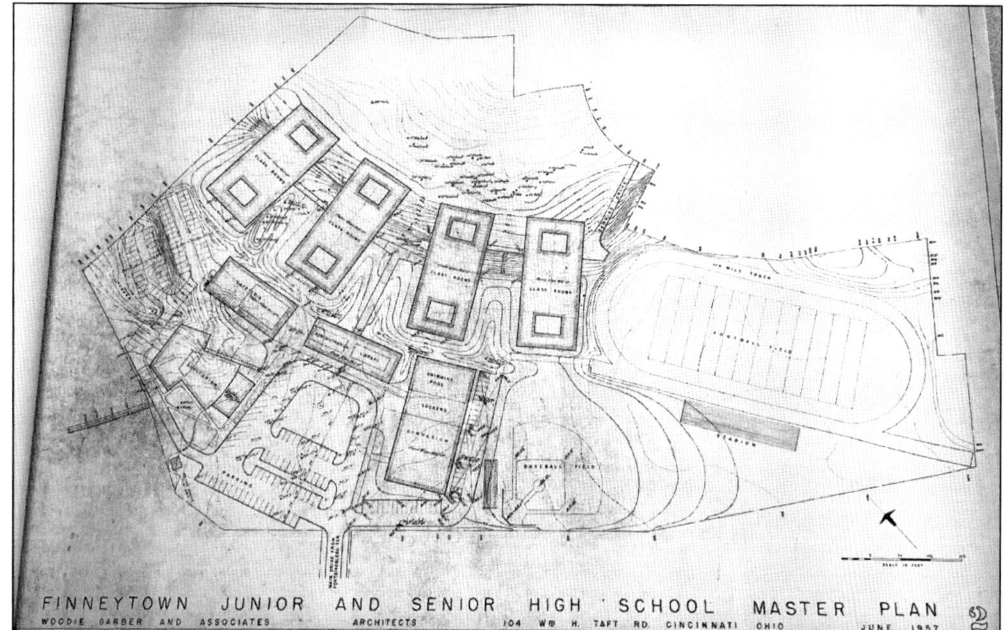

In the 1950s, Garber helped to pioneer "open plan" schools, which included Finneytown High School. The Norwood firm of Holt & Reichard constructed the campus to Garber's specifications (pictured). The proposed swimming pool was never built. Russell Champlin Jr., a Finneytown architect on Garber's team, was heavily involved in the design. (Holt & Reichard.)

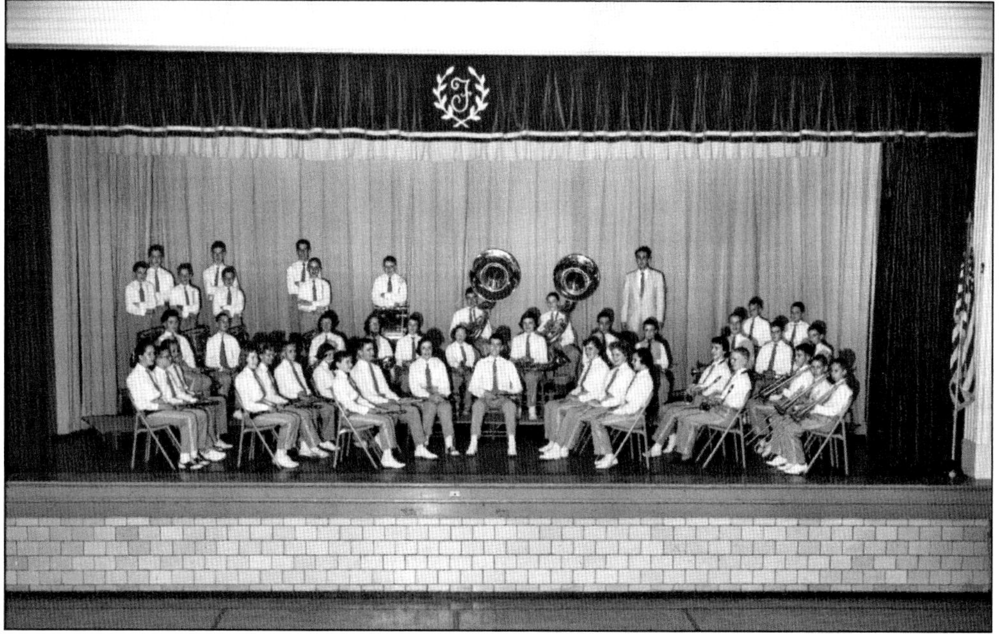

Finneytown's 1958 concert band was organized while the secondary campus was under construction. The district was transforming. Telford Whitaker became superintendent, Mac McNulty became high school athletic director, and a young William Swartzel was hired to create the music programs. Also, the Finneytown School on Winton Road would be renamed Whitaker Elementary School. (William Swartzel.)

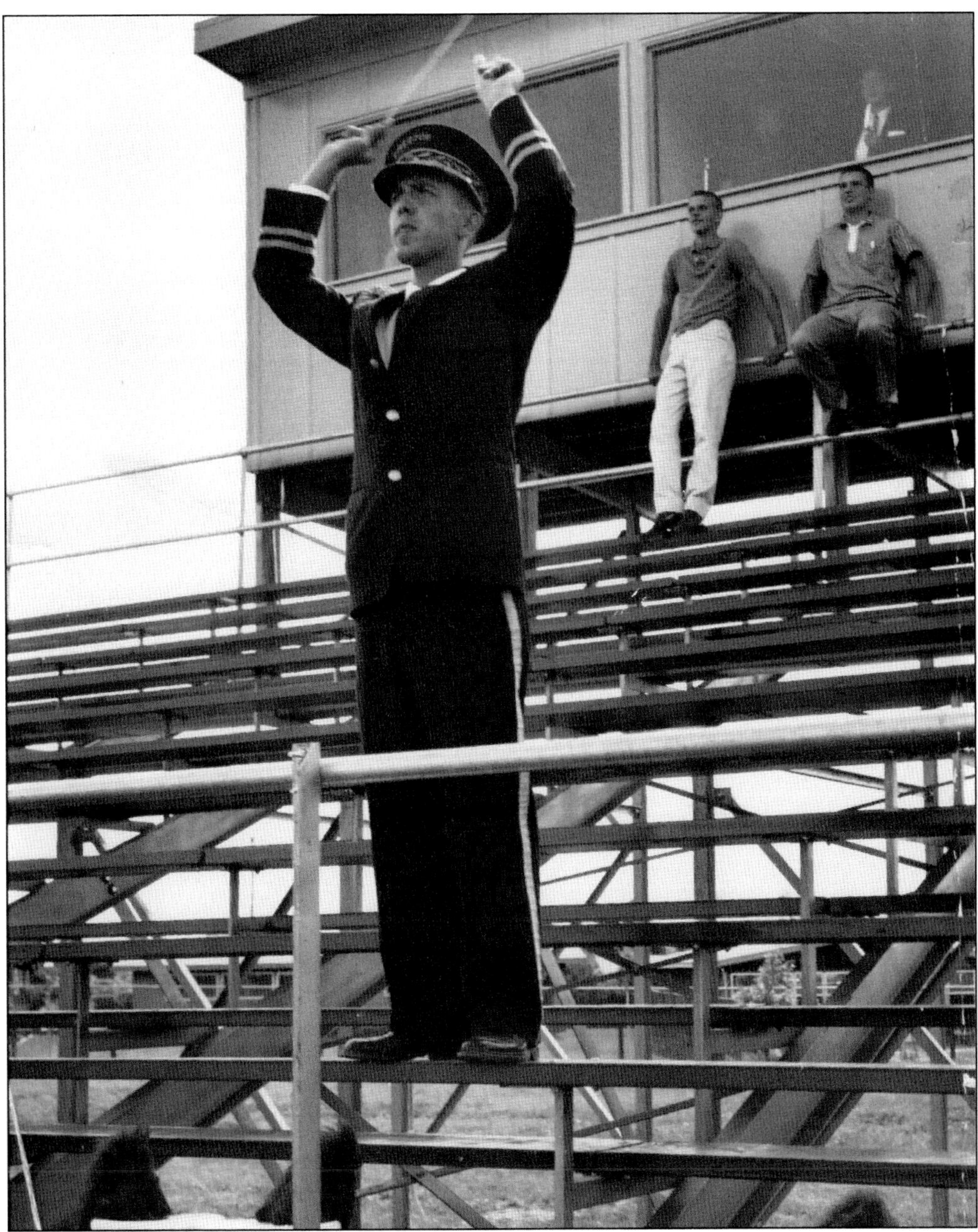

After graduating from the University of Cincinnati in 1956, William Swartzel took his first drive to Finneytown for a job interview. "I headed up old Winton Road, passed the Finneytown Inn, and there were cow pastures," he recalled. "I realized I was in God's country!" Even more attractive to him was the open position for music director at the fast-growing district with a new high school on the drawing board. In 1956–1957, he taught music programs up through the eighth grade. In 1958, with freshmen entering the new high school, he established the marching band, concert band, and choir. "It was exciting because everything we did was new at the time," he recalled. For several years, he was also music director at Faith Lutheran Church. His wife, Janet, often played piano for his various school and community ensembles. He retired from the school in 1986. Finneytown High School's performing arts center is named after him. (William Swartzel.)

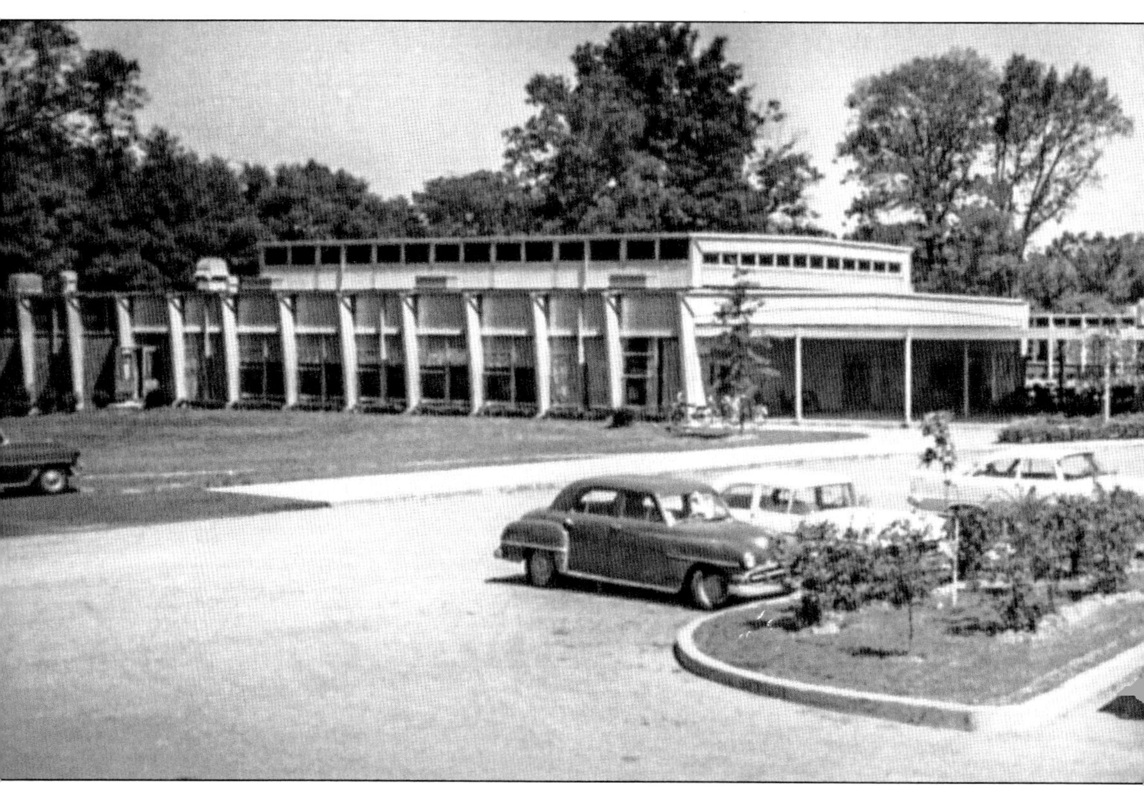

In his design proposal for the new secondary campus, architect Woodie Garber stated his desire to "create an open atmosphere rarely found in schools." However, the design was almost too modern for its own good. After construction had been underway for six months, the state building inspector in early 1958 challenged Garber's radical design. Work was suspended after the inspector refused to issue a building permit. Among his complaints, he objected to classroom walls made of glass. Carl Rubin, Hamilton County's assistant prosecutor, represented Finneytown in the dispute.

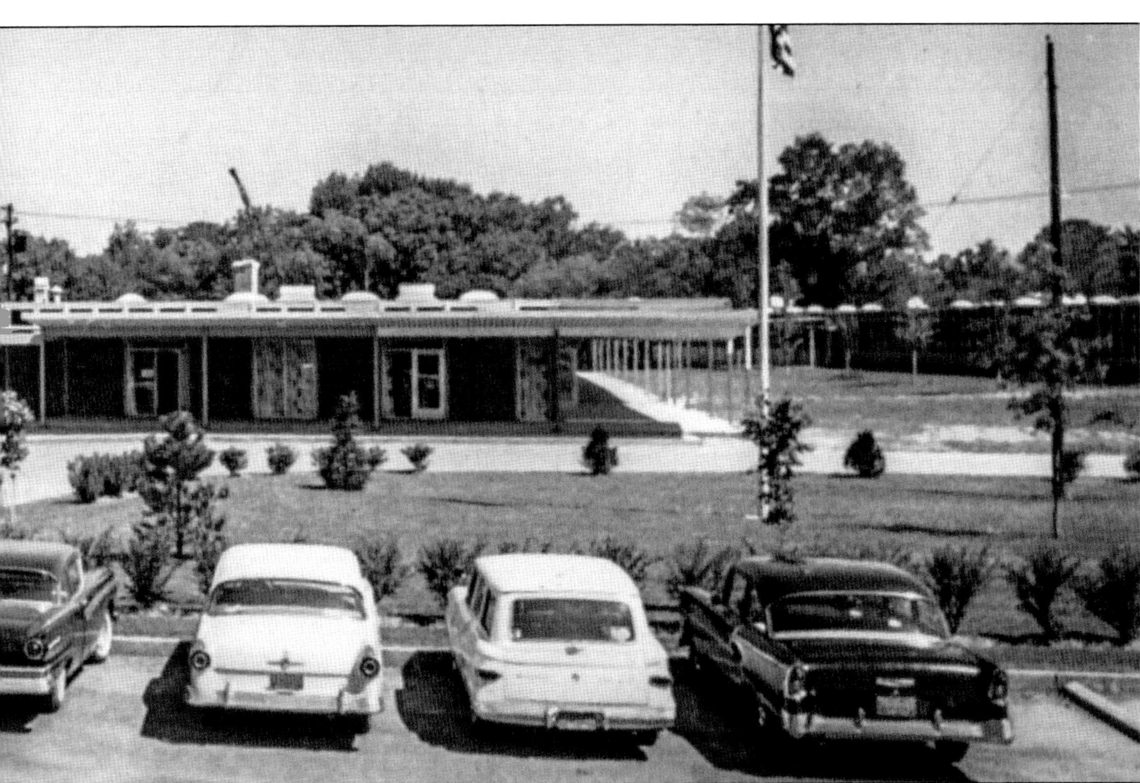

He called the state's argument "a bunch of gobbley-gook." Unable to establish violations of state building codes, the inspector finally relented and construction resumed. In the early 1960s, the design was featured in several architectural magazines. For almost 70 years, the school stood as a monument to 1950s mid-century modern architecture. While its design remained the same, this late 1950s photograph reflects the changing designs of American cars. (Steve Battistone.)

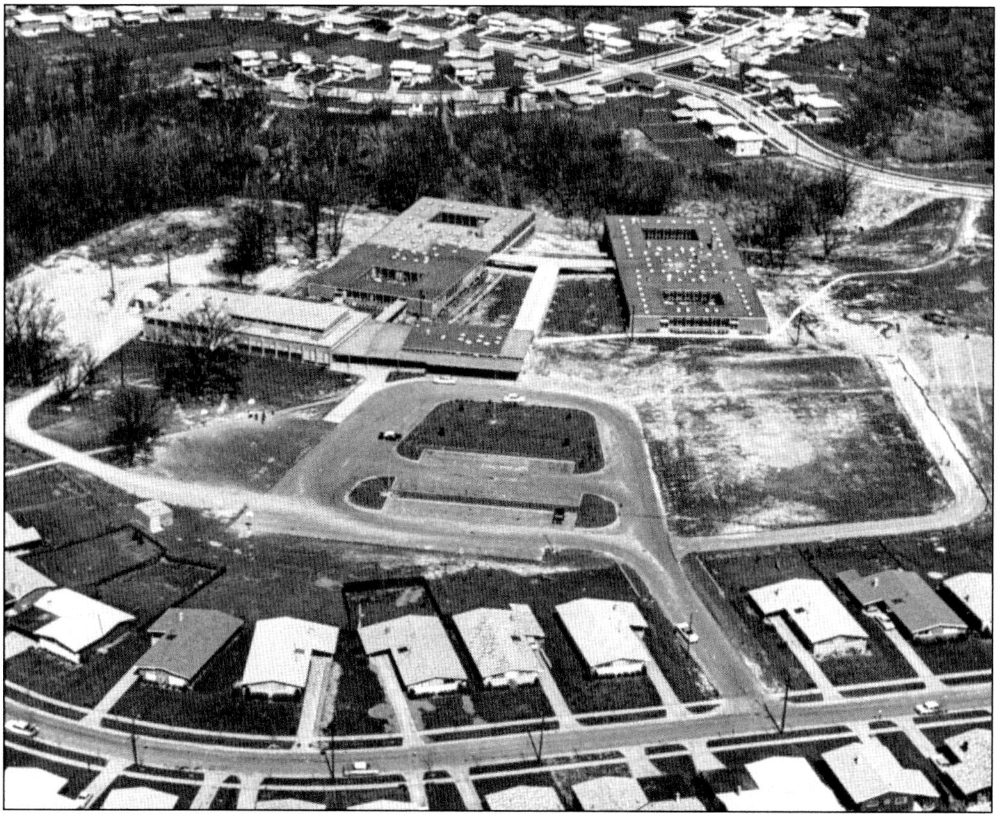

This aerial construction photograph from 1958 reveals Woodie Garber's vision of a school campus with a spacious feel. Covered walkways connect the buildings. The Finneytown middle school and high school buildings were constructed in stages beginning in late 1957 until the early 1960s. The district offered full kindergarten through four years of high school beginning in the fall of 1961. (Steve Battistone.)

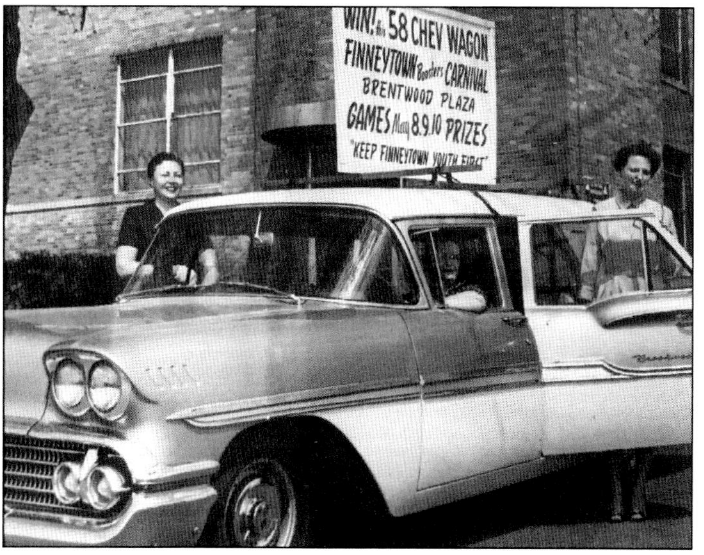

In 1958, members of the Finneytown School Boosters pose with a new Chevy wagon auctioned off at a fundraising event. Founded the year before by John Buckley and C.R. Grimm, Finneytown Boosters started with 13 members paying $3 annual membership dues. By 1958, the organization had grown to 700 and has remained strong ever since in supporting school activities. (Cincinnati Public Library.)

In the 1960s, glossy programs sold at Finneytown High School football games were packed with pages of advertisements from area businesses. Finneytown fielded its first high school football team in 1960. By 1969, they were undefeated league champions, led by coach Carl Seymour and by such standout players as Jeff Steel, Steve Immelt, Pat Leahy, John Howland, Steve Turner, and Keith Pedicord. (Jeff Steel.)

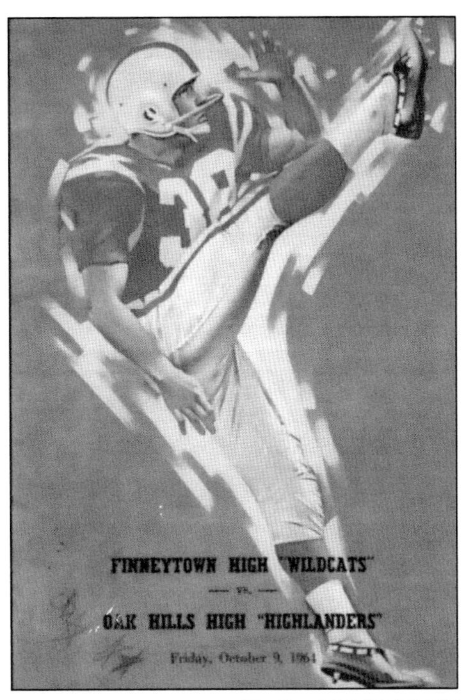

In 1959, the high school band marched in formation down Cottonwood Drive behind Brentwood Shopping Plaza. "People came to Finneytown for the diversity of activities available to students," Swartzel said. "Building up the marching band was a great experience because the school was growing fast and new students poured in." Strong music programs in the Finneytown district continue today. (William Swartzel.)

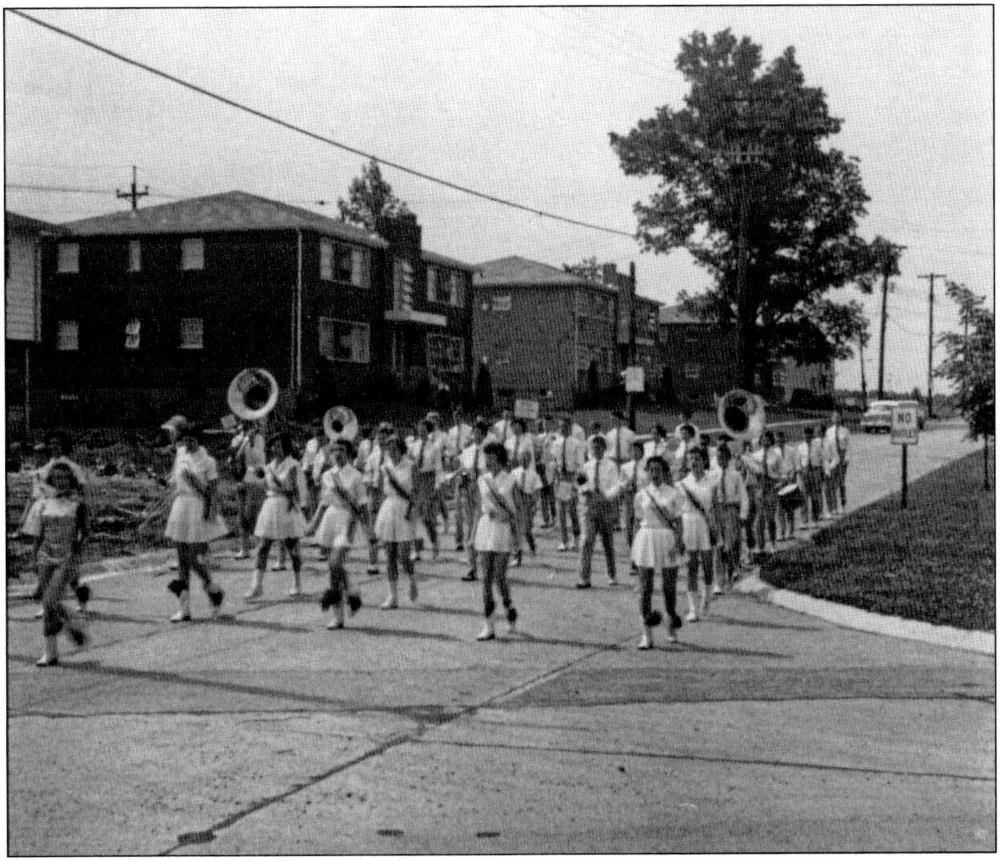

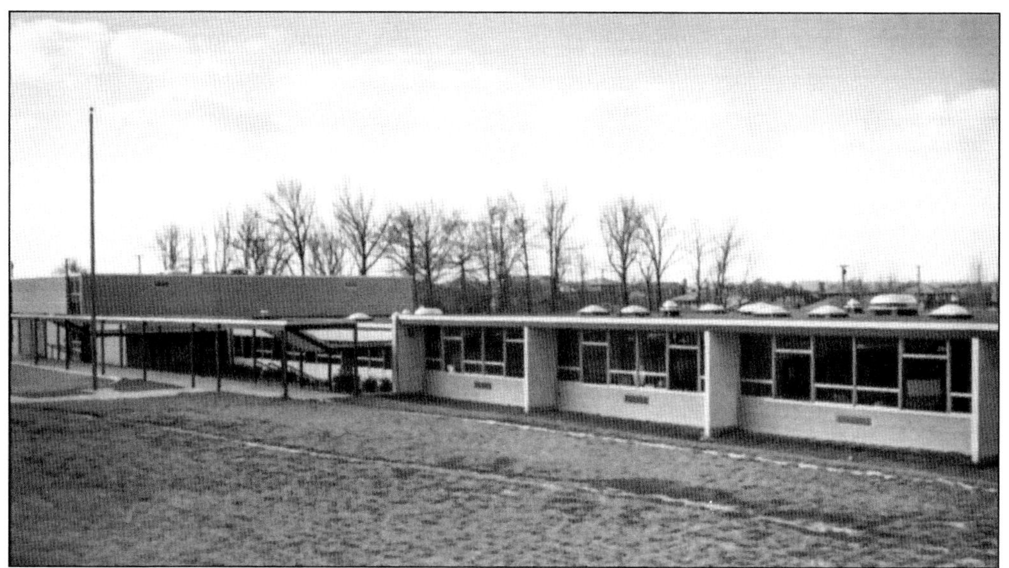

By 1960, burgeoning Finneytown needed more public schools. Behind Brentwood Shopping Plaza, Cottonwood Elementary School opened in 1962 for grades one through six. Designed by local architect Russell Champlin Jr., the building was in the modernist style sweeping the nation. The building was demolished in 2010 after plans were announced for a new elementary school. (Steve Battistone.)

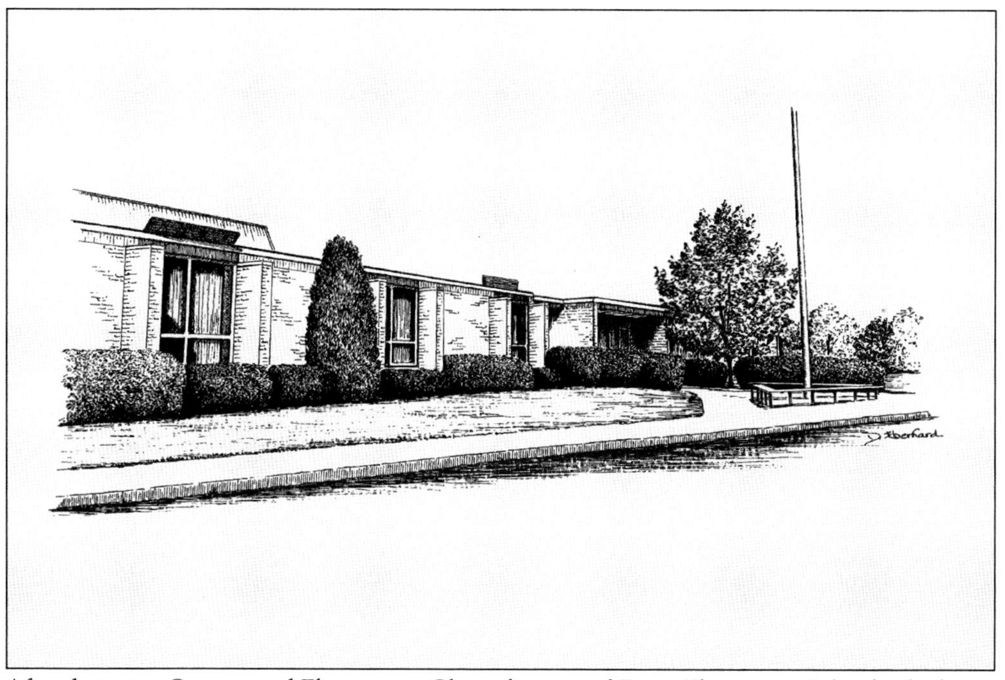

After designing Cottonwood Elementary, Champlin created Brent Elementary School, which was built on Winton Road across from the new high school. The school opened in 1964. Brent's open-style design was similar to Cottonwood and the secondary campus. Popular Cincinnati sketch artist Dee Eberhard produced this drawing in the 1980s. (Rick and Kimberly Payne.)

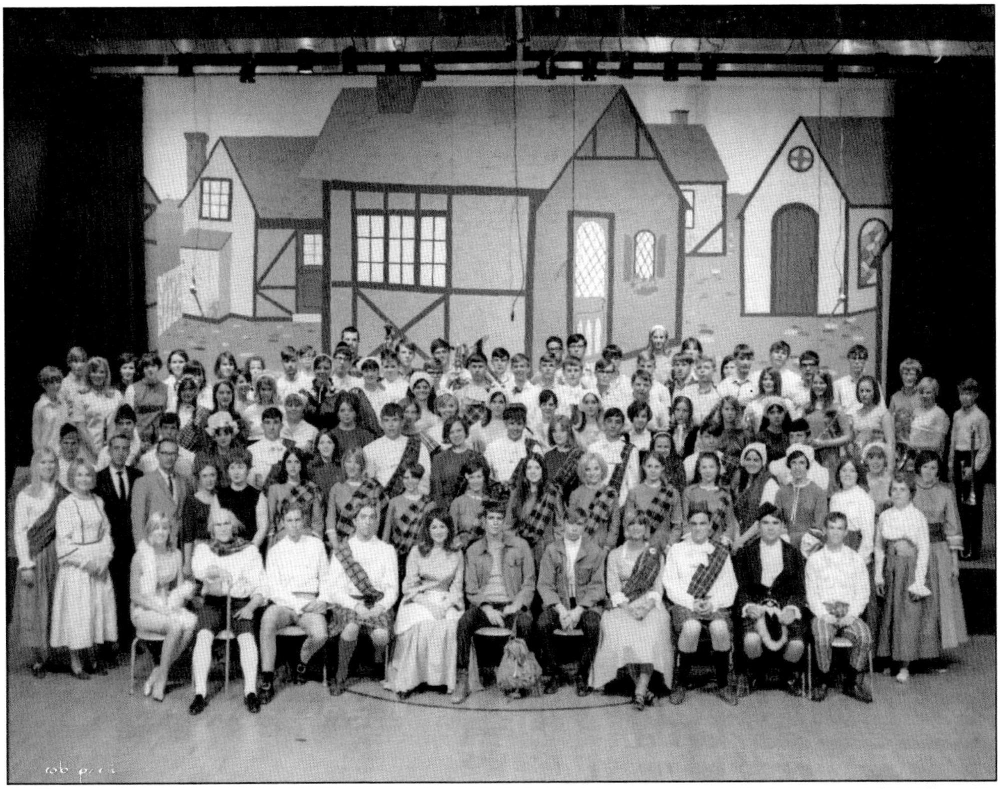

In 1968, Finneytown High School produced its first full-blown musical, The Red Mill. The musical was about two zany American vaudevillians penniless in a Dutch village. Music director William Swartzel worried the big production would make the high school's drama program equally penniless. "I worried we were in over our heads," he recalled. "But the community turnout was tremendous, and ticket sales covered our costs." (William Swartzel.)

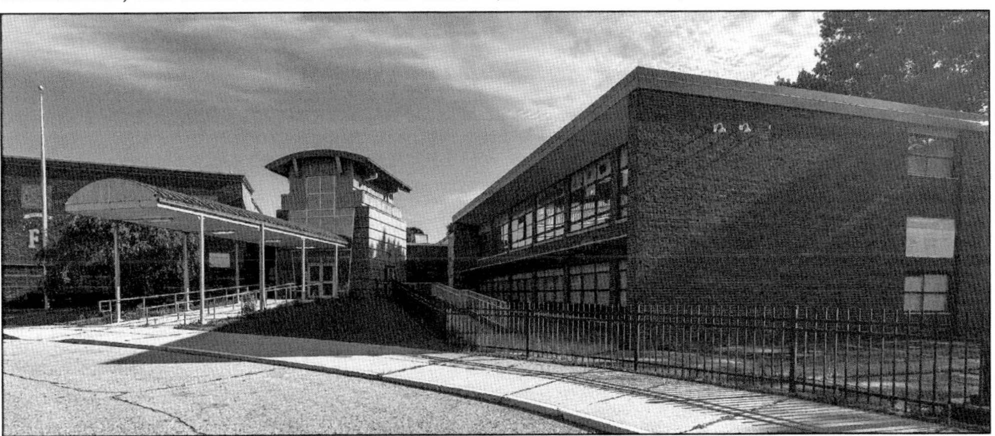

For many Finneytown people, Whitaker Elementary along Winton Road stood on sacred land. After all, on the same property, farmer William Cummings and his son in 1860 constructed Finneytown's first schoolhouse. A school operated continuously on the property until 2022. Whitaker Elementary (called Finneytown School until 1960) underwent several expansions following the construction of a brick school in 1915. Whitaker Elementary was demolished in 2024. (Mark Evans.)

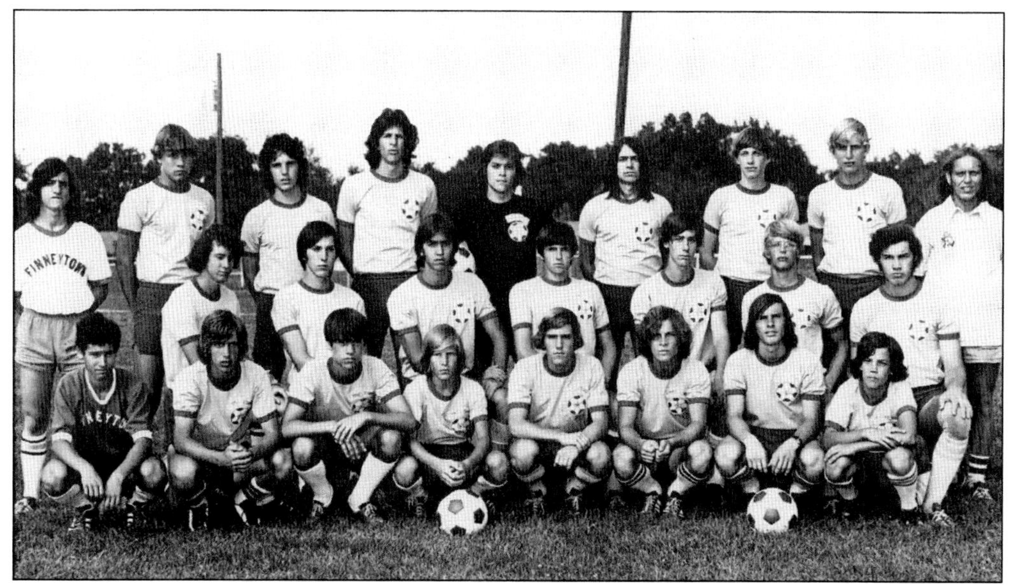

A 1960s youth soccer program in Finneytown spawned a high school sports dynasty. Finneytown's 1974 state soccer champions (pictured) grew out of the 1967 creation of Soccer Association for Youth (SAY). Now a national organization, the first SAY leagues were in Finneytown and Western Hills, and Finneytown's Tom Stevens was president. When these Finneytown soccer kids entered high school, it was lights out. (Bob Muro.)

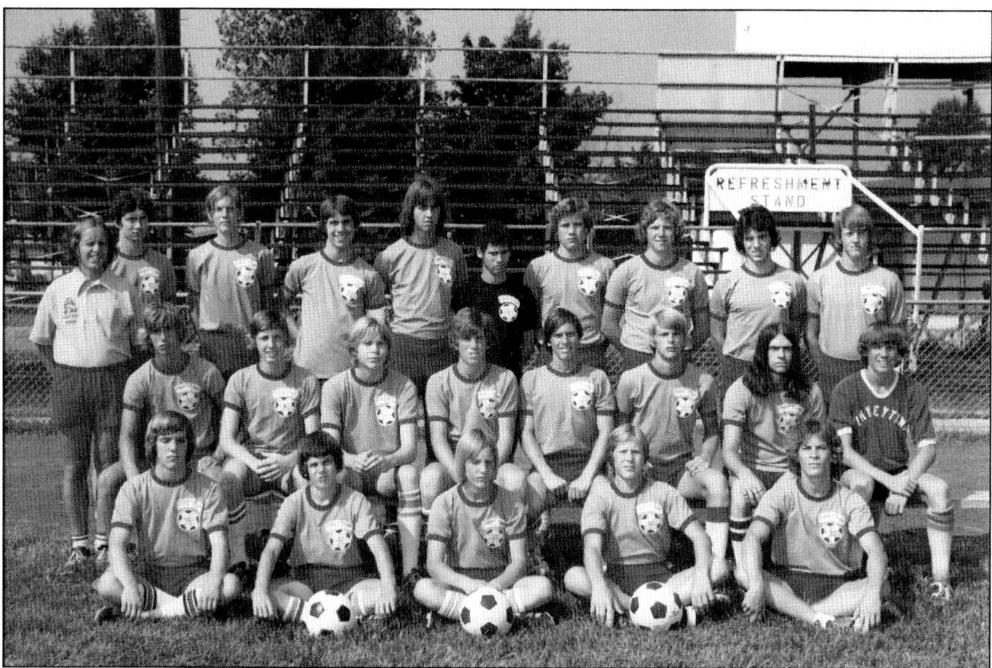

Finneytown's 1975 team, again coached by 27-year-old Bob Muro (far left), resembled the 1869–1870 Cincinnati Red Stockings by playing with the weight of a remarkable win streak on their backs. Finneytown's streak ended at 40 matches (spanning three years) in October 1975. However, after losing in the 1975 district finals, most of these players returned in 1976 to dominate the region and claim another state championship for Finneytown. (Bob Muro.)

Six

St. Xavier High School Bombers Arrive

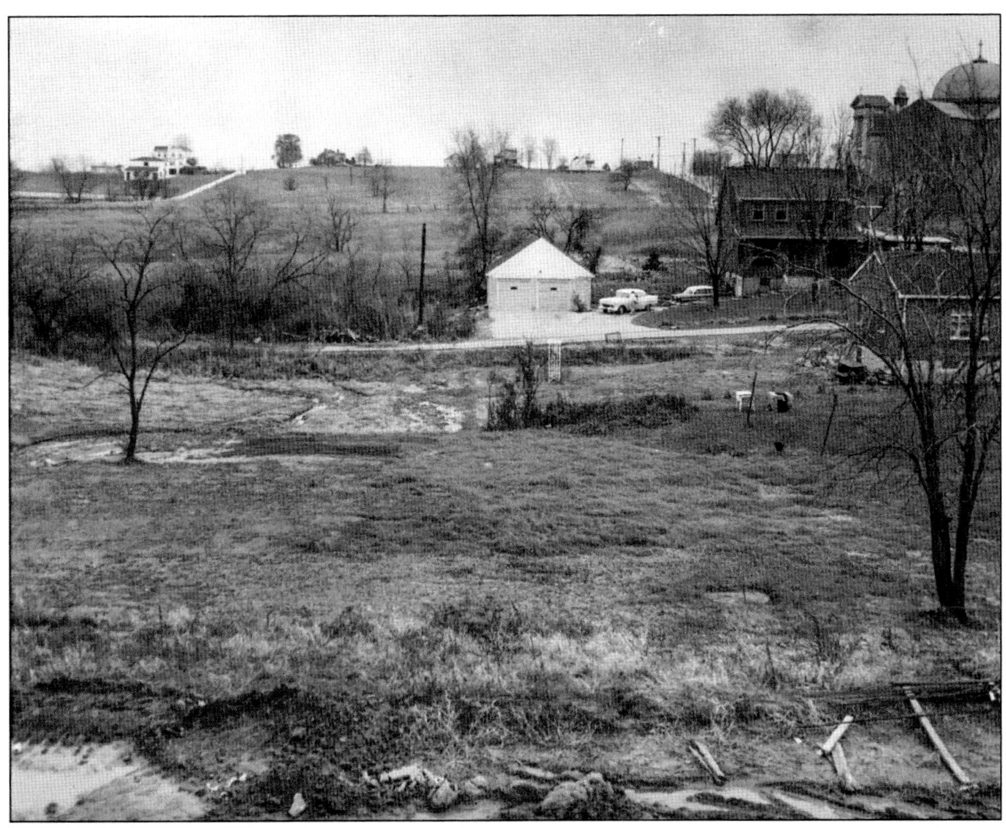

In May 1955, the Society of Jesus (Jesuits) from the Archdiocese of Cincinnati bought 61 acres along North Bend Road (top of photograph) and across the road from Girls Town (far right). St. Xavier High School, which the Jesuits had operated downtown since 1831, was out of space. Moving the all-male school to this new site was a significant event in Finneytown history. (St. Xavier High School.)

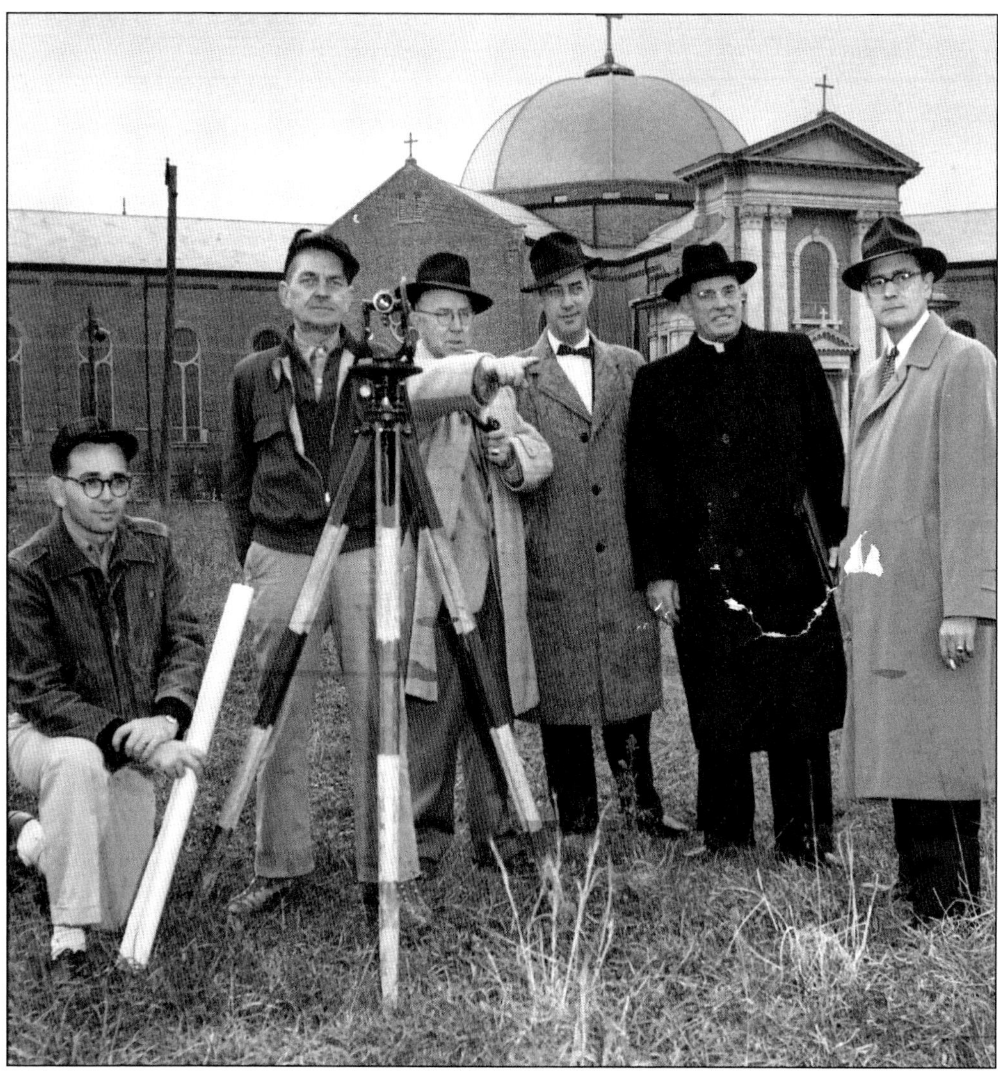

In 1955, the local media continued to speculate where the Jesuits would move St. Xavier High School, one of the region's oldest and most respected educational institutions. Because the school had been a downtown Cincinnati fixture for more than a century, interest ran high. Even though the Jesuits had invested $65,000 to purchase the acreage next to Girls Town in a remote section of Finneytown, the Archdiocese of Cincinnati also assessed other locations. In November 1955, news photographers captured the Jesuits surveying the Finneytown site. With Girls Town looming behind them, the surveying team consisted of, from left to right: surveyors Wilbur Test and David Murphy, St. Xavier High School supporters J.R. Kinsella and Fred Sullivan, St. Xavier High School president and rector Rev. John J. Benson, and St. Xavier High School supporter Phil Overbeek. The decision to relocate to Finneytown was still almost two years away. (St. Xavier High School.)

In 1957, after the Jesuits selected Finneytown, they hired local architect Albert Walters (left) to design a new school. He examined a model of his proposed campus design with Rev. Daniel Foley, a St. Xavier High School faculty member. For years, Walters was the main architect for Xavier University building projects, including his iconic design of Bellarmine Chapel. (St. Xavier High School.)

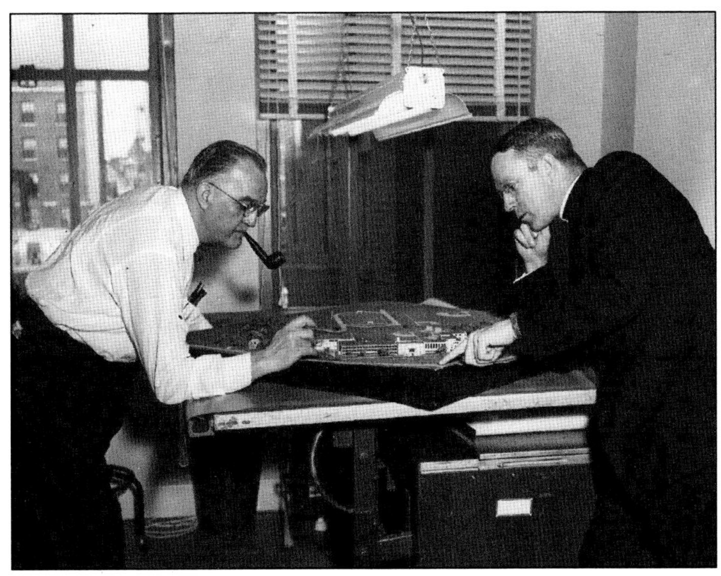

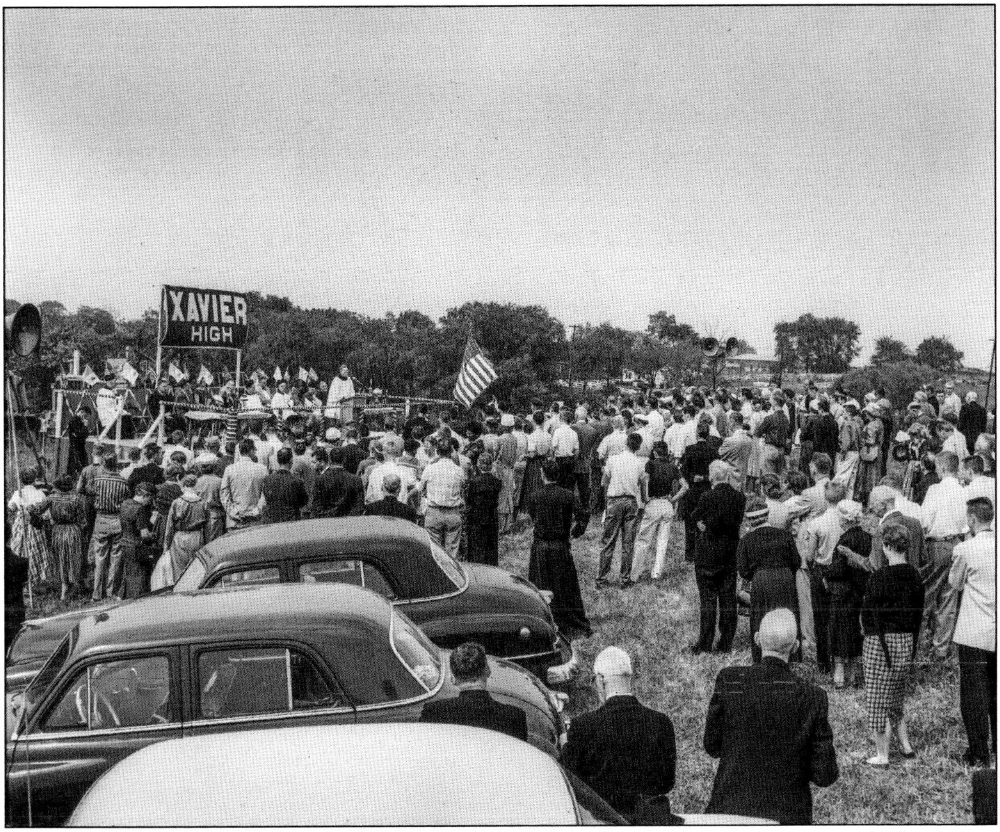

The St. Xavier High School ground breaking on May 25, 1958, attracted a large crowd. The Jesuits located the school in Finneytown because they believed the area would be a future population center in Greater Cincinnati. The school made Finneytown more attractive to the considerable number of Catholic families already living there, though St. Xavier High School drew students from the entire area. (St. Xavier High School.)

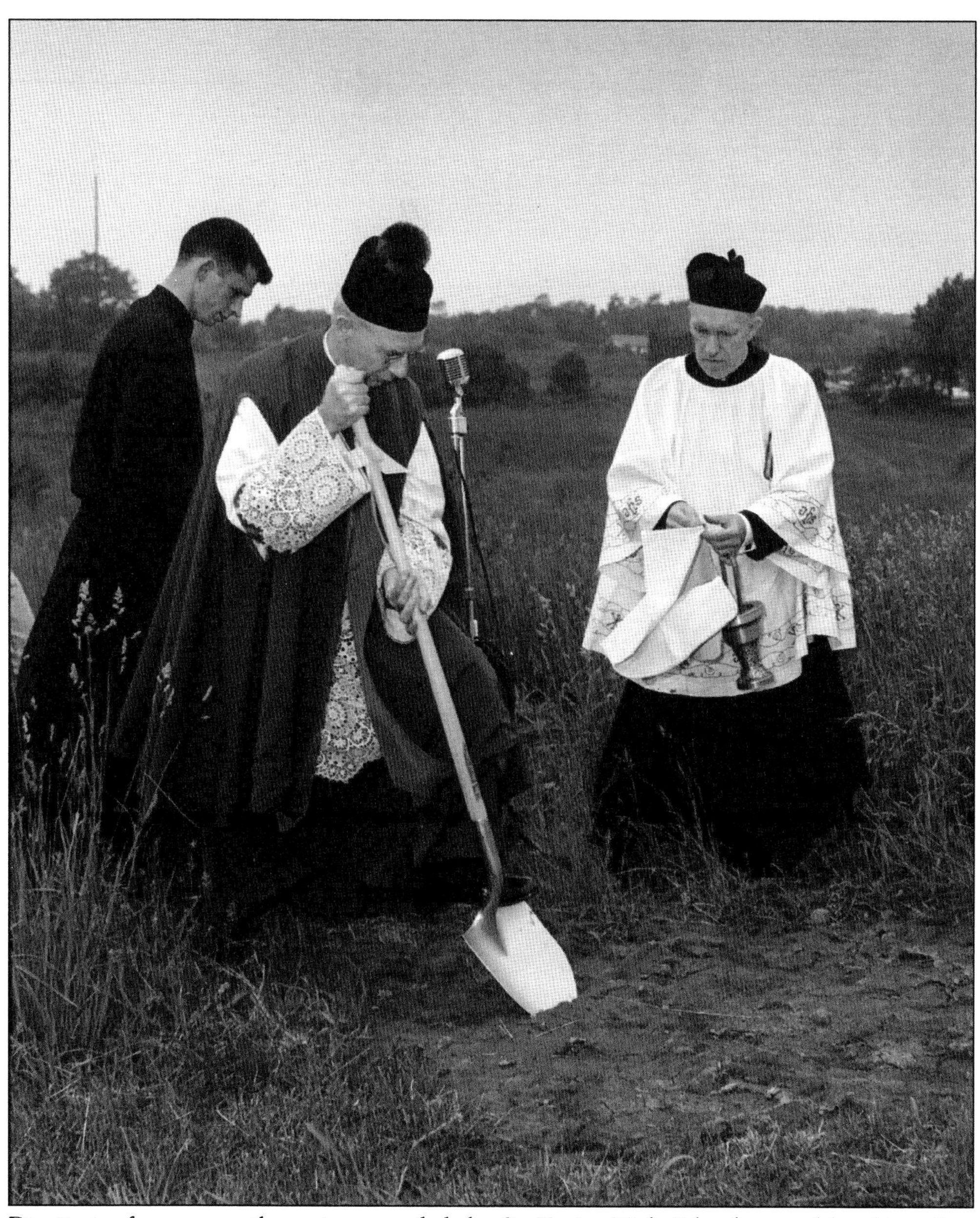

Dignitaries from across the region attended the St. Xavier High School ground breaking. Rev. Carl Ryan (center), Archdiocese superintendent of parochial schools, turned the first spade of dirt during a ceremony in an open field soon transformed into a solid learning facility for young men. St. Xavier High School faculty members Rev. James Singer (left) and Rev. L.A. Majerowski (right) assisted. St. Xavier High School was one of three new Catholic high schools constructed in the late 1950s in the Archdiocese of Cincinnati. Reverend Majerowski was a beloved leader at St. Xavier High School, where he had taught Latin and religion since the mid-1930s. For years, he dressed as Santa Claus during Christmas for the school's local missions that served children. In the 1950s, he oversaw St. Xavier High School's global missions with a focus on Japan. As the Catholic Church grew in postwar Japan, he attracted local attention to the Jesuit's financial needs in Japan and hosted fundraisers. (St. Xavier High School.)

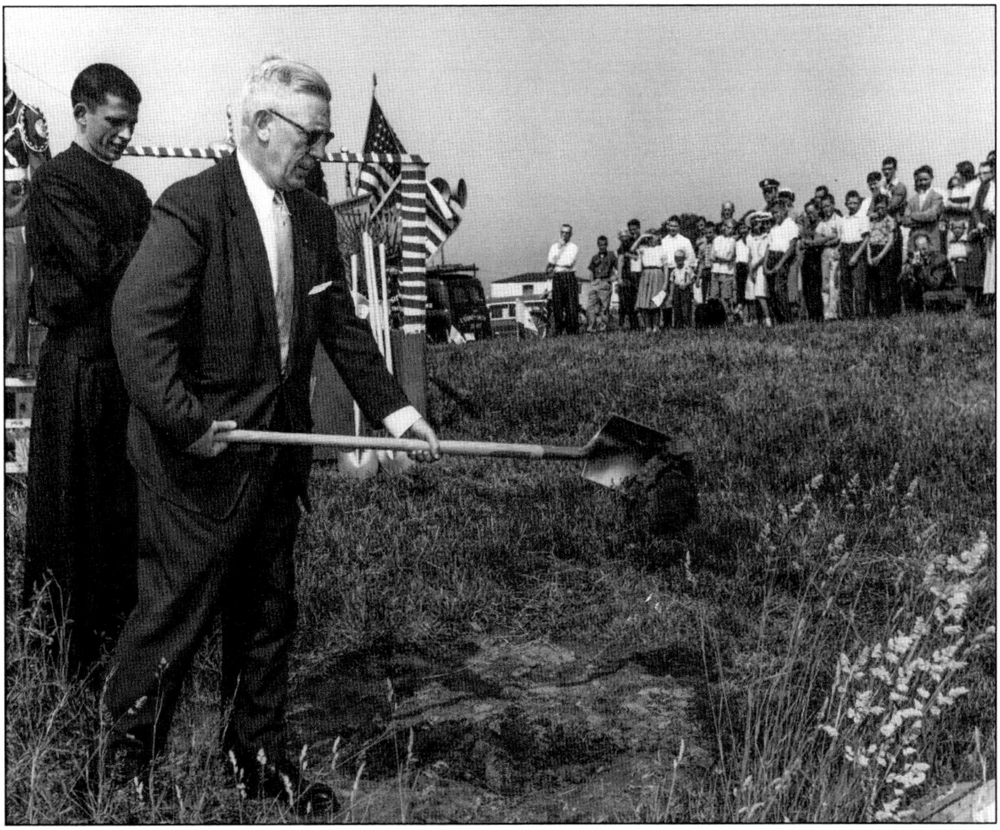

Harry Gilligan, chairman of the Archdiocese's Building Fund, tosses dirt at the ground breaking. A longtime funeral director and St. Xavier High School supporter, Gilligan was active in politics—a family tradition. His son John Gilligan (a 1939 St. Xavier High School graduate) served as Ohio governor from 1971 to 1975. Harry's granddaughter, Kathleen Sebelius, was the Kansas governor from 2003 to 2009. (St. Xavier High School.)

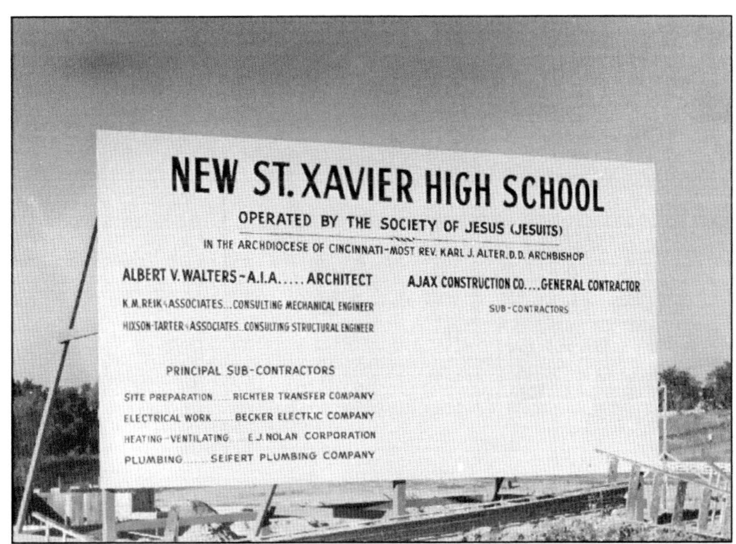

In 1958, the Jesuits erected a sign at the St. Xavier High School construction site. At the time, the newspapers described how supporters lightheartedly referred to the new school as "the Finneytown Hilton." The Jesuits moved fast. By mid-year, they had awarded more than $2.4 million in construction contracts for the new school. (St. Xavier High School.)

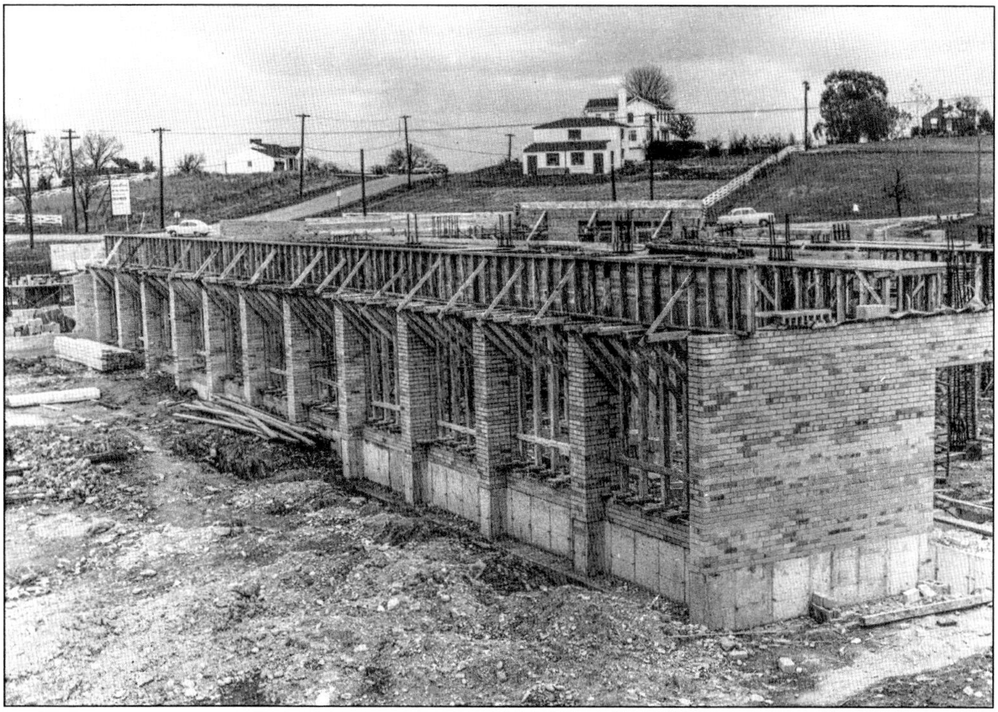

The photograph above from 1958 captures the construction of the school's faculty building. In the background, North Bend Road and View Place connect at the southeast corner of the school campus in a rural setting different from today. The photograph below from 1959 shows the progress made in one year. The image was taken from the roof of the convent house at Girls Town across North Bend Road. Architect Walters designed the campus to accommodate 1,200 students, which reflected the upsurge in the birthrate, particularly among Catholics, in the post–World War II era. Rev. John Benson, St. Xavier High School president and rector, oversaw the school campus construction. (Both, St. Xavier High School.)

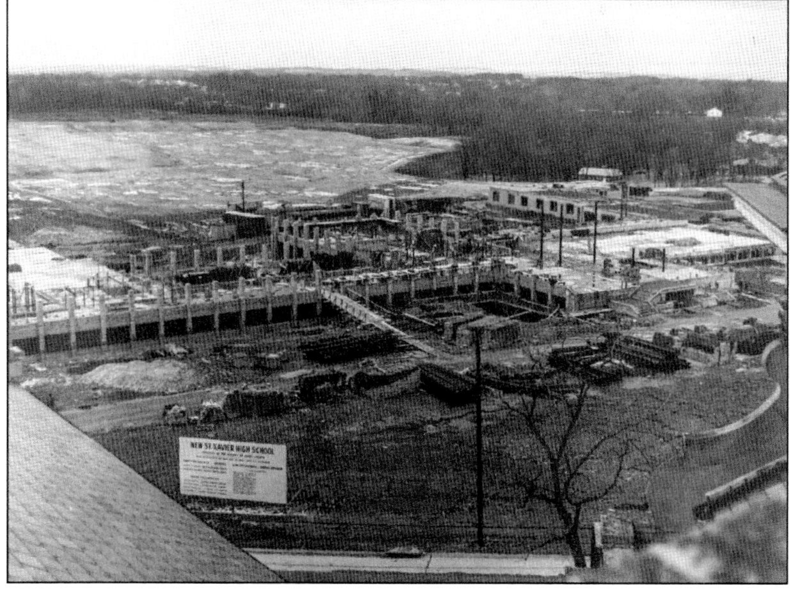

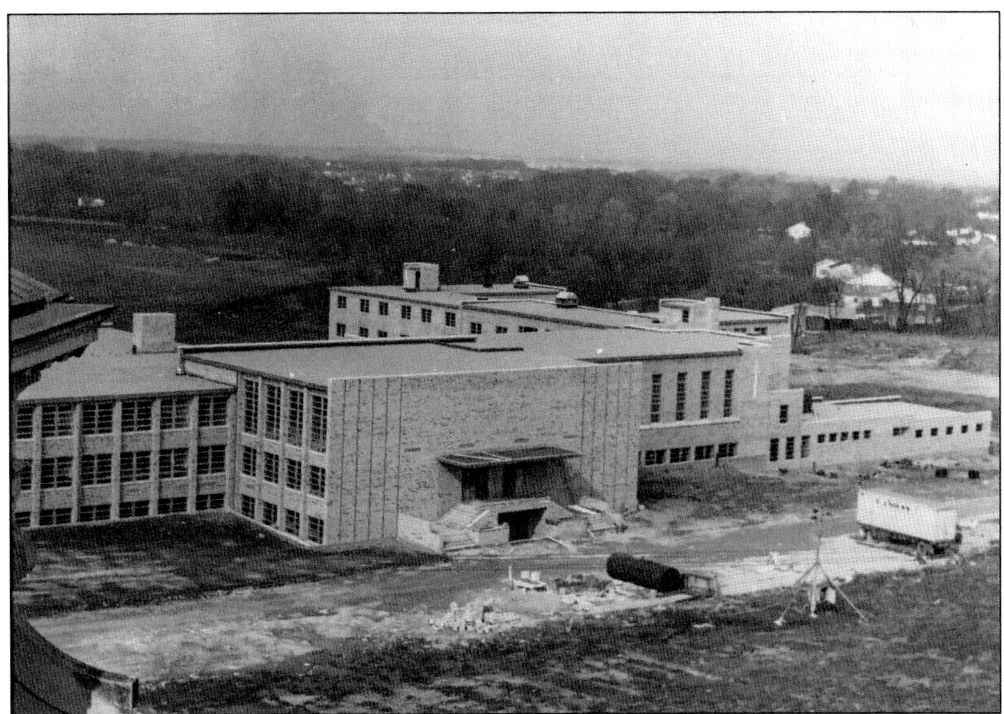

What a difference a year made. The photograph above from 1959 is the school's distinct front entrance, and the photograph below from mid-1960 highlights the near-complete, brick campus facing eastward. In designing the high school, architect Albert Walters said he pursued "a contemporary design and function" while providing "a distinct personality." The local architect, who died in 1993, left a lasting mark on Catholic-affiliated buildings in Cincinnati. In addition to the St. Xavier High School campus and Xavier University buildings, Walters developed St. Francis-St. George Hospital in Western Hills. Ultimately, the Jesuits would invest almost $4 million to complete the new school. (Both, St. Xavier High School.)

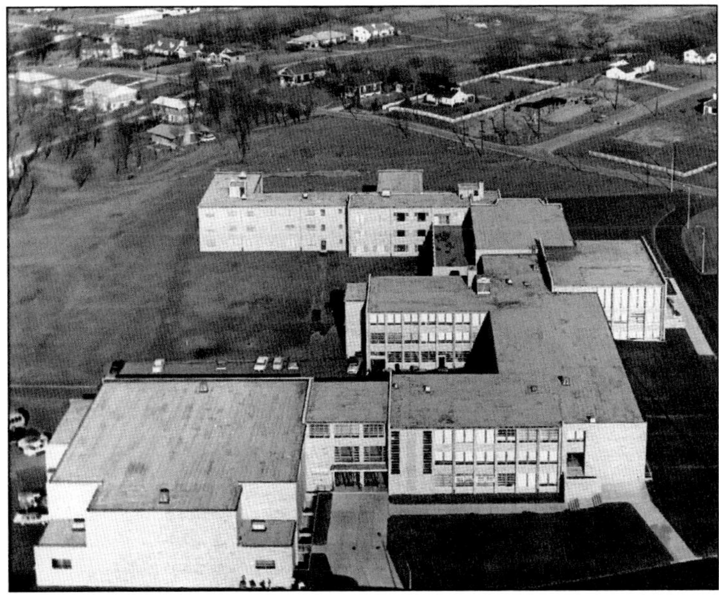

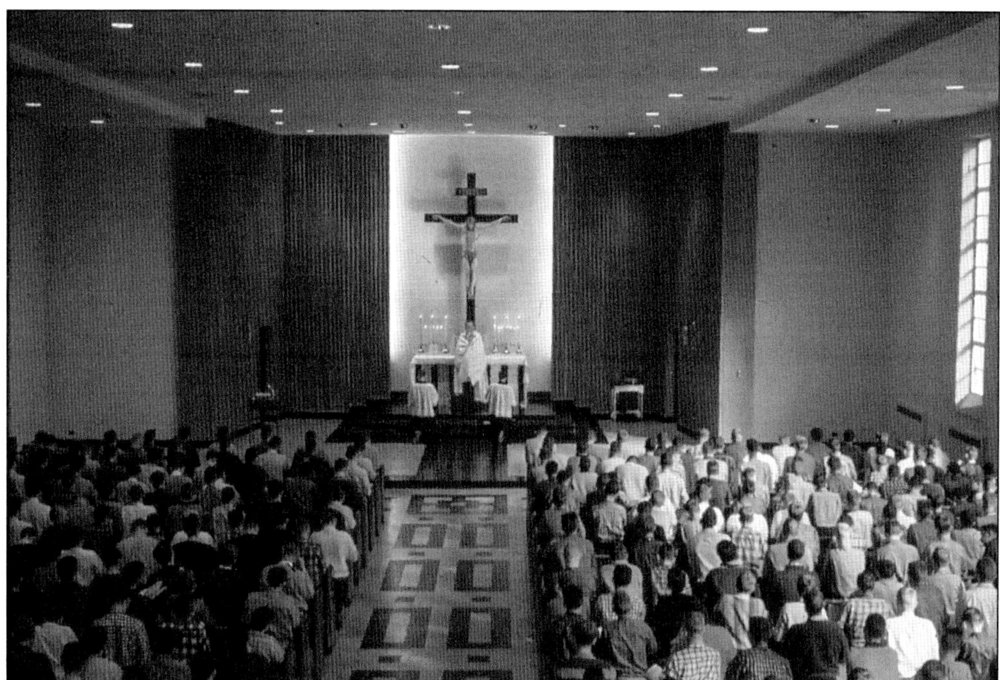

A distinct feature of the new campus was a modern chapel capable of serving hundreds of students. The images above and below capture a mass from December 1960, three months after the school opened. Over the next four decades, the chapel held countless masses and special liturgical events. In 1998–1999, the St. Xavier High School campus underwent a major expansion, which included a new chapel, technology laboratories, and sports facilities. Stained-glass works from the original chapel, including a rendering of Francis Xavier from the Girls Town chapel across the street, were transferred to the new chapel, called the Chapel of the Holy Companions of St. Ignatius Loyola. (Both, St. Xavier High School.)

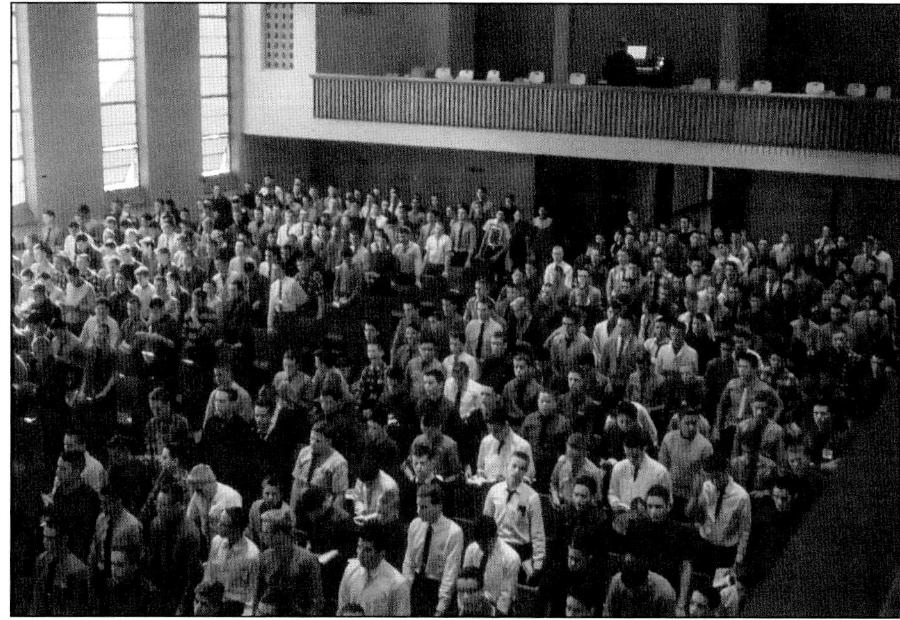

Students in this early 1961 photograph gather on the front steps of the new school. St. Xavier High School opened the previous September with 1,100 students. The completed campus included 33 classrooms. For several months, the Jesuits considered possible uses for the vacated St. Xavier High School campus downtown but ultimately tore it down. (St. Xavier High School.)

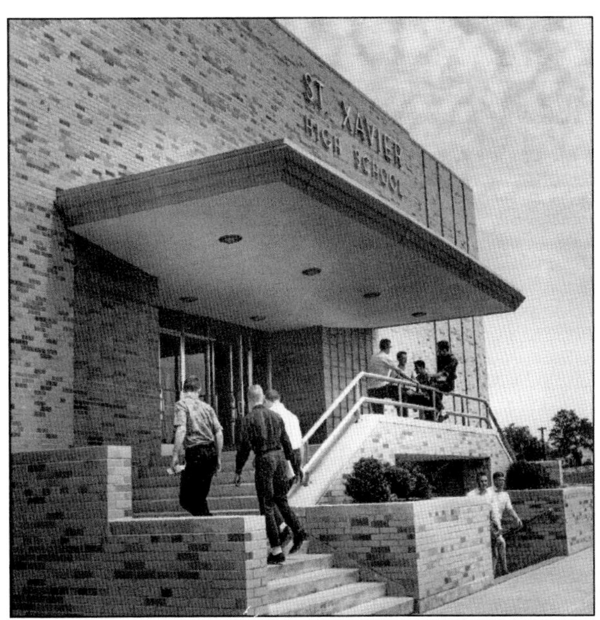

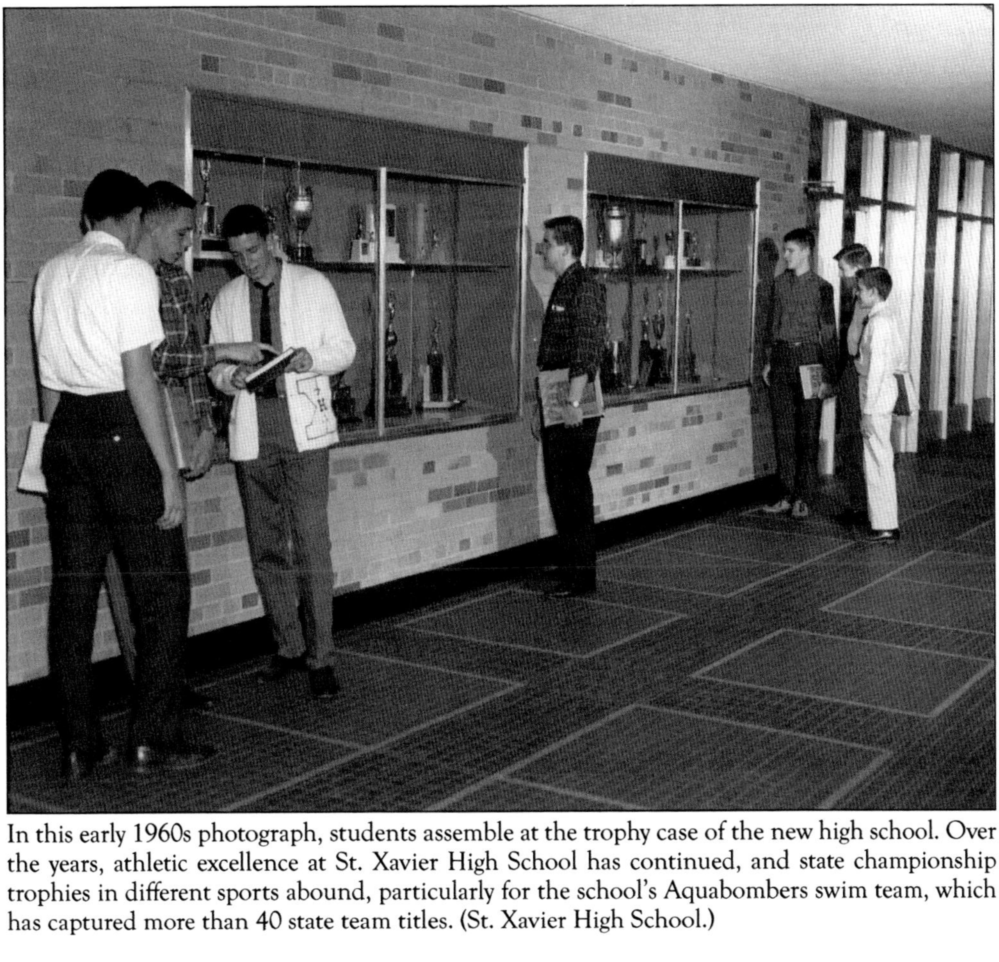

In this early 1960s photograph, students assemble at the trophy case of the new high school. Over the years, athletic excellence at St. Xavier High School has continued, and state championship trophies in different sports abound, particularly for the school's Aquabombers swim team, which has captured more than 40 state team titles. (St. Xavier High School.)

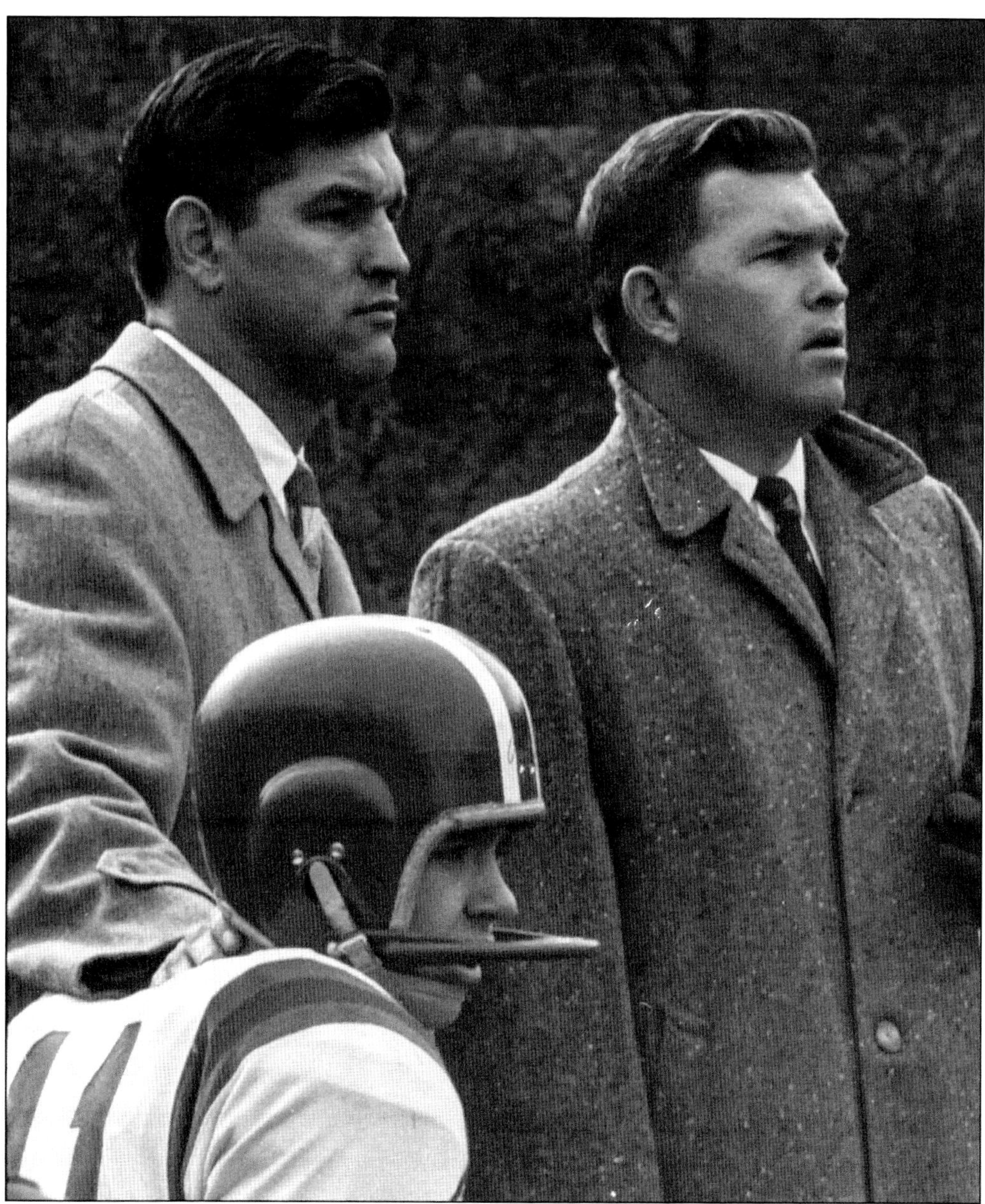

Few high schools can claim a coaching duo like Thomas Ballaban (left) and Richard Berning (right). Ballaban was St. Xavier High School's head football coach from 1953 to 1997, compiling 142 wins and nine Greater Cincinnati League Championships. He was awarded Cincinnati Football Coach of the Year in 1957, 1958, and 1970. Eight years after St. Xavier High School moved to Finneytown, Ballaban led the Bombers to its first undefeated season. In 1955, he encouraged the school to hire Berning as head basketball coach. During his 1955 to 1994 tenure, Berning's career 568 wins made him the basketball coach with the most victories in Cincinnati high school history. His teams won numerous titles and reached the state finals in 1965. For several seasons, Berning also was Ballaban's assistant football coach. The local sports world was stunned when Berning died at age 65 in 1995, one year after his final season. Ballaban died in 2014. Today, the Bombers play football on Ballaban Field and basketball in Berning Gymnasium. (St. Xavier High School.)

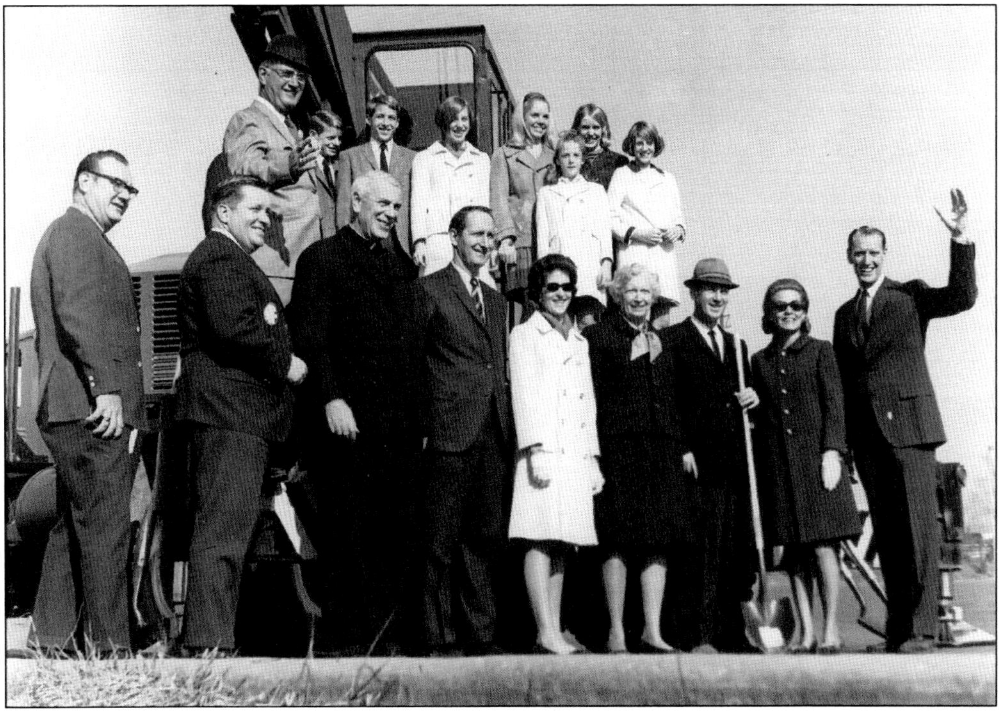

In this photograph from March 1969, St. Xavier High School supporters and their families celebrate the groundbreaking for Keating Natatorium at the school campus. Attorney Charles Keating Jr. (waving at far right) and brother William Keating (fourth from left) financed the facility as a memorial to their father, Charles Keating Sr. The natatorium became home to both the storied Aquabombers swim team and the Cincinnati Marlins. (St. Xavier High School.)

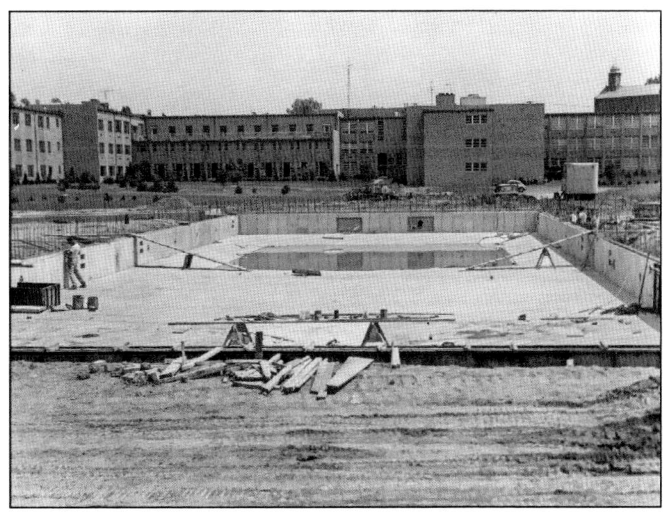

While constructed in 1969, Keating Natatorium was touted as Ohio's most modern indoor swimming pool. At 50 meters in length, the natatorium was part of Charles Keating Jr.'s vision for Cincinnati to become a national swimming center. A longtime Finneytown resident, Keating was an NCAA national swimming champion in 1946 at the University of Cincinnati. Several of his children were great swimmers. (St. Xavier High School.)

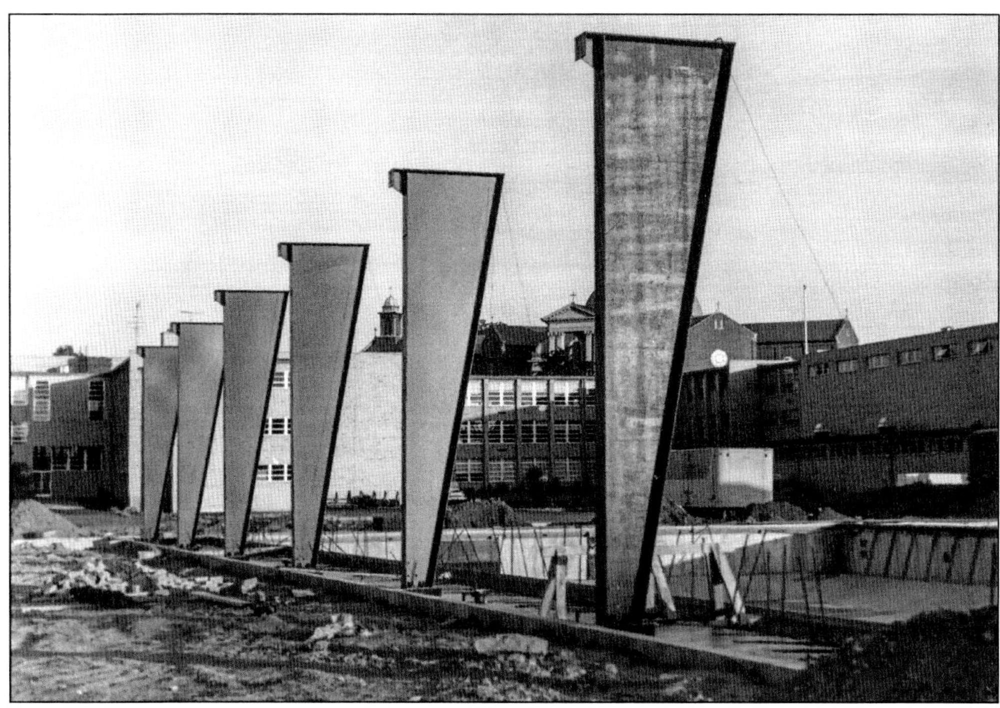

No time was wasted in getting the Keating Natatorium into operation. Before it was completed, St. Xavier High School and Cincinnati Marlins swimmers were in the water. As president of the Pepsi-sponsored local Marlins club, Charles Keating Jr. secured a huge prize: the 1970 AAU (Amateur Athletic Union) Senior Men's and Women's Swimming Championships at Keating Natatorium. In April 1970, Olympic champions Debbie Meyer, Gary Hall (future husband to Keating's daughter Mary), and Mark Spitz arrived in Finneytown to compete in the AAU meet. Spitz promptly hurried back to Indiana University for a chemistry test. Also that year, the St. Xavier High School Aquabombers won the state championship. Numerous Olympic champions have graced the Keating pool, including St. Xavier High School graduate Joe Hudepohl, who won gold medals in relay events at the 1992 and 1996 Olympics. (Both, St. Xavier High School.)

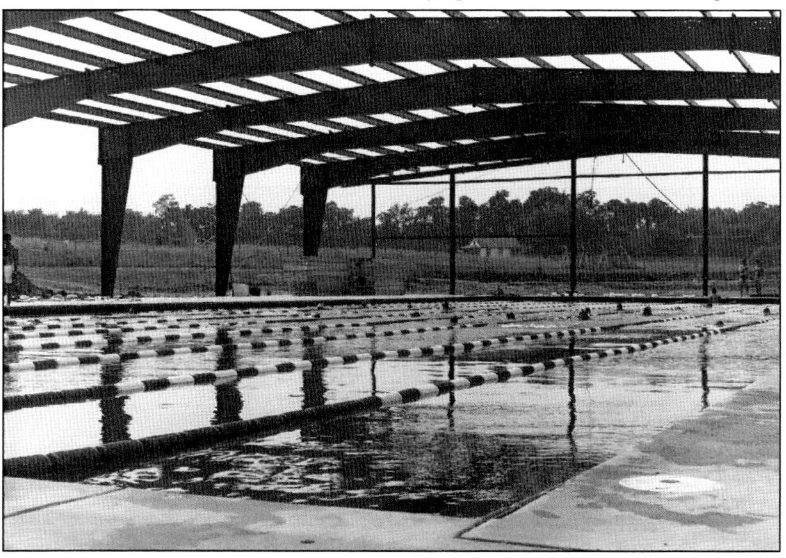

Seven

A Few Good Men

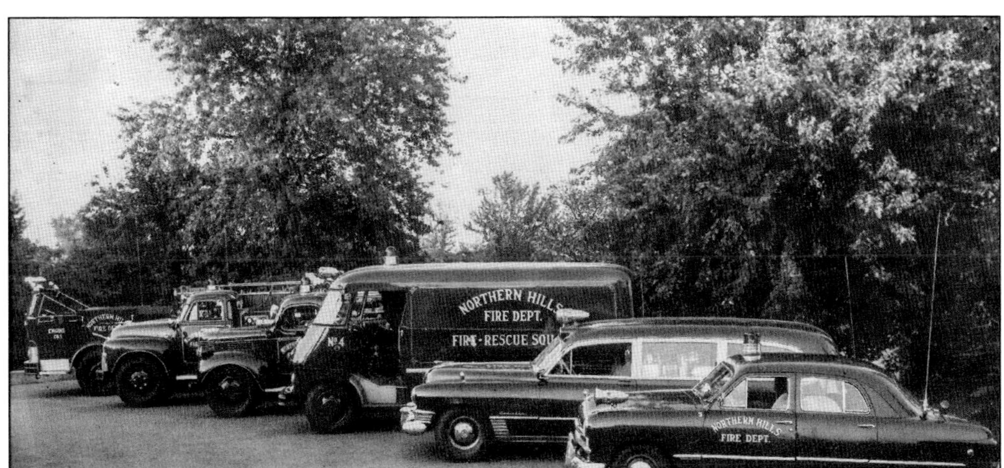

No organization better exemplified the civic spirit of mid-century Finneytown than the Northern Hills Volunteer Fire Department. It was created during World War II with one fire truck "pumper" and a handful of volunteers. By the late 1950s, when this image was captured, the department's 15 volunteers operated six vehicles and a fire station on Winton Road. (Springfield Township Fire Department [STFD].)

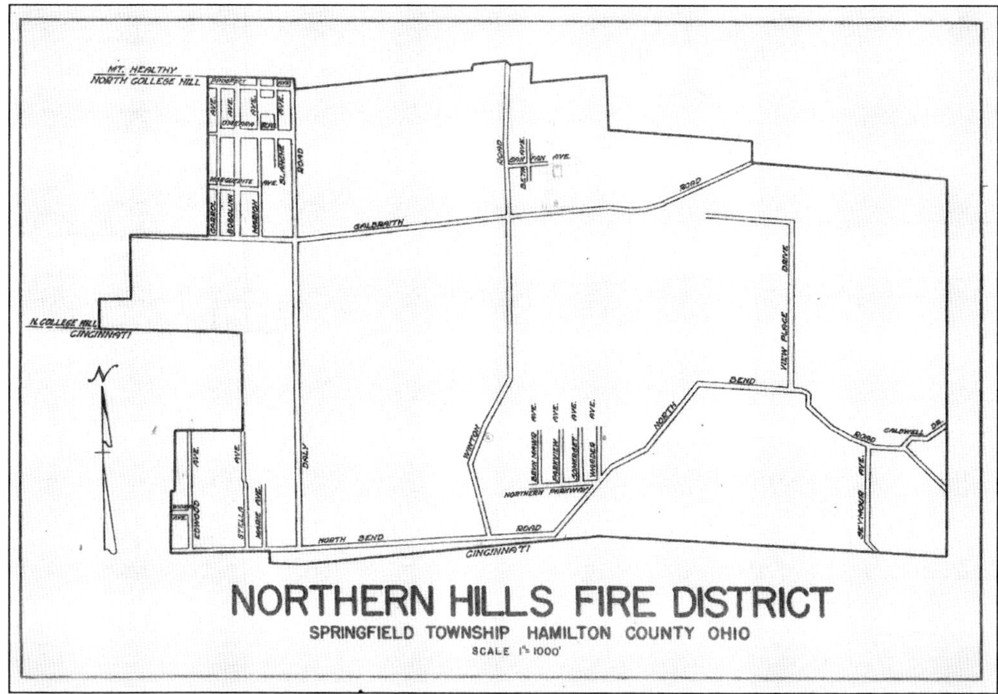

In 1944, Springfield Township Trustees created Northern Hills Fire District (pictured), which encompassed Finneytown and neighboring areas. That same year, the community passed a tax levy to finance a pumper for the group of men comprising the department. Several Finneytown civic leaders, including Telford Whitaker, William Kuhlmann, and L.C. Gartner, led a campaign committee supporting the levy. (STFD.)

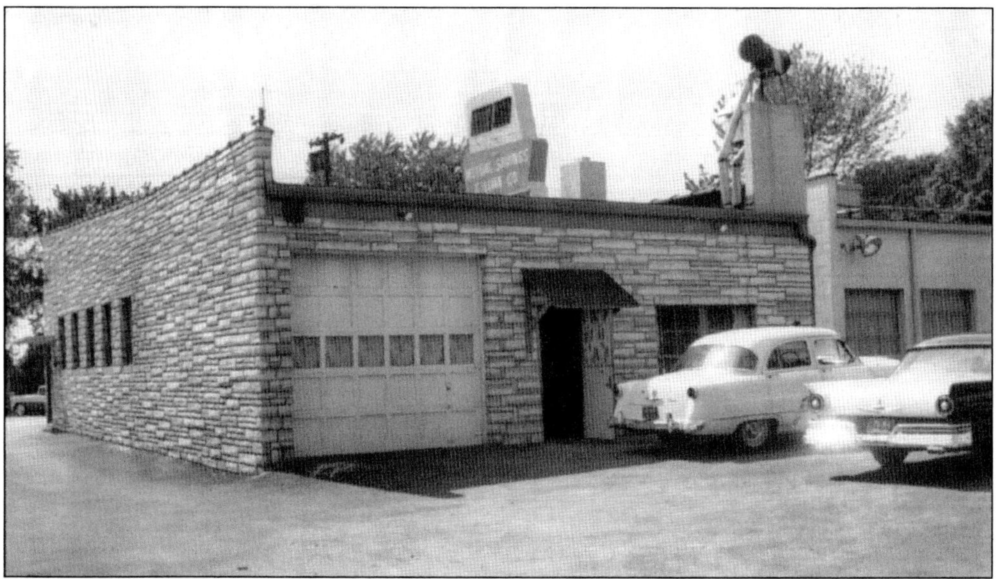

By the late 1940s, the volunteer firefighters operated from this small fire station along Galbraith Road east of Winton Road. The department's ability to effectively support a fast-growing Finneytown played a major role in the community's refusal in the early 1950s to be annexed into the city of Cincinnati. (STFD.)

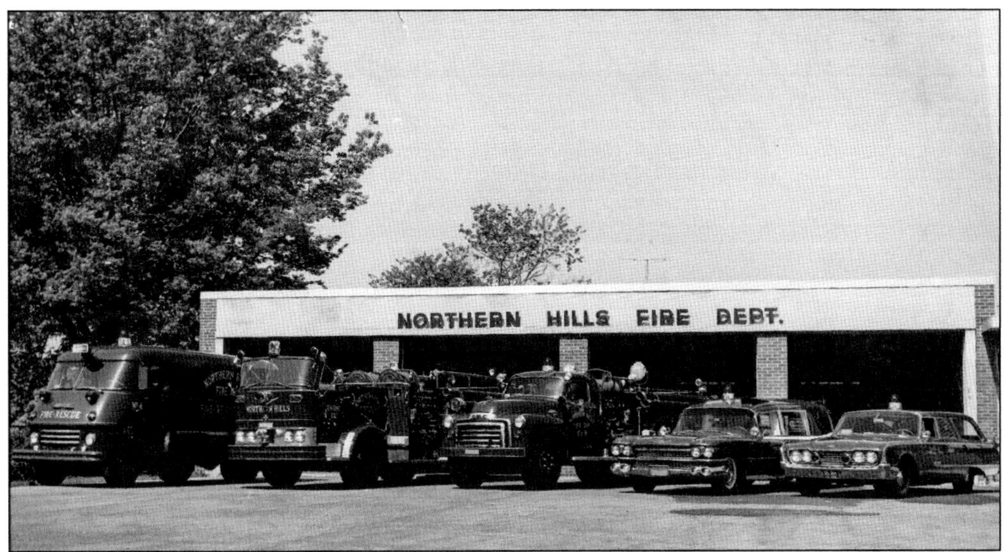

By 1960, the department operated from a larger firehouse on the west side of Winton Road, immediately south of Brentwood Shopping Plaza. The facility, shared with the township, served as department headquarters for decades. The firehouse, photographed here in 1961, was community-oriented. Firefighters held open houses and other events to promote fire prevention. (STFD.)

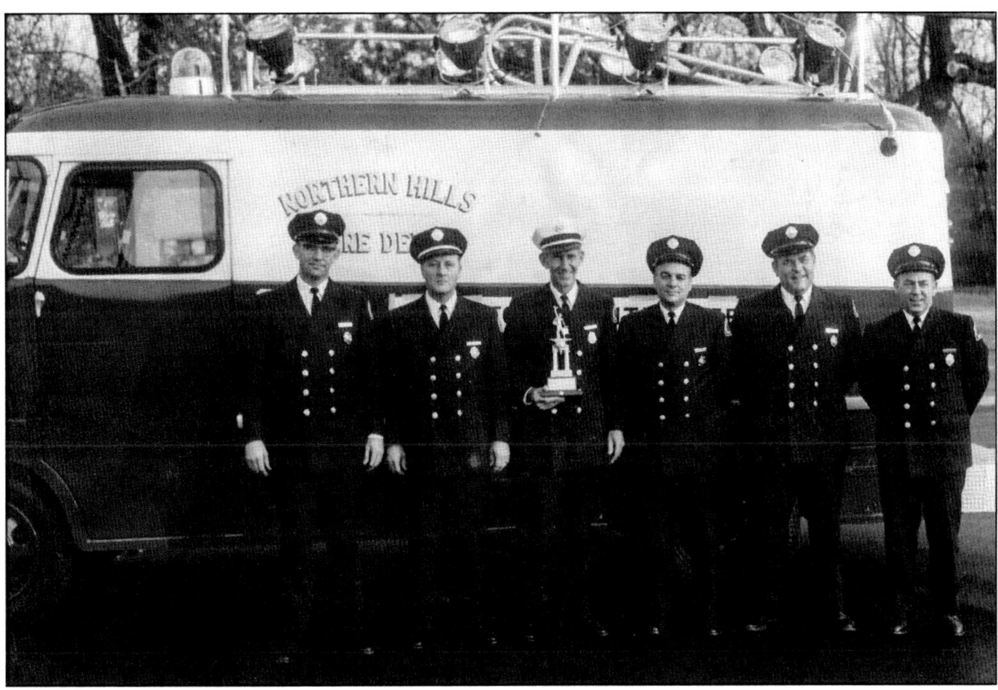

In 1963, the rescue squad displayed a trophy won at an annual competition held by the International First Aid Association. The rescue squad members are, from left to right, Willis Hoeweler, Leroy Weber, Bob Fangmeyer, Bill Gross, Jerry Sirk, and Don McMillion. "The trophy looks like an Oscar," Fangmeyer told local reporters. (STFD.)

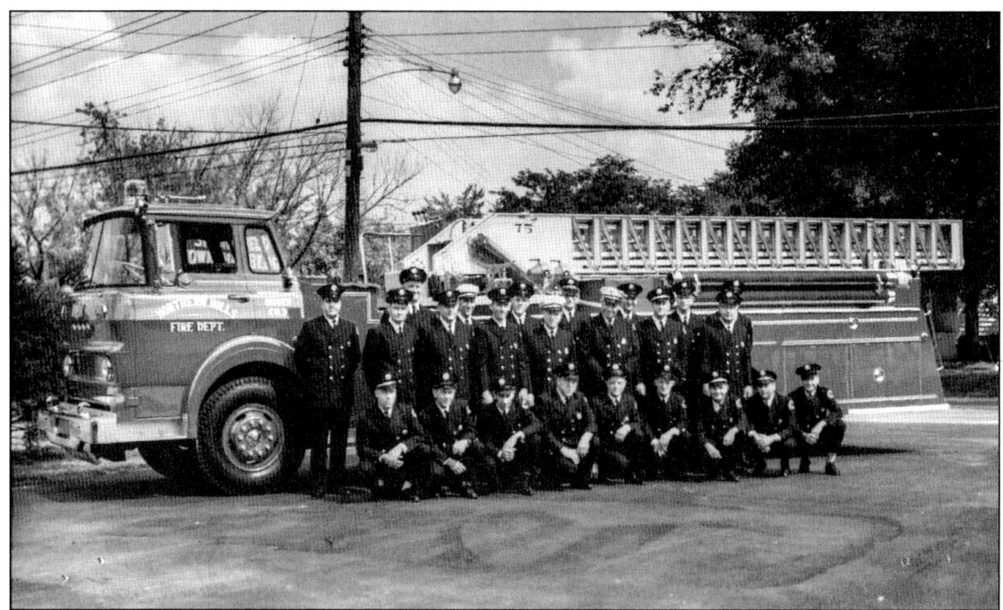

In 1963, the fire department members lined up for a photograph. Members included, in no particular order, Herb Lambert, Don McMillion, Bill Holman, Bill Gross, John Welch, Joe Colonial, Harold, Crossland, Bob Cory, Bob Bowen, Jerry Sirk, Ralph Tuttle, Nat Bond, Leroy Weber, Robert Coy, Francis Scherpenberg, Bob Fangmeyer, Bob Rook, Bill Schroyer, and Willis Hoeweler. (STFD.)

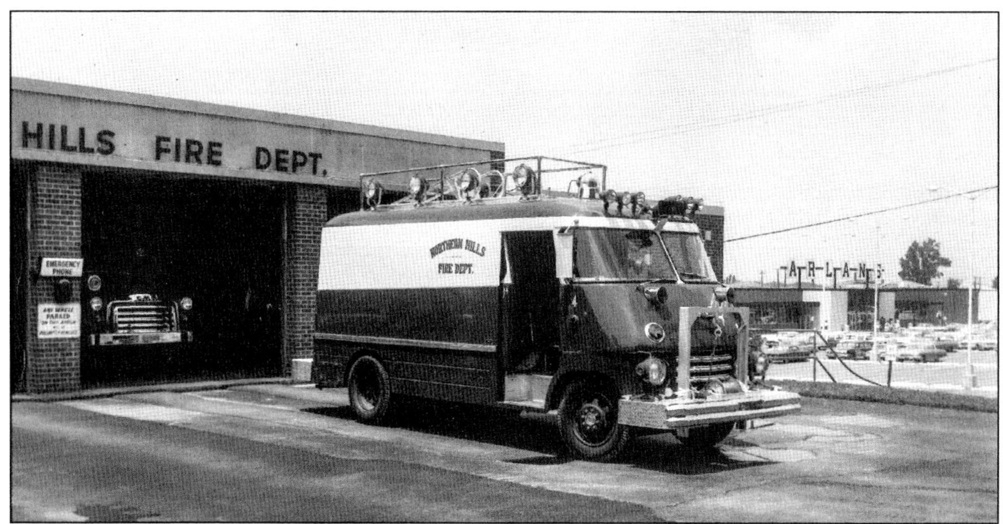

In the early 1960s, a rescue vehicle is parked at the Winton Road firehouse. To the right is Arlan's, a popular discount store at Brentwood Shopping Plaza. Several retail stores operated at the same location after Arlan's closed in the 1970s. Today, it is the site of a Kroger supermarket. (STFD.)

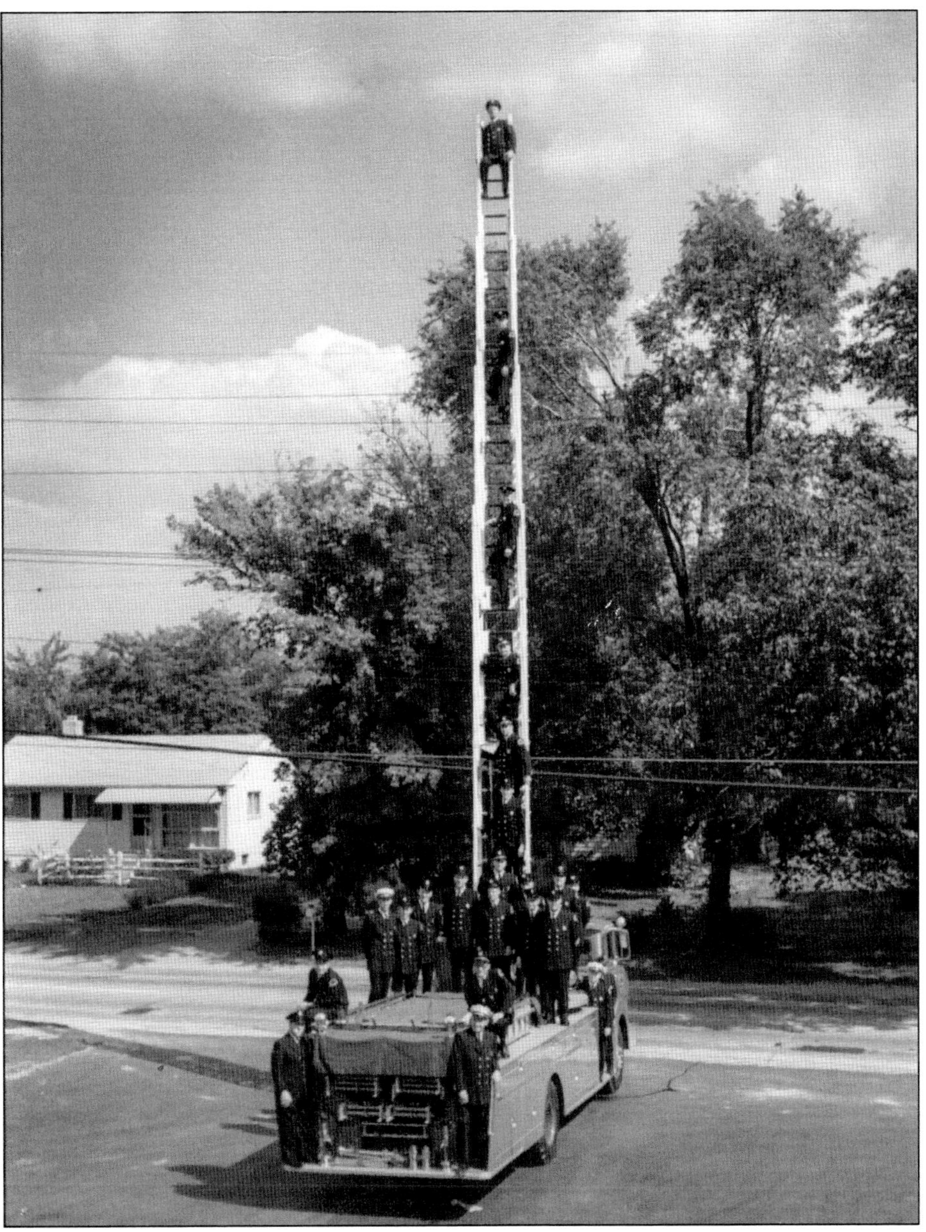

In this 1963 photograph, two decades after a handful of Finneytown guys began training as volunteer firemen, 22 uniformed members of the Northern Hills Fire Department, including several brave souls sitting on the 85-foot ladder, pose on one of its fire engines. The growth reflected the transformation in Finneytown, which has more than doubled in population between 1953 and 1963. From the ladder, firemen could see Brentwood Village, Wintondale, North Hill Estates, Brentwood Acres, Finneytown High School, Xavier High School, and Brentwood Shopping Plaza—subdivisions, schools, and businesses that did not exist a decade before. When this photograph was taken at the firehouse, Winton Road (behind the fire engine) was two lanes. By 1969, Winton Road grew to four lanes, and many houses along it gave way to commercial development. Today, this once casual spot in the heart of Finneytown is a rock's throw from Ronald Reagan Highway. (STFD.)

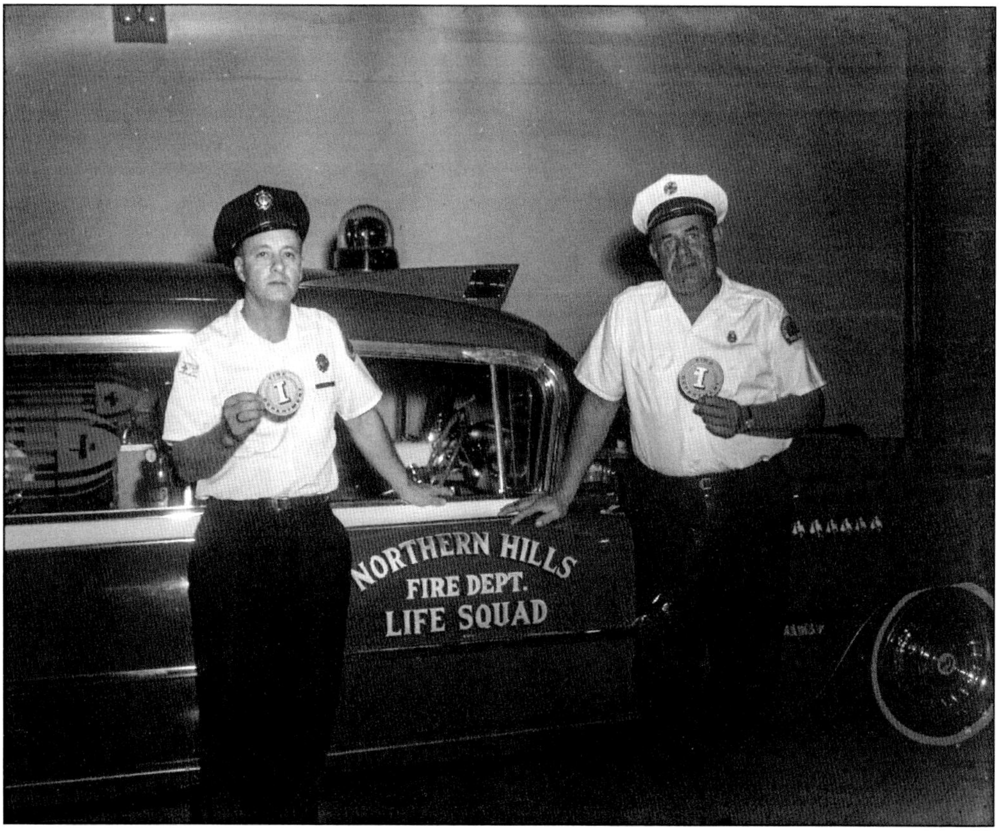

Leroy Weber, captain of the life squad (left), and Nat Bond, fire chief (right), were department leaders for decades. A former football player at the University of Notre Dame, Bond was an owner in the contracting firm of Bond & Sheehan. He served as fire chief from 1952 to 1983. The stork decals on this 1959 ambulance represent babies born in the vehicle. (STFD.)

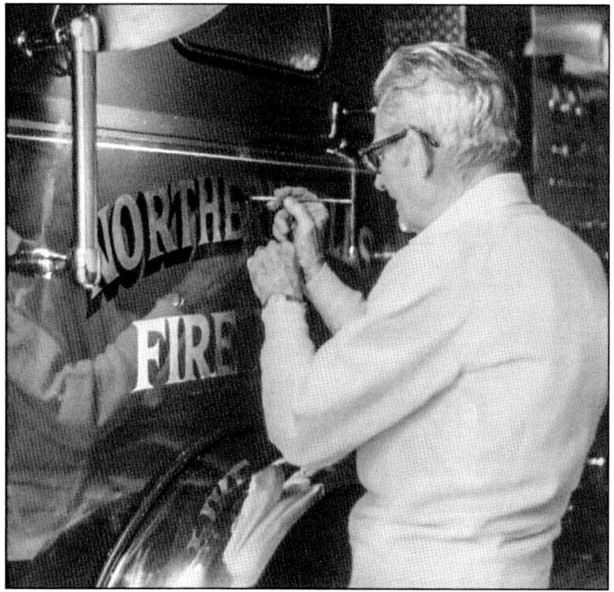

In the 1960s, an artist painted the side of a fire engine using gold leaf, a very thin sheet of gold. Applying gold leaf is a time-consuming process. For more than a century, gold-leaf lettering was an essential feature of a fire engine's decorative appeal. Today, applying gold-leaf lettering is becoming a lost art form. (STFD.)

During 1964–1965, the department created two substations to respond to a growing number of fire runs in a growing community. The north substation (pictured) was created on Winton Road near the Powel Crosley Jr. YMCA. The south substation was on North Bend Road near Parkview Heights. Both were situated on residential property. (STFD.)

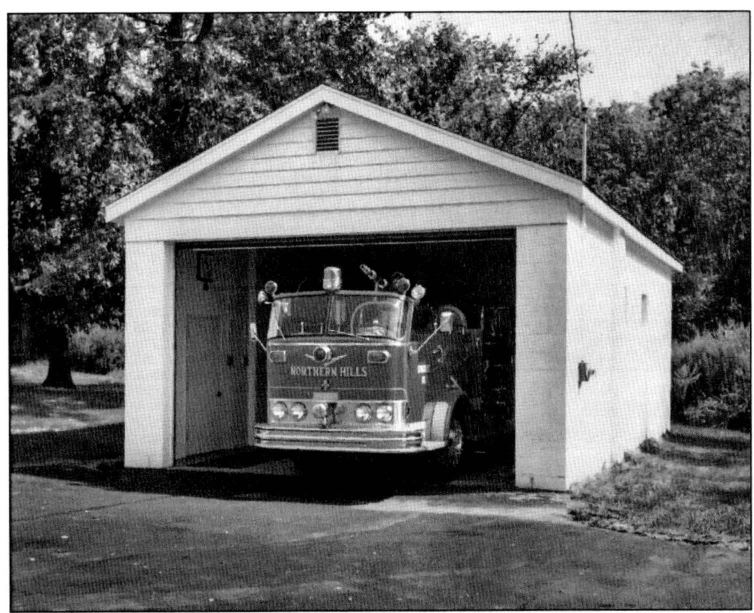

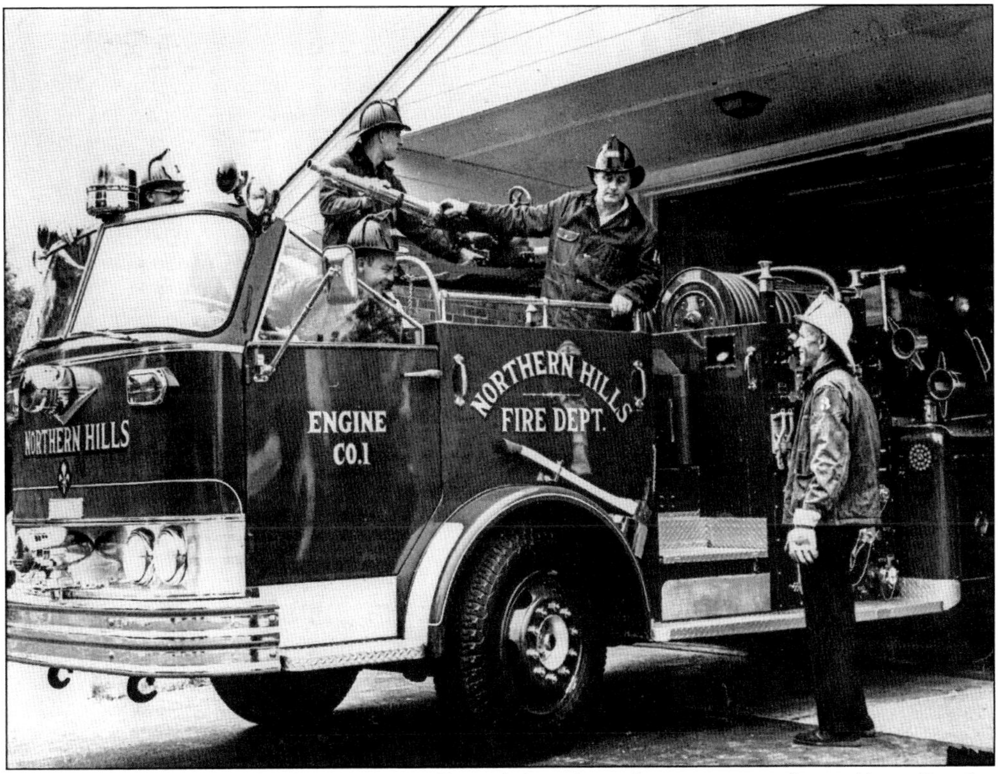

In 1965, Assistant Chief Bob Fangmeyer (far right) smiles at his crew on a classic Ahren-Fox fire engine at the north substation. The department stayed headquartered at the main facility on Winton Road, shared with township officials. By the mid-1960s, the fire department and rescue squad reached 35 members. (STFD.)

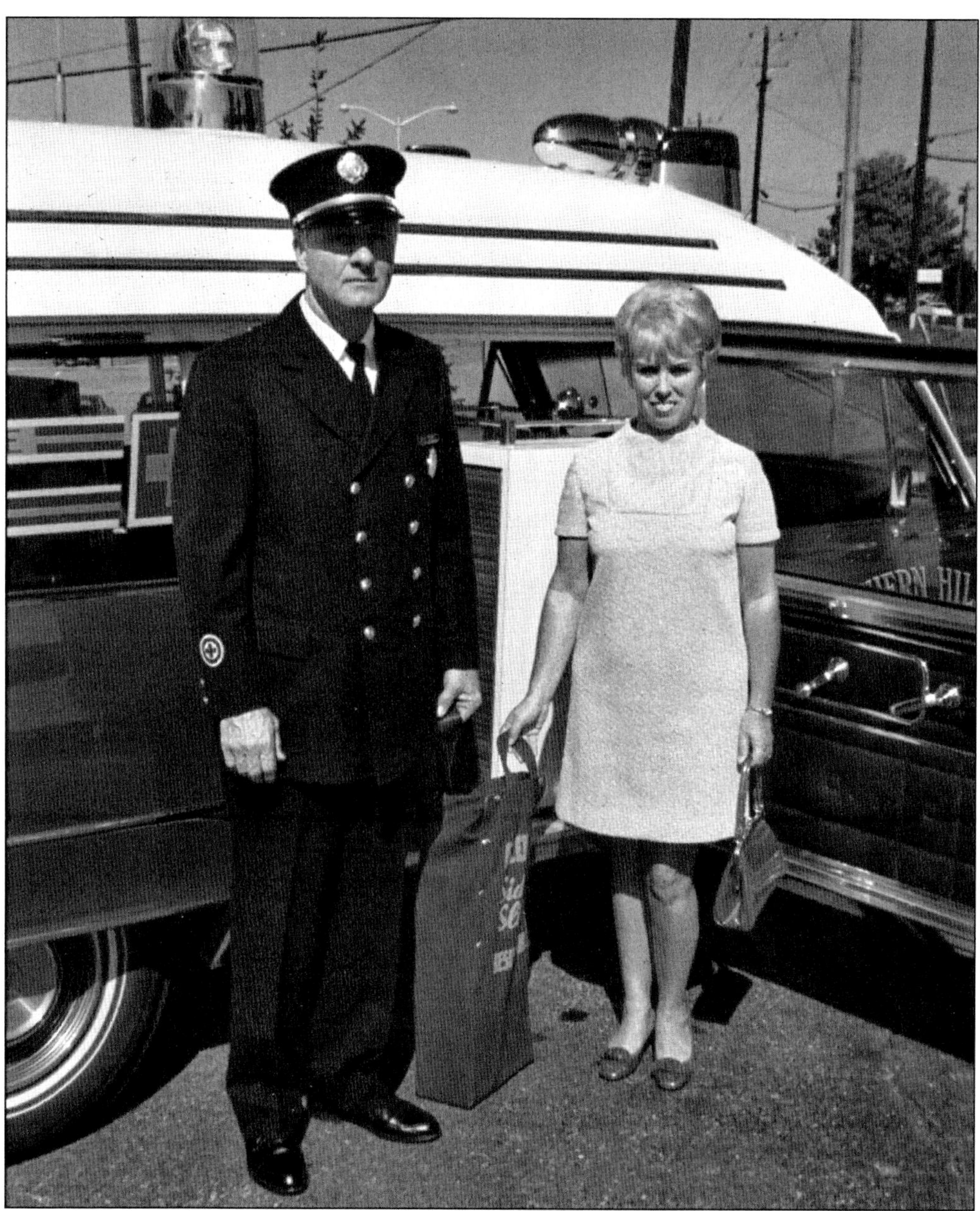

The fire department stayed closely connected to Finneytown's civic organizations. In this 1969 photograph, Leroy Weber of the rescue squad received a $300 portable resuscitator from Mary Ballentine of the Finneytown Junior Woman's Club. The resuscitator provided resuscitation, inhalation, and respiration capabilities for the ambulance. For decades, the fire department operated as a nonprofit organization and contracted its services with the township. "For a volunteer fire department, Northern Hills was among the most progressive in the state in terms of practices and equipment," said Rob Leininger, who joined as a volunteer in 1981. "Among the volunteers, we had so many different trades, from roofers to electricians, and they all used their skills with the department. It was amazing how these guys could do anything needed," added Leininger, who became the first chief of the Springfield Township Fire Department when it was established in 1996. (STFD.)

On February 16, 1965, firefighters responded to a blaze at Loughead Cleaners and Shoe Repair on the Hempstead Drive side of Brentwood Shopping Plaza. The fire caused smoke damage to neighboring stores, including Don Seta Beauty Salon, Harry's Barber Shop, Jack Eckerle Jewelry, Brentwood Savings, Central Trust Bank, and Kroger. (STFD.)

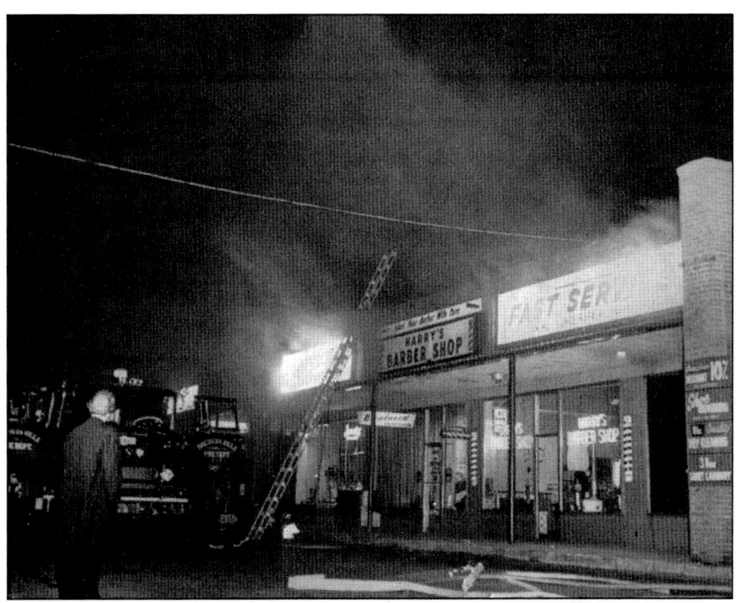

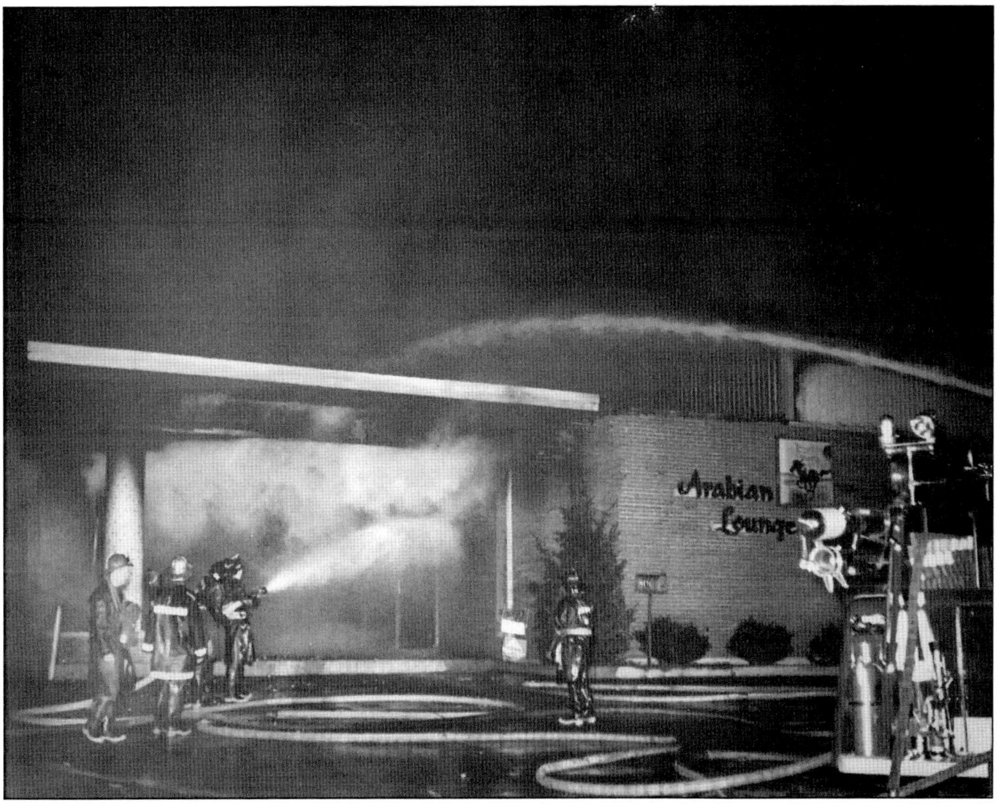

On a sad night for Finneytown's hip nightlife crowd, a fire severely damaged Brentwood Bowl's Arabian Lounge on April 16, 1967. The bowling alley's owners commended the firefighters for saving the facility. However, Arabian Lounge, which for seven years featured exotic drinks, live music, "Go-Go Girls," and an Arabian snake dancer, would be no more. It reopened as the Black Lantern Lounge. (STFD.)

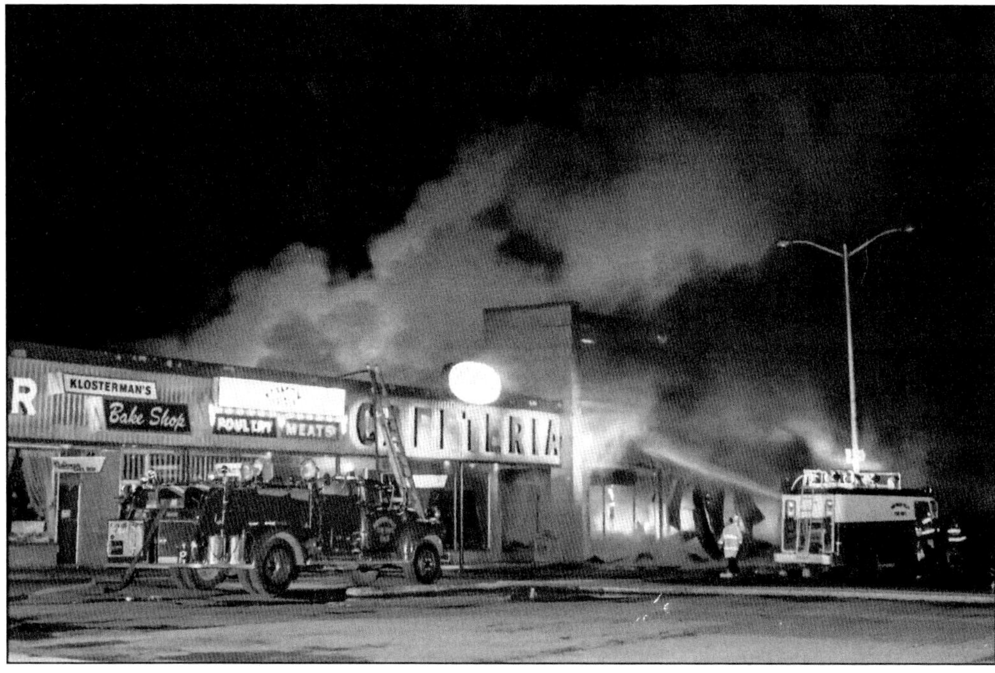

In one of the most dramatic fires in Finneytown, 100 firefighters from Northern Hills and eight neighboring departments battled a blaze in the early morning of March 15, 1972, at the W.T. Grant store at Brentwood Shopping Plaza. Facing strong winds, firefighters kept the fire largely contained within the Grant store, which was destroyed (below). Also damaged were neighboring Perkins Cafeteria, Gray's Drug Store, and Klosterman's Bakery. Springfield Township patrolman Robert Fangmeyer discovered the fire at 3:40 a.m. A former volunteer firefighter, he responded quickly. The fast convergence of fire engines and firefighters, combined with Grant's heavy firewalls, prevented the fire from spreading throughout the plaza. (Both, STFD.)

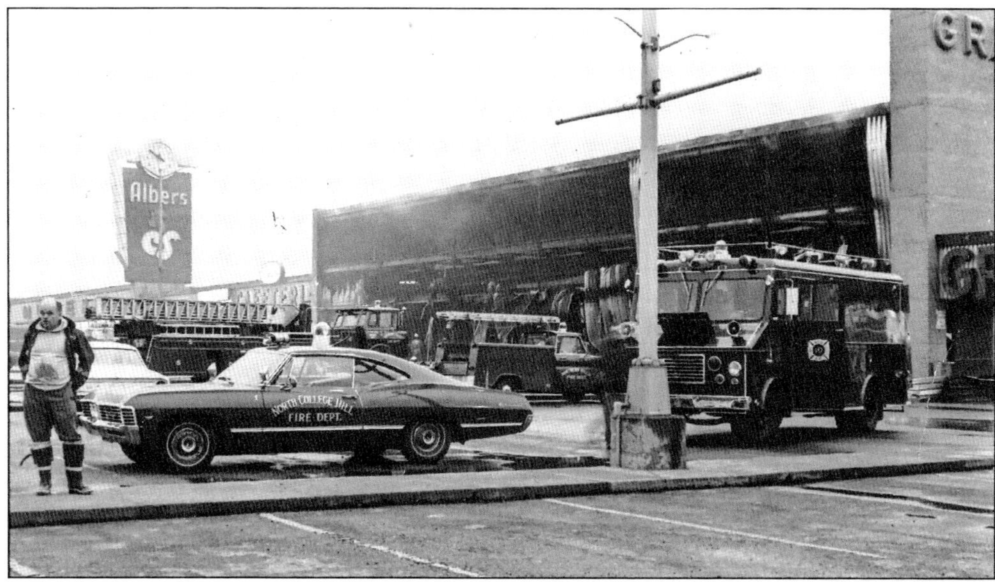

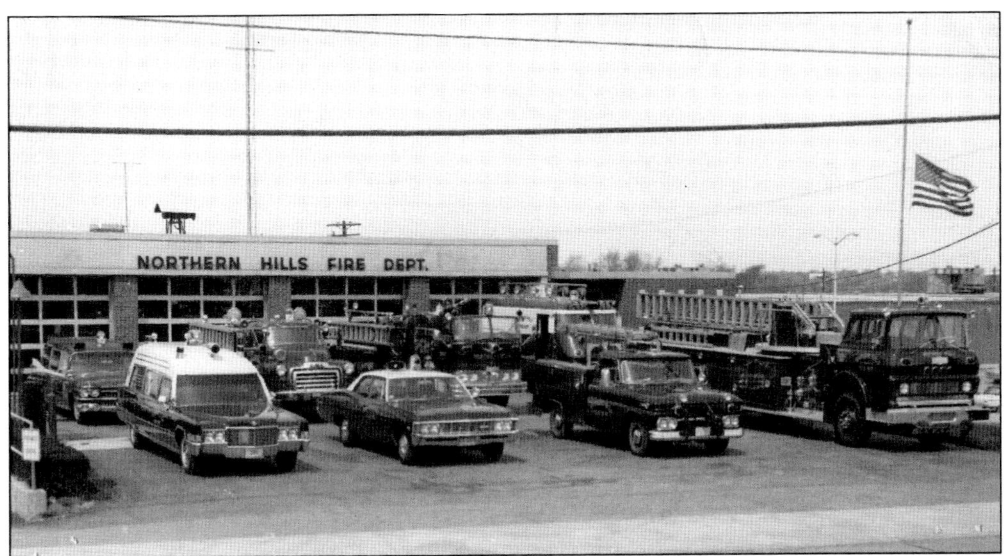

Firefighters love to display their vehicles. In 1969, the department celebrated its 25th anniversary with its fleet in formation. Members and families gathered at the township complex and fire station on Winton Road. Today, a Chipotle restaurant operates at the former fire station site. By this juncture, Fire Chief Nat Bond led a department of 40 members, three stations, and eight fire and rescue vehicles. (STFD.)

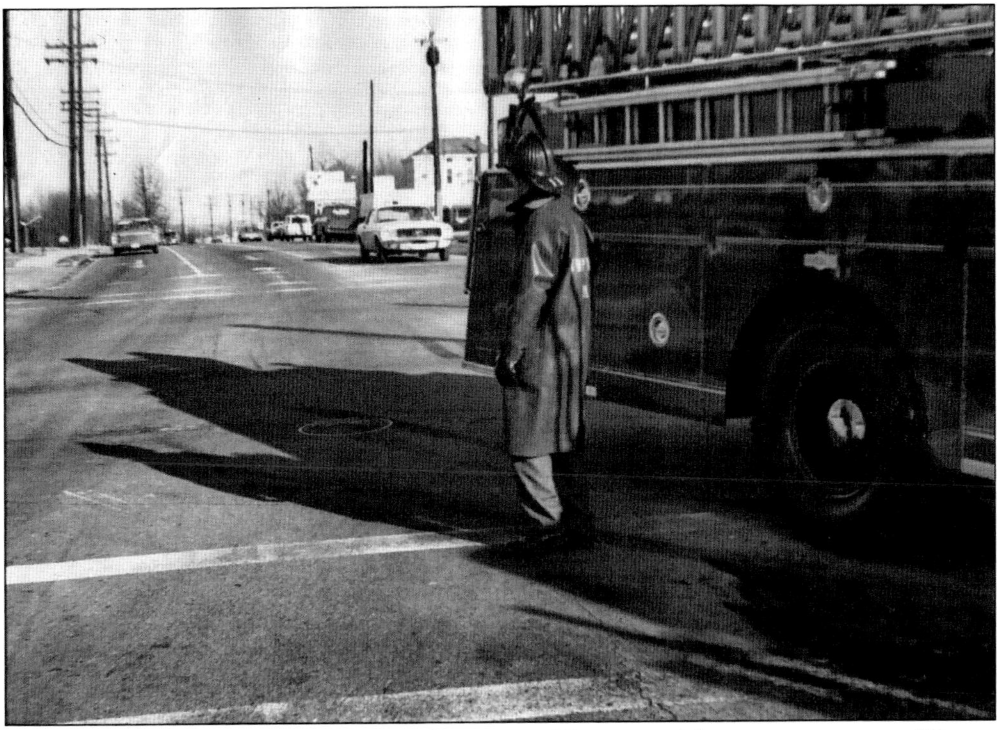

In 1969, a volunteer firefighter directs traffic at one of Finneytown's busiest intersections, Winton and Galbraith Roads, which was walking distance from the main fire station. By this time, Winton Road had expanded beyond two lanes. The volunteer organization operated another 27 years before the township established its own fire department. (STFD.)

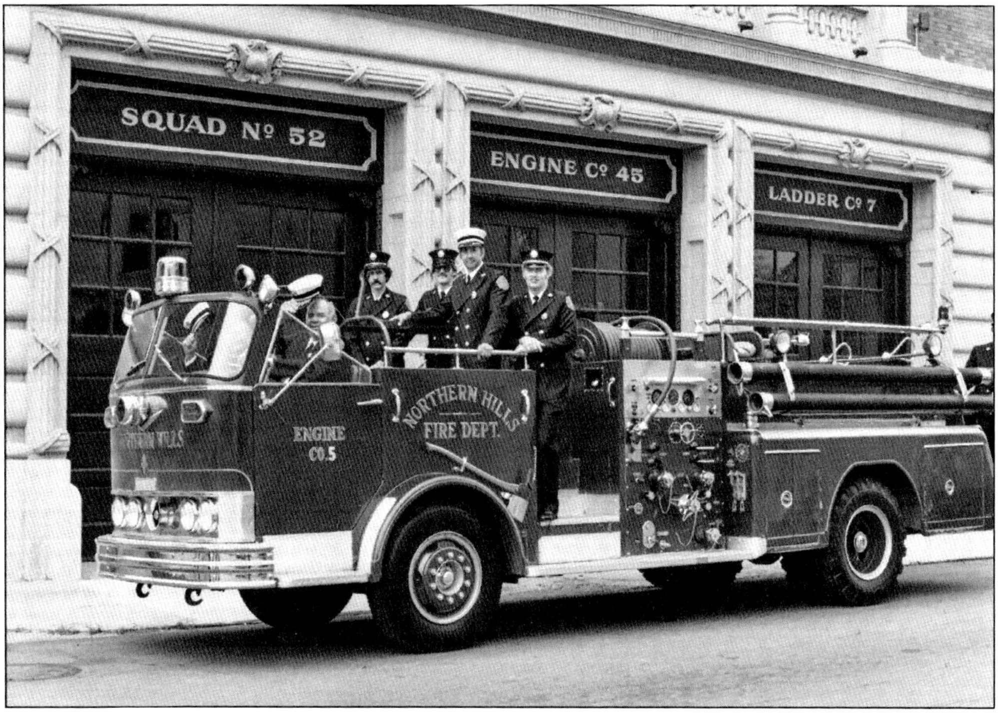

As the beloved volunteer department recedes into history, its legacy lives at the Cincinnati Fire Museum. In 1981, the department donated its 1957 Ahrens-Fox fire engine to the downtown museum after operating the Cincinnati-made vehicle for 23 years. The museum celebrates Cincinnati as the birthplace of US professional firefighting. (STFD.)

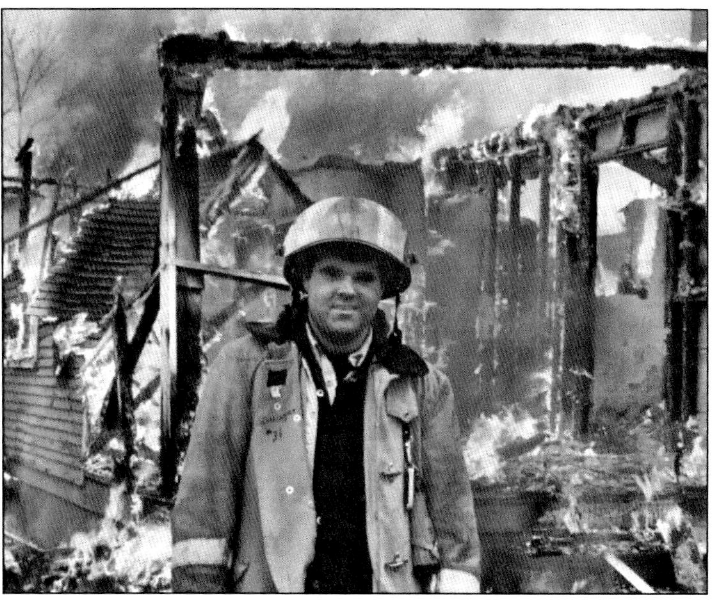

Rob Leininger would link the fire department of old to the new. In 1981, he joined the Northern Hills volunteers and became fire chief in 1989. In 1996, when the Springfield Township Fire Department was formed from the Northern Hills, New Burlington, and Edgemont volunteer groups, he became fire chief. In this 1980s photograph, Leininger can smile—because the fire was a training exercise. (STFD.)

Eight

NATURE'S STORYTELLER

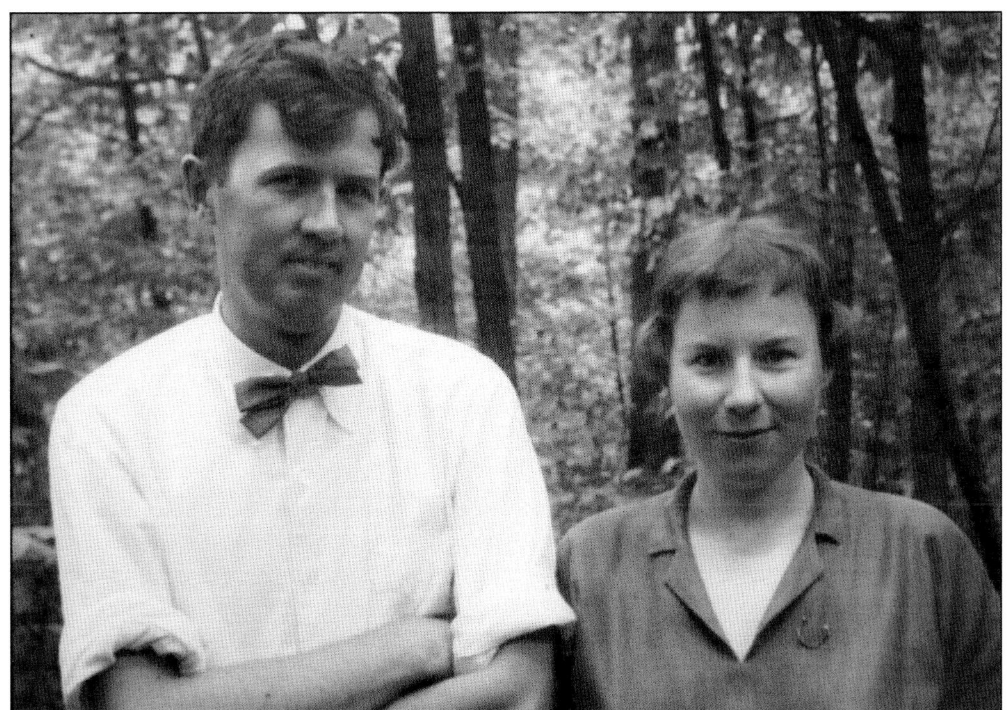

Artists Charley and Edie Harper met on the eve of World War II at the Art Academy of Cincinnati. A decade after marrying in 1947, they moved to Finneytown with their young son, Brett. Over the next 50 years living in the community, Charley painted tirelessly and became one of America's most prolific and recognizable illustrators with his unique and minimalist portrayals of nature. (Brett Harper.)

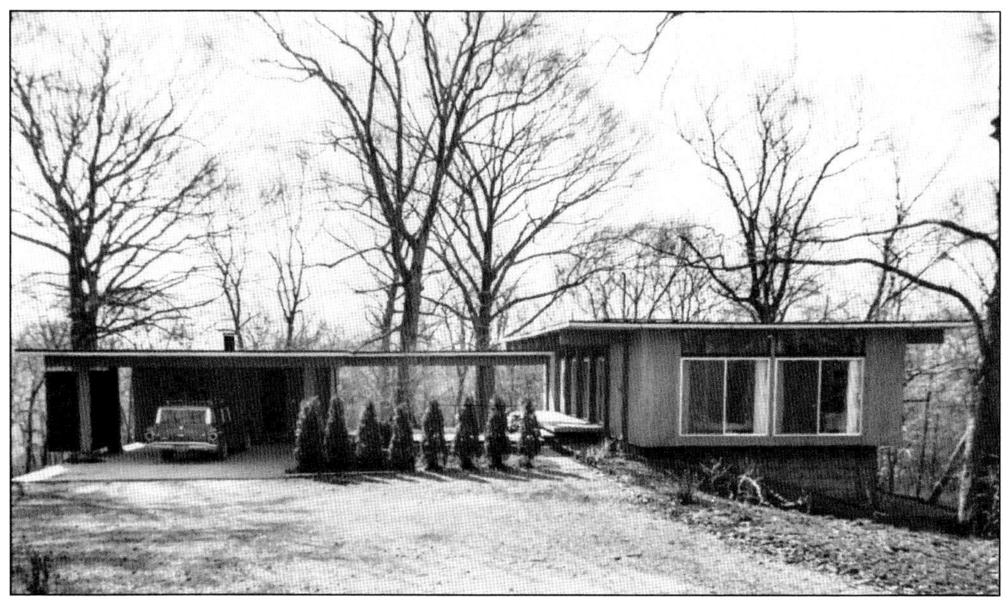

In 1956, Cincinnati architect Rudy Hermes (1927–2016), designed for his friend Charley Harper a "modernist" home, which was built in secluded Finneytown woods. The two friends collaborated on concepts to reflect the Harpers' love of nature: cypress siding and large expanses of glass to reveal the wooded outdoors. "After Dad took his radical design to the bank, he worried about securing a loan [for the project]," said son Tyson Hermes. "But Charley's reaction was 'We are right on track!' " Seen below near the front entrance is one of Charley's trademark images: a ladybug. The design by Hermes, who created classic mid-century modern homes in Finneytown and across Cincinnati, gave Charley and Edie the perfect atmosphere in which to create memorable works. (Both, Tyson Hermes.)

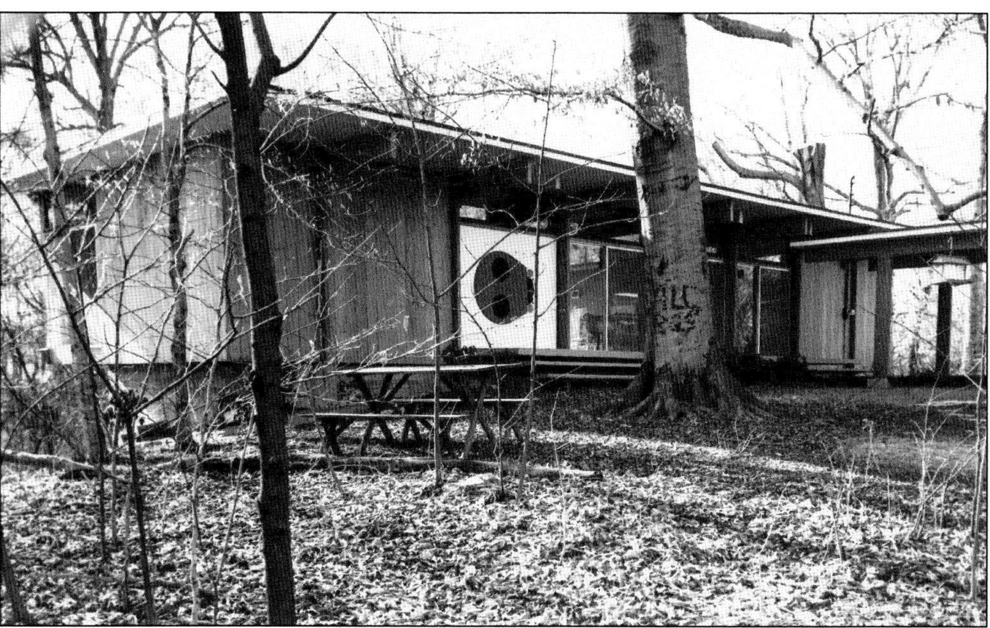

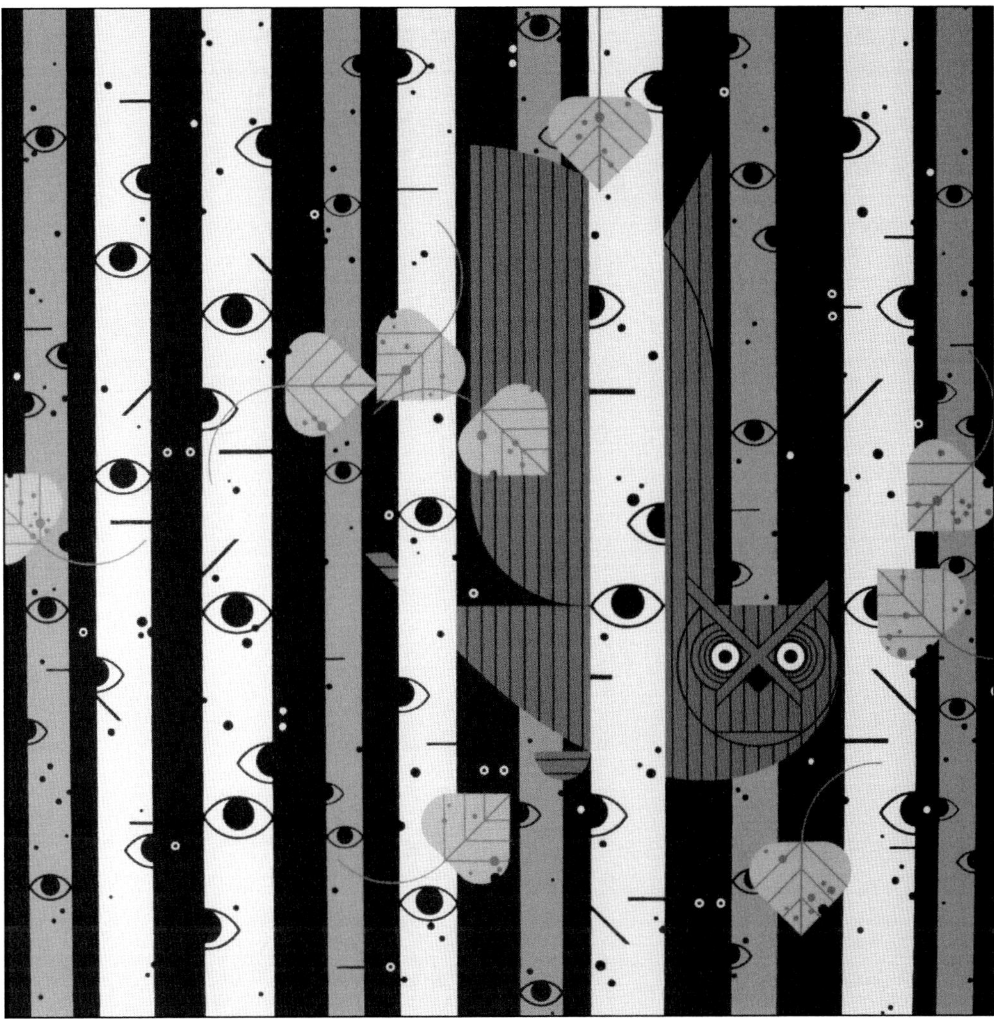

In describing this silk-screened print called "Bark Eyes," Charley Harper wrote, "The night has a thousand eyes, and you can count them all in an aspen grove." Growing up on a farm in West Virginia, Harper developed a profound love for nature. World War II interrupted his college studies when he served in a US Army Intelligence and Reconnaissance Platoon in Europe. "I was constantly assailed by the senselessness and overwhelming horror of war," he wrote, though he sketched in the field. After the war, he graduated from the Art Academy of Cincinnati, where he later joined the teaching staff. Living in Finneytown, he illustrated popular books and produced 1,200 works during his 37 years with *Ford Times*, a monthly publication of Ford Motor Company. Ford encouraged him to sell his minimalist nature prints in the magazine. He charged $4.95 per print, plus 50¢ postage. His work soon sold nationwide. (Frank Rapien.)

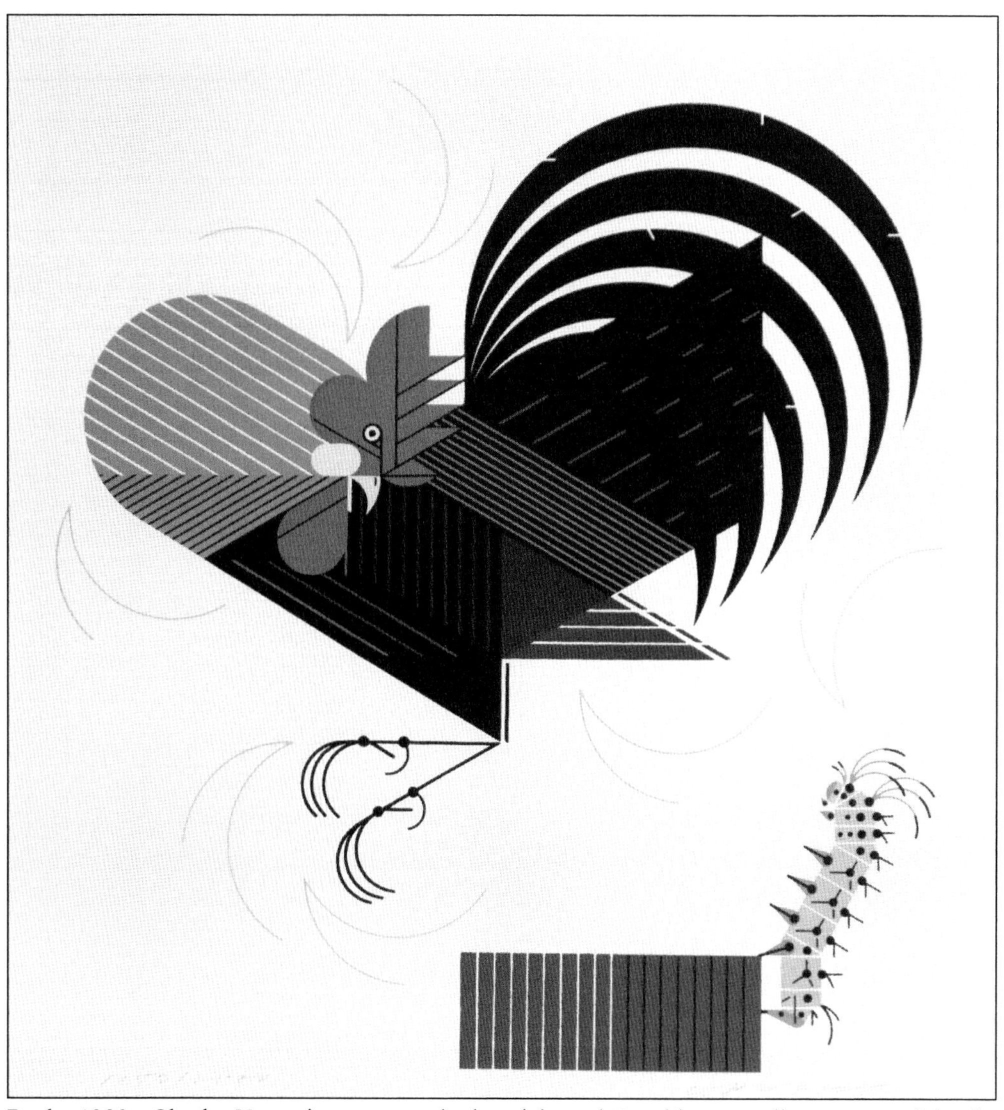

By the 1980s, Charley Harper's unique art had proliferated. In addition to illustrating such books as *The Golden Book of Biology*, the *Betty Crocker Cookbook*, and *Ranger Rick* magazine, he created nature posters for the National Park Service, Cincinnati Zoo, and Delta Airlines. His original works and silkscreened prints, such as the above "Crawling Tall," were widely distributed. "I concentrated on trying to simplify the great natural forms and symbolize the design underlying the surface clutter," he wrote. Harper often accompanied his work with clever titles and a side story. For "Crawling Tall," he wrote, "Learn a lesson from the larva of the Royal Walnut Moth. Look mean, hang tough, and crawl tall." He was called "an artist, humorist, and naturalist," though his war memories followed him. "His work was an antidote that kept his thoughts of the war at bay," said son Brett. (Frank Rapien.)

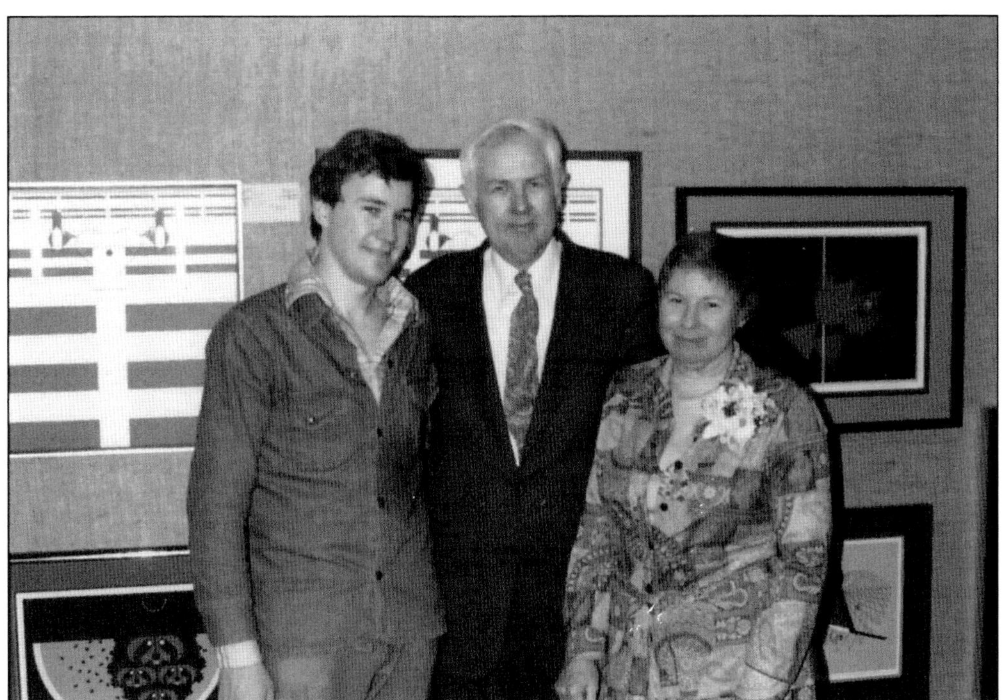

A trio of Harper artists: Brett, Charley, and Edie. The only child of Charley and Edie, Brett grew up in the 1950s and 1960s attending Finneytown's public schools. An accomplished artist, Brett has also devoted his life to growing his father's legacy. Owner of Charley Harper Studio, Brett sells his father's works and his own works. He has displayed Charley's art across the United States and Europe. (Brett Harper.)

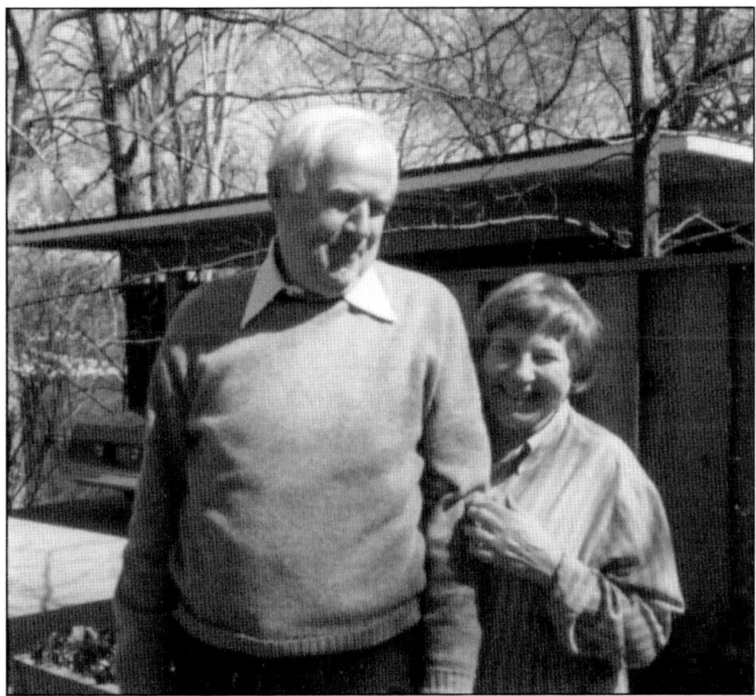

Charley and Edie, pictured later in life at their Finneytown home, were friendly, approachable people. While overshadowed by her husband's stature, Edie enjoyed success as an artist and was best known for her minimalist portraits of cats as well as Christian imagery. Charley died in 2007; Edie followed in 2010. (Brett Harper.)

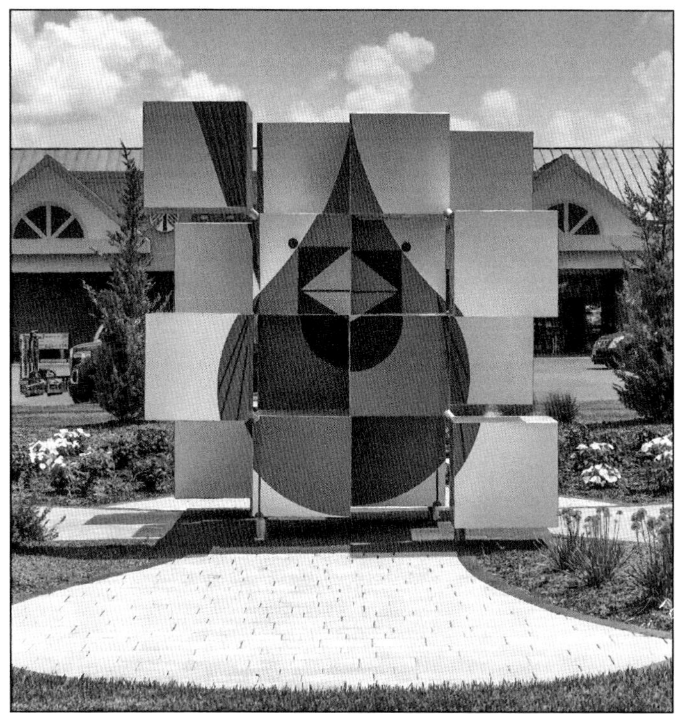

With each passing year, Charley Harper's legacy grows. His signed prints and original works command thousands of dollars, and his images appear on everything from jewelry and housewares to Christmas ornaments. In 2022, Springfield Township honored him with a sculpture at Finneytown's busy corner of Winton and Galbraith Roads. At the gas station catty-corner from the sculpture, Harper's cardinal stares at you. (Mark Evans.)

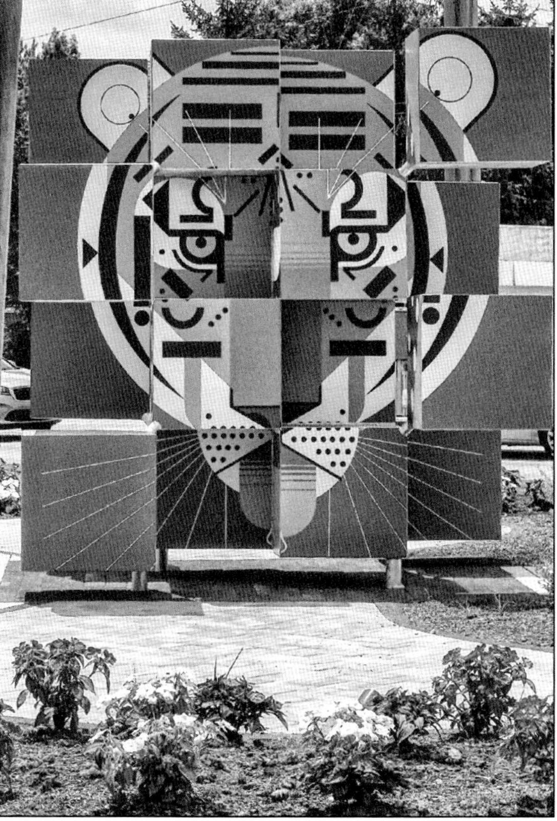

"The Many Sides of Charley Harper" is an innovative sculpture by Micah Landers. It celebrates Charley's unique ability to express nature through "minimal modern realism." What appear initially as simply colorful blocks, actually produce at specific angles for passing cars, representations of his most iconic images, including a Bengal, Cincinnati's NFL team mascot. (Mark Evans.)

Nine

MID-CENTURY MARVELS

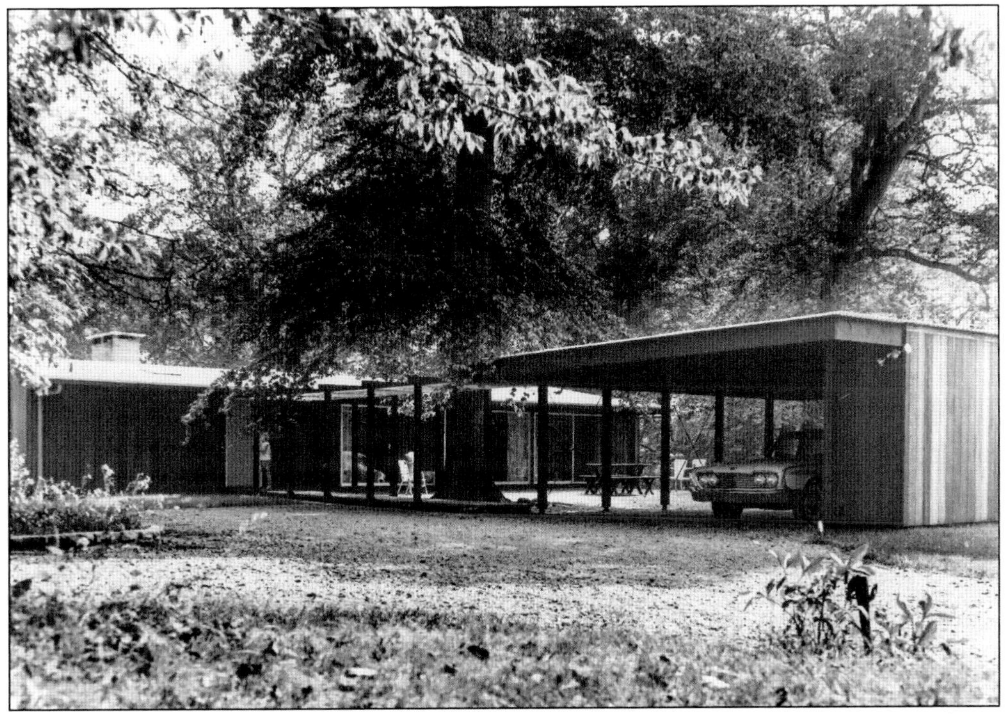

Rudy Hermes designed this Finneytown home in 1956 (next door to Charley Harper's home) in a modernist style now coined "mid-century modern." Inspired by the designs of Frank Lloyd Wright, this architecture flourished from the 1940s into the mid-1960s. Greater Cincinnati was a center of activity for mid-century modern designs, and the neighboring communities of Finneytown and Wyoming were hotspots. Several influential modernist architects designed Finneytown homes. (Tyson Hermes.)

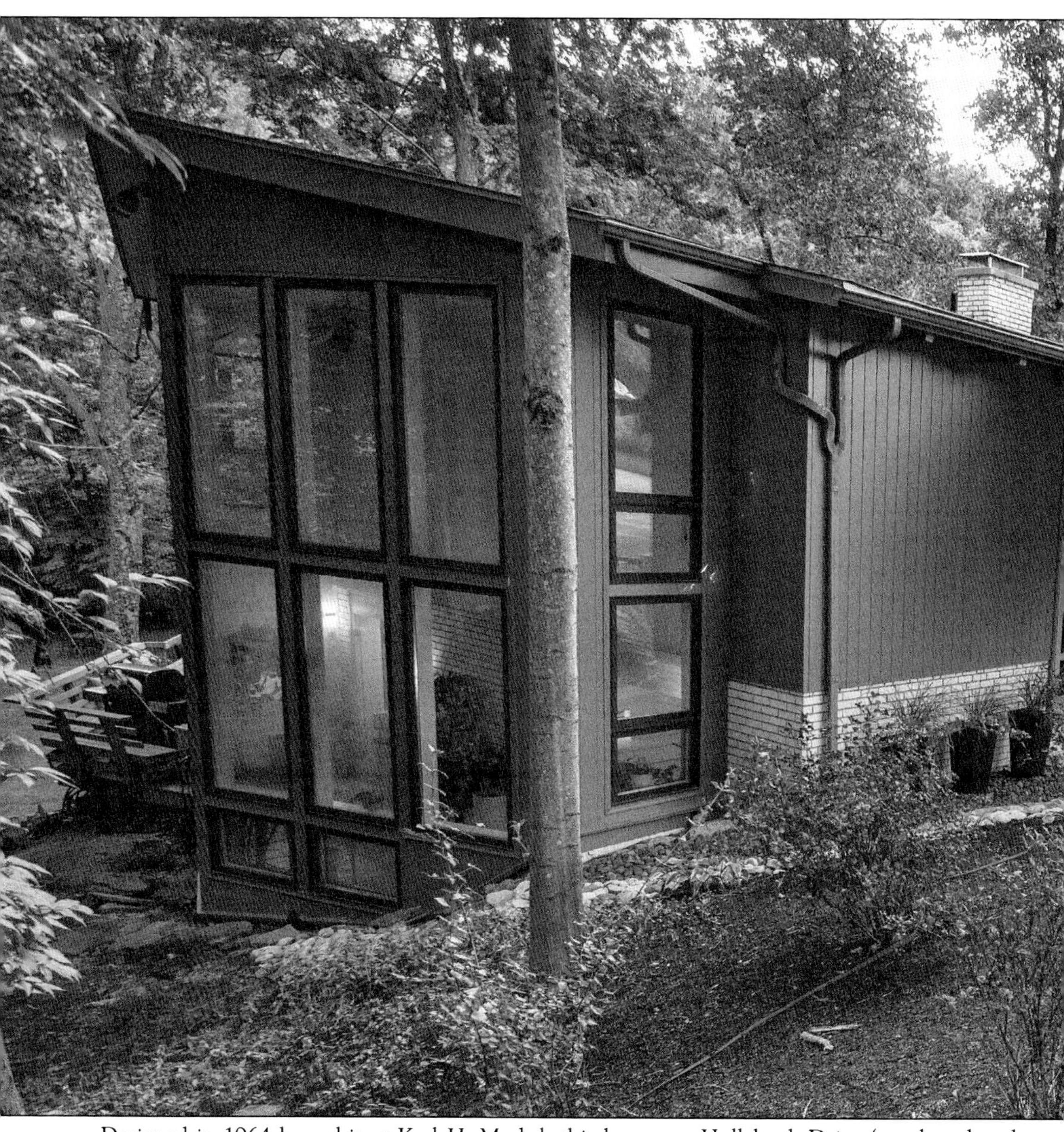

Designed in 1964 by architect Karl H. Merkel, this home on Hollyhock Drive (purchased and restored in 2022 by the Seilkops) displays the hallmarks of mid-century modern architecture: clean lines, angled roofs, open spaces, large windows, low footprint, and a close connection to nature. With this home, Merkel outdid himself: The house and garage are detached, but connected by a single roof. An open spot in the roof allows rain to fall on an outdoor garden. Merkel, a longtime

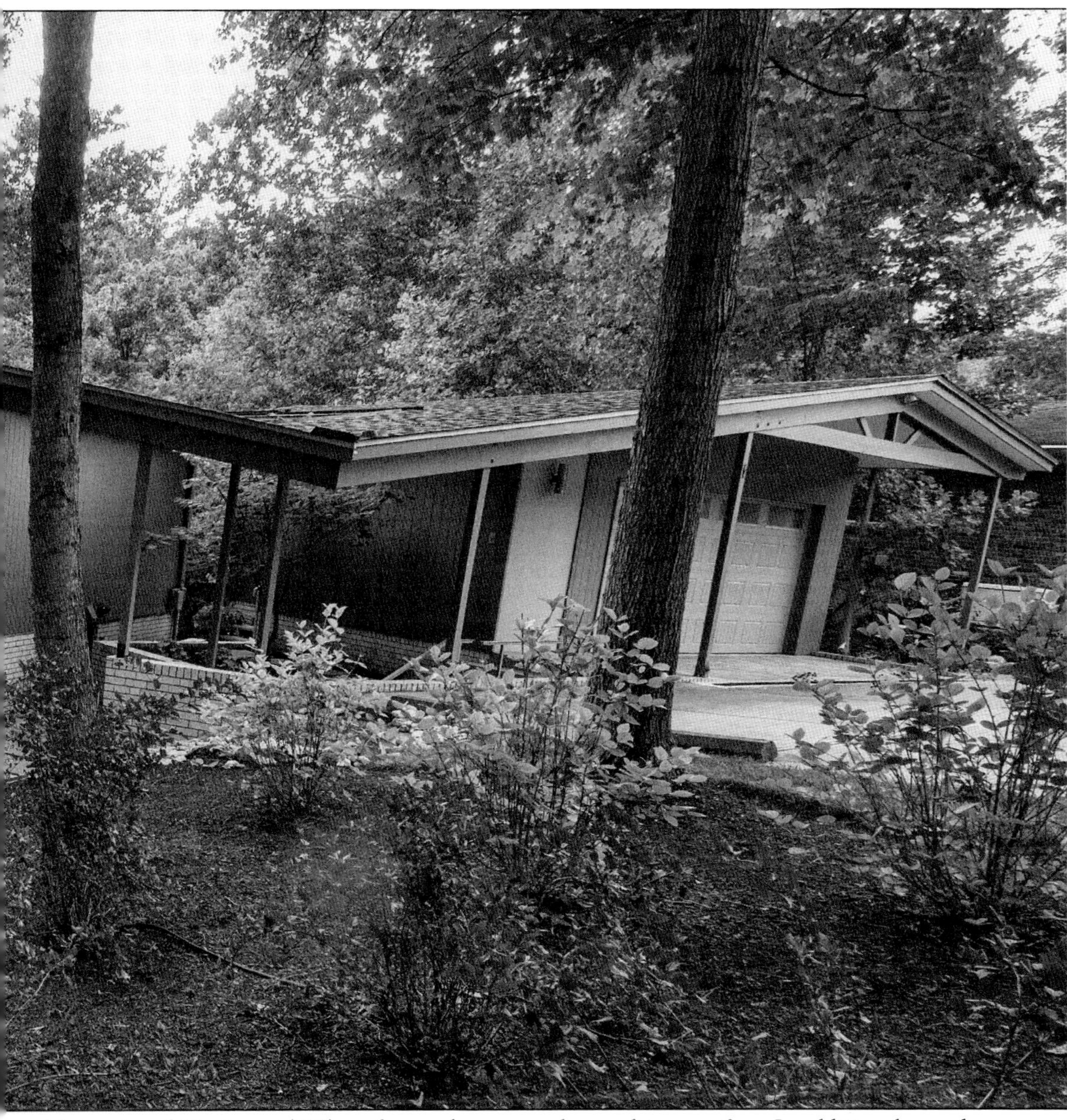

University of Cincinnati (UC) professor, also operated an architecture firm. In addition, he used his expertise in the service of his country at the height of the Cold War. In 1964, Merkel teamed with fellow UC architecture professor Jim Alexander, an important designer in the mid-century modern style, to create modular and portable "fighter bases" for Wright-Patterson Air Force Base. (Mark Evans.)

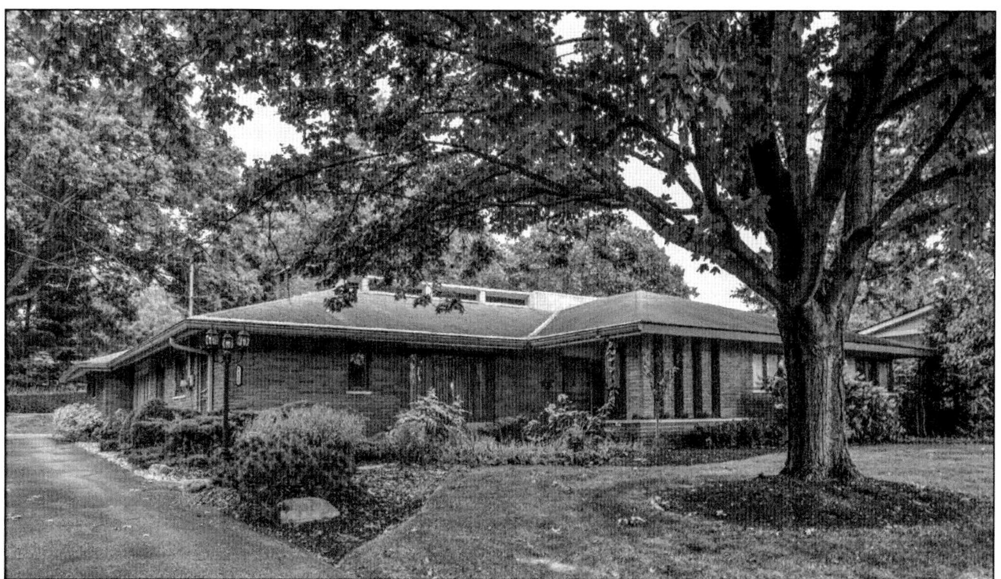

North Hill Estates, a subdivision created in the early 1960s by developer Don Lang, featured a variety of modern designs produced by different architects and builders. This home on Pinemeadow Lane was built in 1960 for architect Thomas R. Graham. Among its interesting features are large windows, brick columns, and a skylight ceiling. (Mark Evans.)

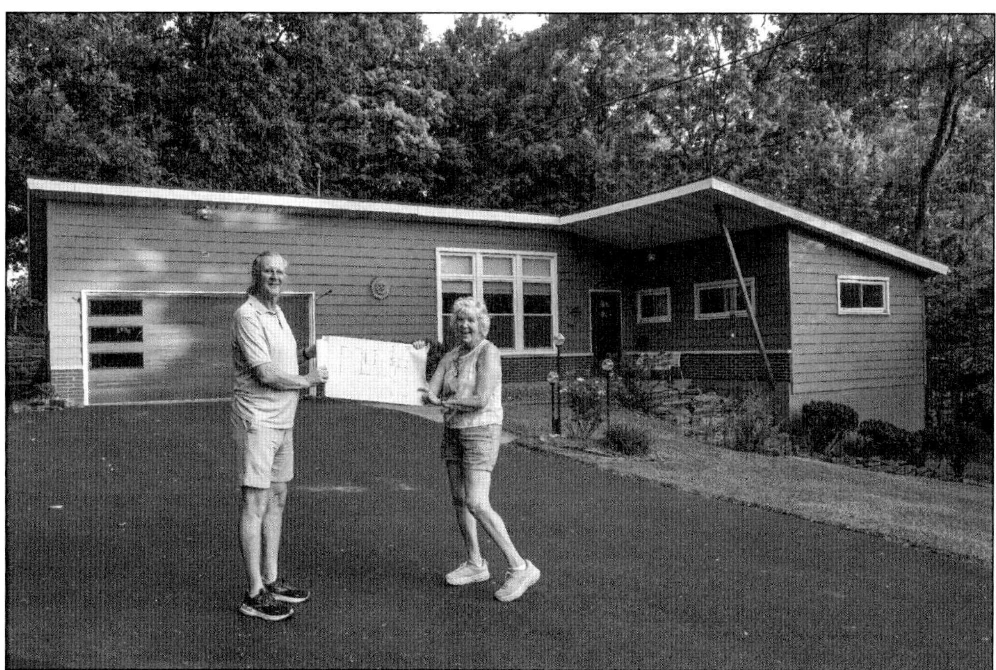

Jeff and Patty New hold the 1953 drawings for their home at the end of wooded Long Lane. A classic treatment with many early 1950s homes was the use of a bracket to hold up an extended roof to create a front porch. As with many of Finneytown's mid-century modern homes, the back of this home is larger than the front. (Mark Evans.)

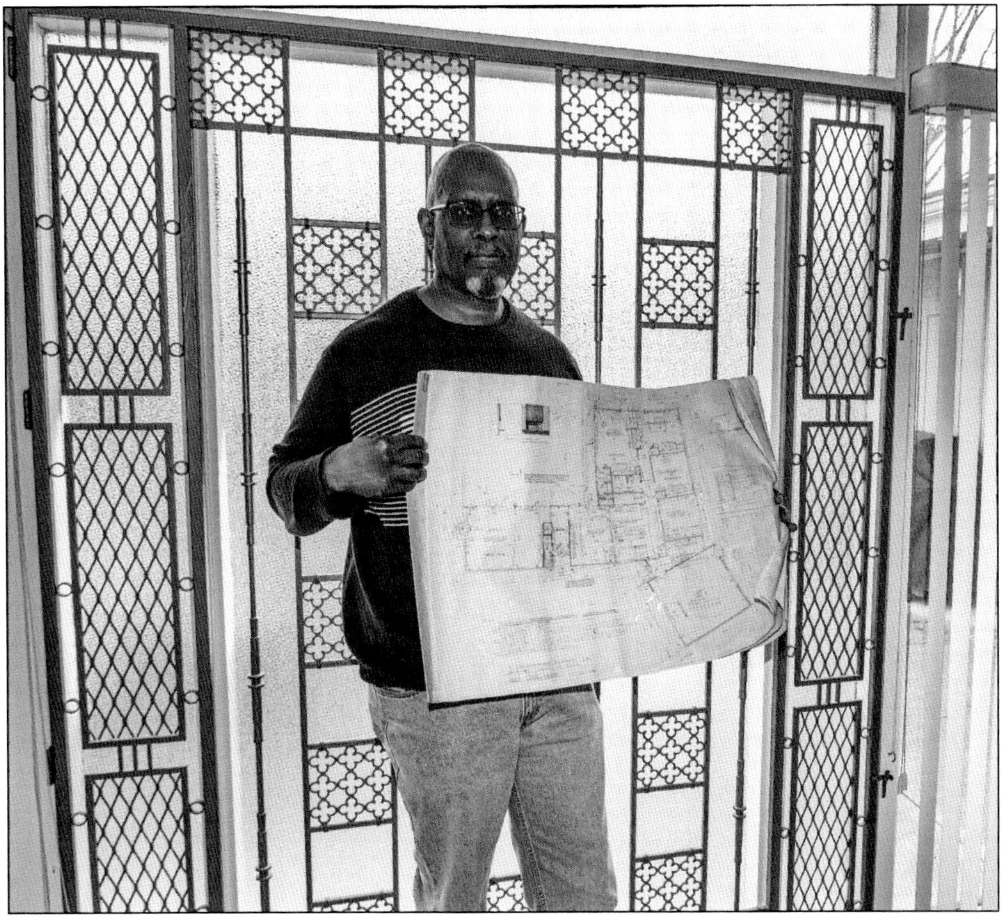

In 2003, when Bert Lewis (pictured) bought this home on Bluecrystal Court, it came with the original 1961 drawings by Cincinnati architect Richard Calef. Lewis was taken by Calef's clever use of space, especially the back patio (below). While Lewis and Calef never met and were of different generations, they had similar life experiences. Both grew up in Cincinnati and were war veterans: Calef in Europe during World War II and Lewis in the Vietnam War. Both earned technical degrees at UC. Lewis studied civil engineering and spent his career with the City of Cincinnati. In the late 1960s, after Calef's wife died suddenly at a young age, he moved to Texas and left an enduring legacy of unique buildings across Cincinnati. He died in 2000 at age 79. (Both, Mark Evans.)

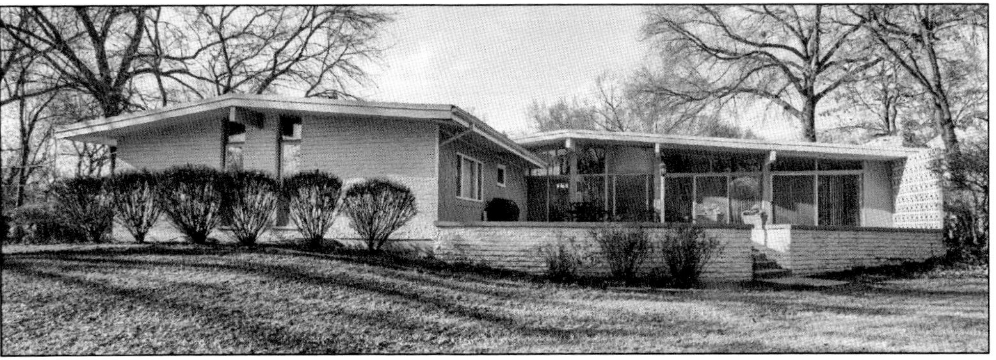

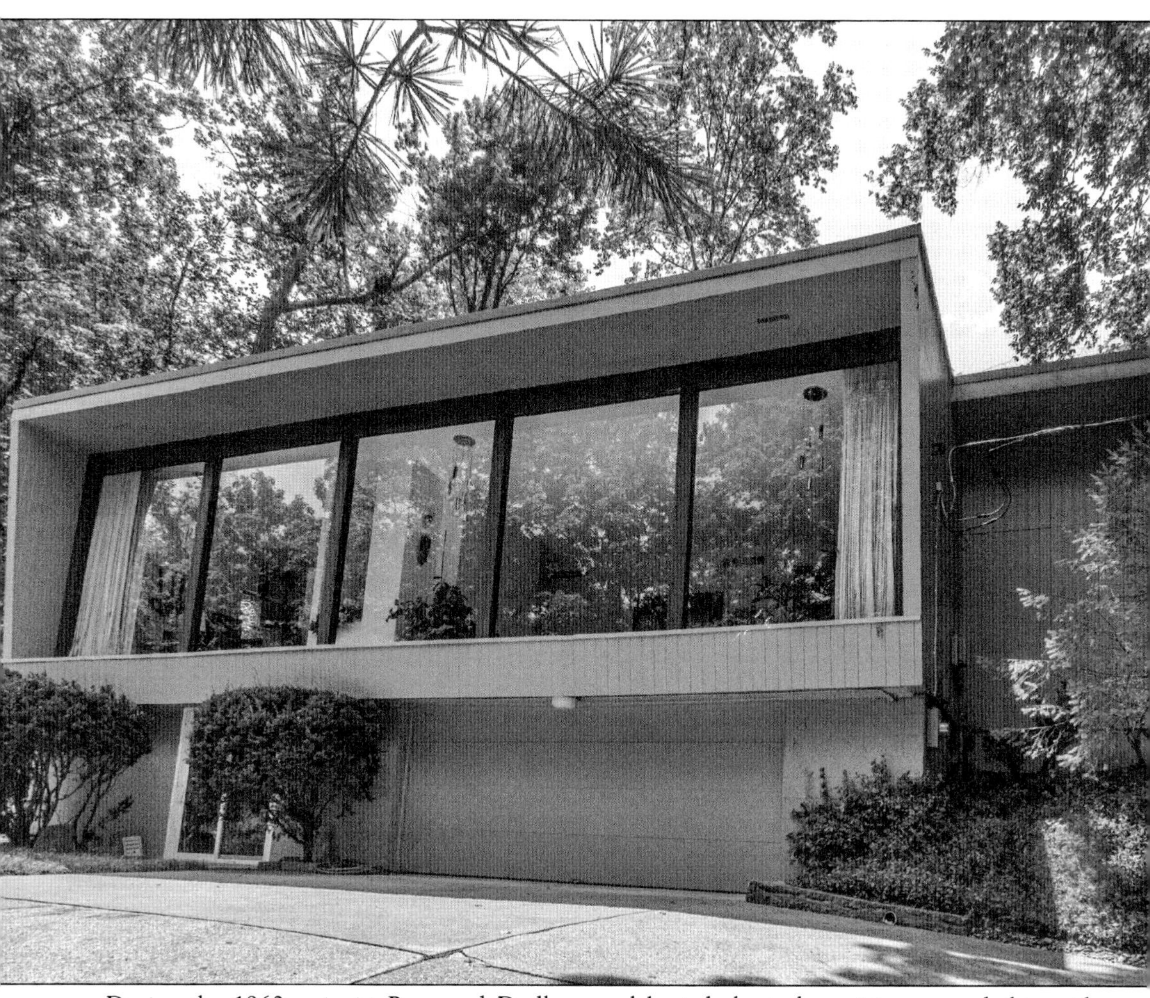

During the 1960s, pianist Raymond Dudley, a celebrated classical musician, owned this mid-century modern home at the end of Commonwealth Drive. While teaching at UC's College-Conservatory of Music from 1964 to 1979, he recorded for major labels and performed across the United States and Europe. At this home, built in 1963, he practiced on a grand piano in the living room near this massive front window. Dudley's greatest musical contributions were his recorded interpretations of Hayden piano sonatas. In 1967, he was the featured soloist at Cincinnati's Music Hall on the historic night that Boston Pops Orchestra conductor Arthur Fiedler debuted with the Cincinnati Symphony Orchestra. Dudley was a close friend of fellow Canadian and classical pianist Glenn Gould. When the Dudley family moved from Finneytown, the home was sold to dentists Robert and Eva Ringgenberg. They lived there for more than a half-century. (Mark Evans.)

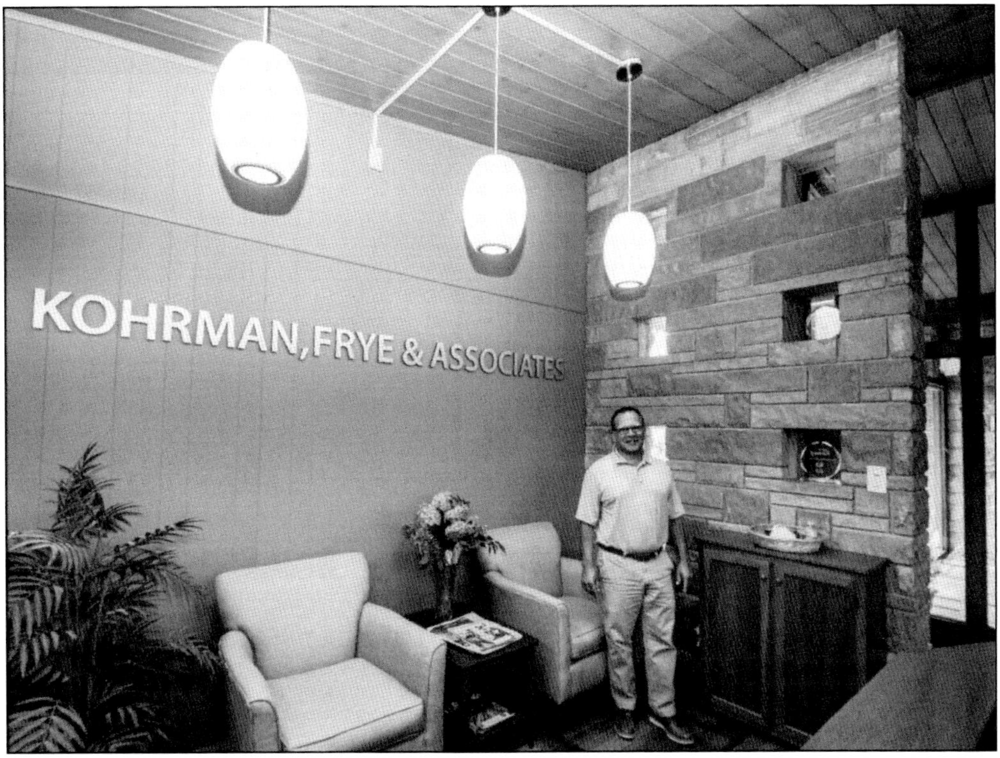

Mike Frye (pictured), a partner in Kohrman, Frye & Associates, stood in the lobby of the accounting firm's restored office building on Hempstead Drive. The firm acquired the building in 1990 and faithfully preserved its original features. In 1958, physicians Ray Lippert and Carl Thompson built this mid-century modern office for their medical practice across the street from Brentwood Shopping Plaza. The building's architects, Garrod, Killiam & Garrod, used stone cut from a specific Indiana limestone quarry to create this interior wall. True to the mid-century modern era, the roof (below) is angled and the exterior materials include stone, metal, and glass. As a result, the building is one of Finneytown's most distinct commercial buildings. (Both, Mark Evans.)

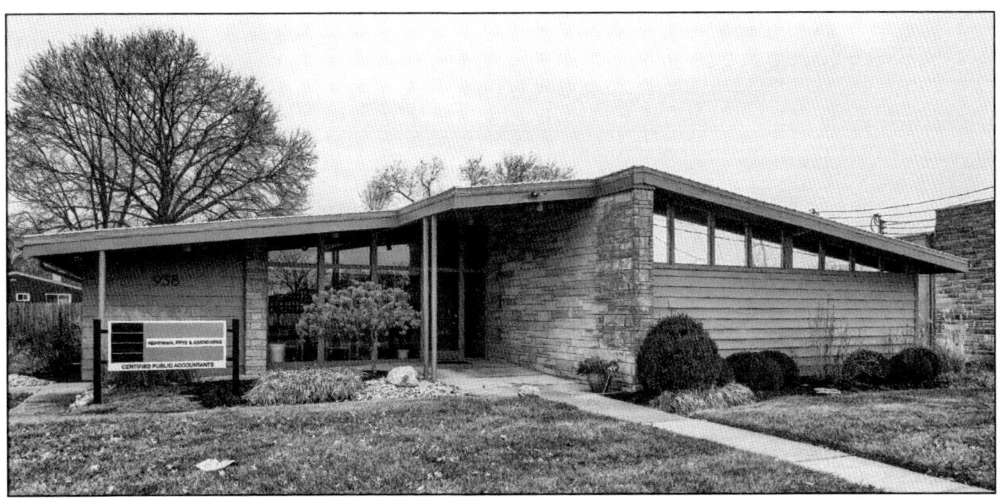

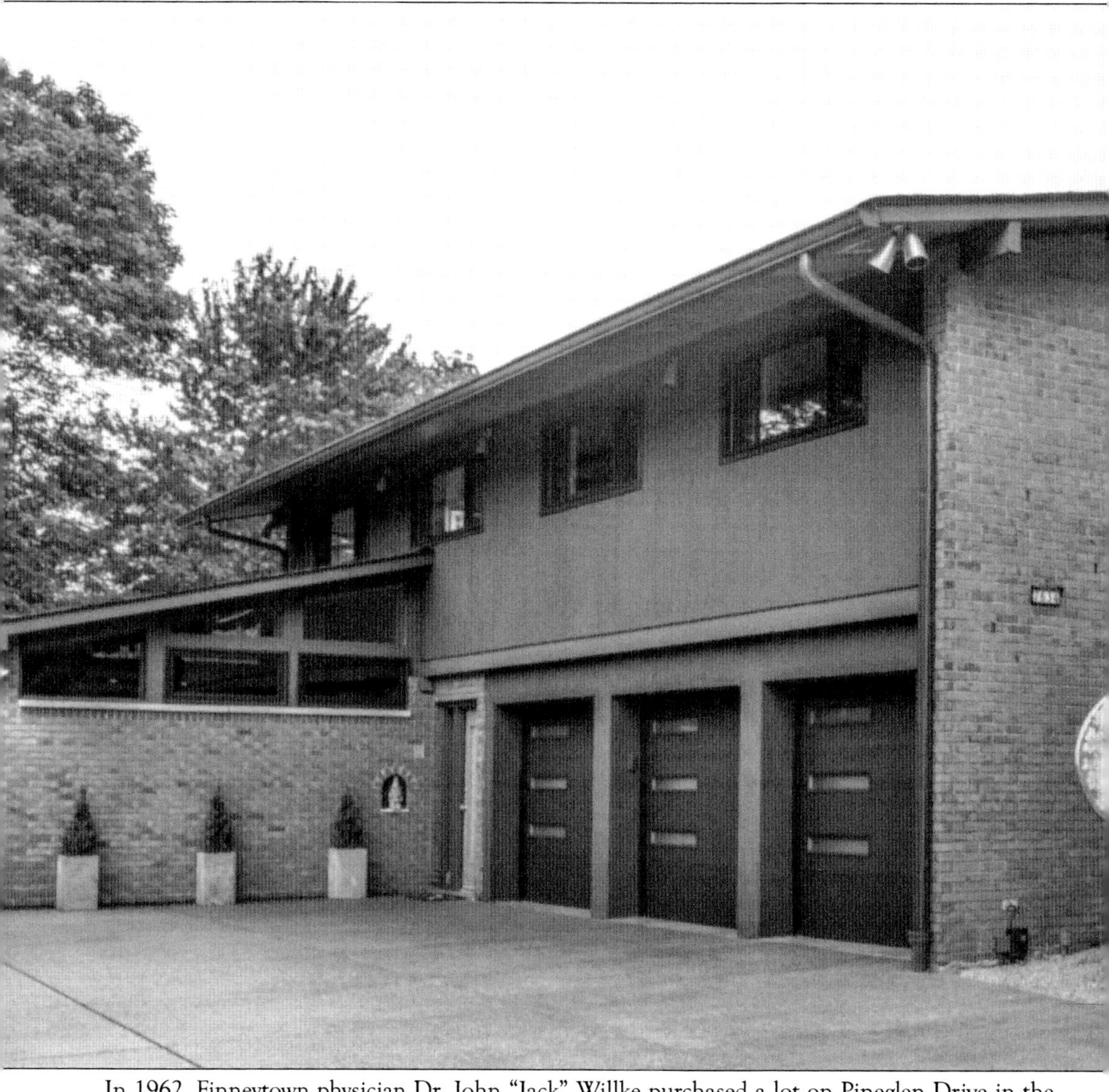

In 1962, Finneytown physician Dr. John "Jack" Willke purchased a lot on Pineglen Drive in the North Hill Estates development. The wooded property reflected its previous history as part of the massive Nieman Nursery. To complement the setting, he hired architect Rudy Hermes to design a home resembling a lodge with a three-car garage. John's specifications included an open-floor design, heavily wooded interiors, and dramatic ceilings. As a modernist architect, Rudy brought a

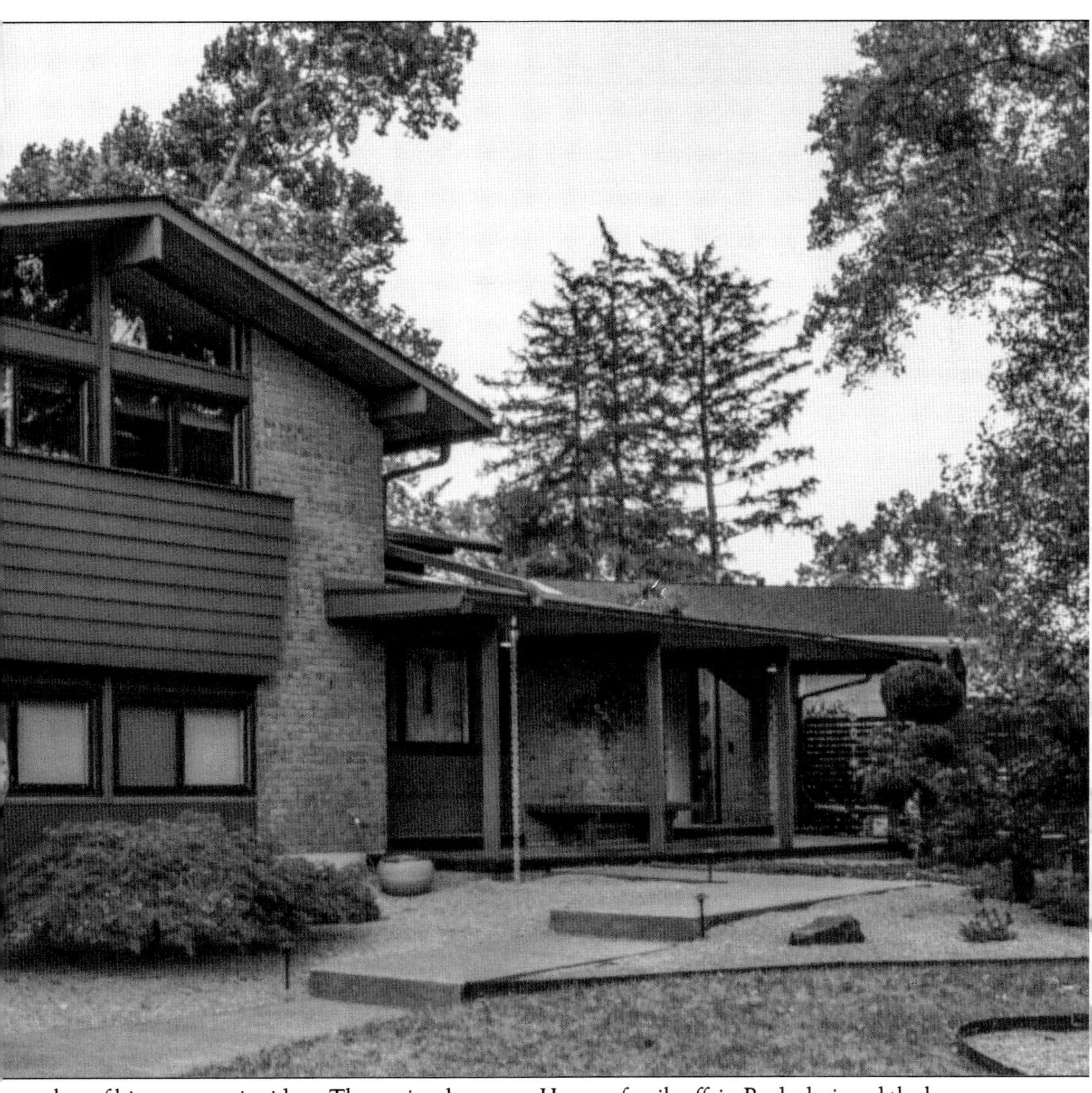

slew of his own creative ideas. The project became a Hermes family affair: Rudy designed the house, his father's construction company built the house, and his wife, Carole, an interior decorator, collaborated with John and his wife, Barbara. The result is one of Cincinnati's most stunning mid-century modern homes. After acquiring the home in 2015, Tim Dutton and Amy Flesher restored the house and accented the modern look with additional outside décor. (Mark Evans.)

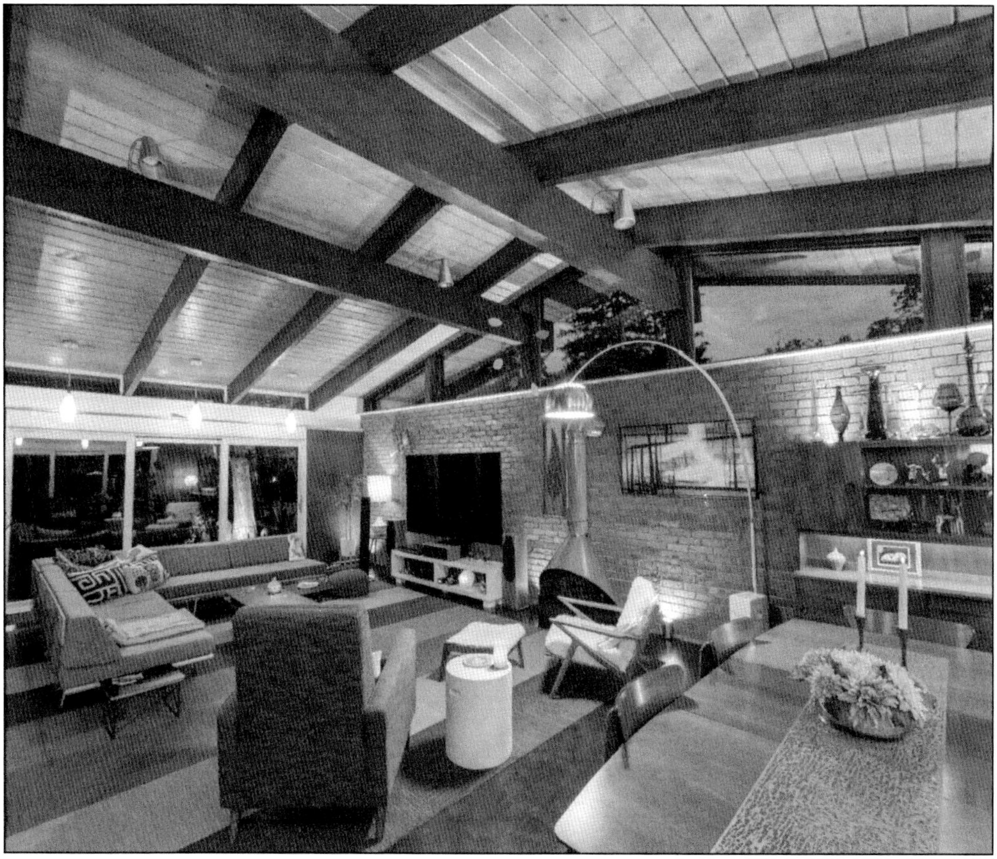

Tim Dutton and Amy Flesher acquired the Willke home through CincinnatiModern, a real estate agency co-owned by Arlen and Susan Rissover. Beginning in the early 2000s, the Rissovers helped to create a rebirth of interest in vintage mid-century modern homes across Cincinnati, including many in Finneytown. In 2015, soon after acquiring the Willke home in Finneytown, Tim and Amy hosted cf3 (Cincinnati Form Follows Function, a local modern advocacy nonprofit) and Rudy and Carole Hermes in their home, which Rudy designed in the early 1960s. As an interior decorator during the modernist era, Carole shared with Amy ideas for further enhancing the interior décor (pictured). Tim and Amy also restored the home's backyard, which includes a pool (below) built in 1968. Rudy died in 2017, and Carole followed in 2021. (Both, Mark Evans.)

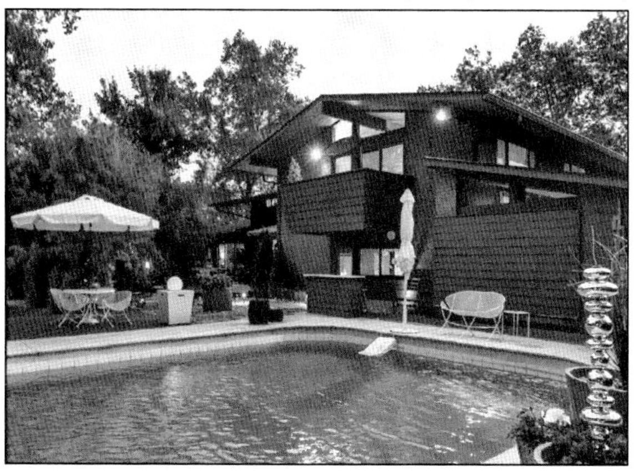

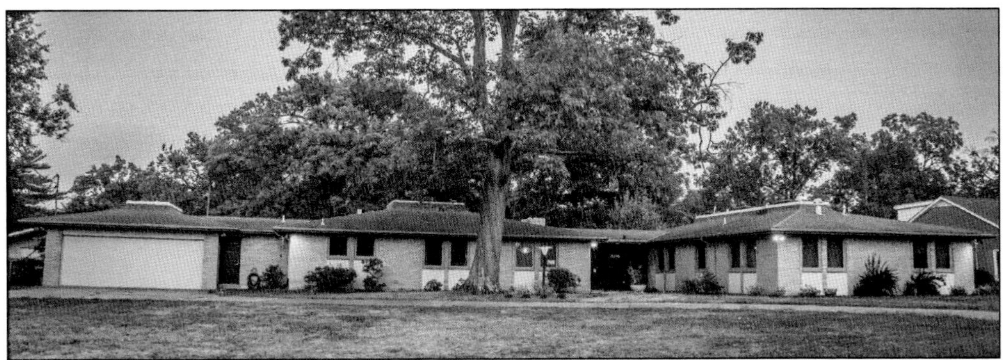

Completed in 1965, family physician Omer J. Feldhaus and his wife, Ruth, built this sprawling, single-story home in North Hill Estates. Glaser, Myers & Associates designed the 12-room home to Ruth's specifications, which reflected her admiration for the Prairie-style architectural design of Frank Lloyd Wright. They lived in the house for the rest of their lives. Tony and Dawn Gast became the home's second owners in 2020. (Mark Evans.)

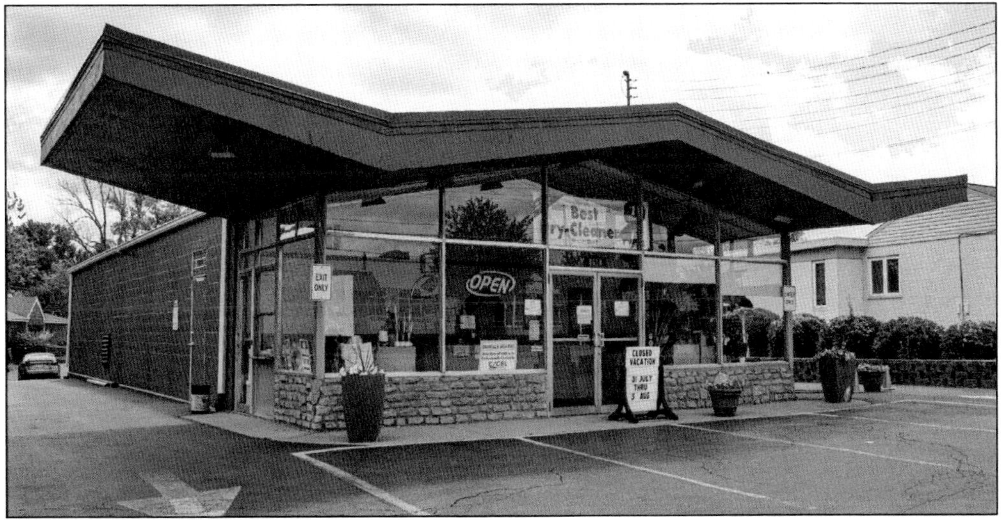

Constructed in 1960, the Apparel Care building on Winton Road, a dry-cleaning operation for decades, is a rare example in the Midwest of "Googie" architecture. Inspired by car designs, the Atomic Age, and space flights, Googie-style commercial buildings peaked in the 1950s and early 1960s, mostly in southern California. The Googie name originated from the Googie's Coffee Shop in Hollywood. (Mark Evans.)

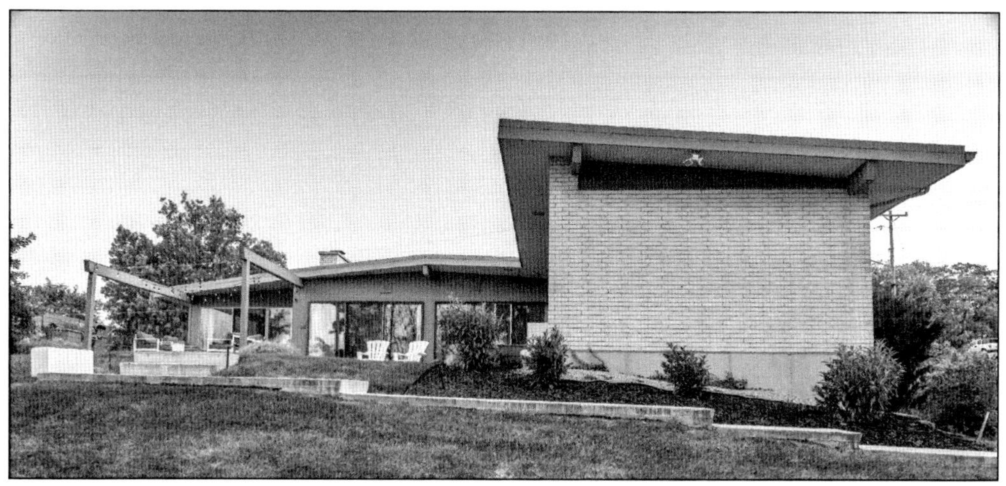

Deanview Drive in View Place subdivision is arguably Finneytown's mid-century modern epicenter. The influence of modernist UC architecture professors, combined with Finneytown's topography of wooded enclaves and hills, fostered a home design movement, said Susan Rissover of CincinnatiModern. This 1960s home atop Deanview reflects the mid-century modern philosophy of designing homes to the contour of the land. (Mark Evans.)

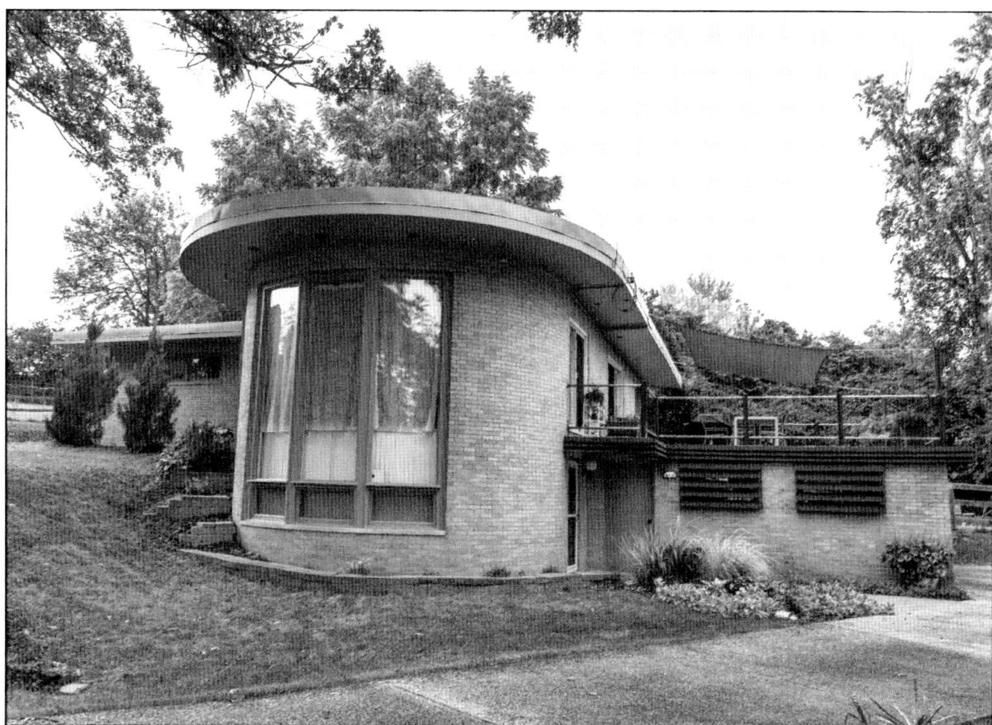

In the 1950s and 1960s, Deanview Drive attracted young homebuyers from GE and P&G interested in futuristic designs with bold exterior statements. Situated at the bottom of the street, this 1963 home catches the eye with its unusually large front window. By the early 1970s, the rising price of building materials made many mid-century modern designs cost-prohibitive. (Mark Evans.)

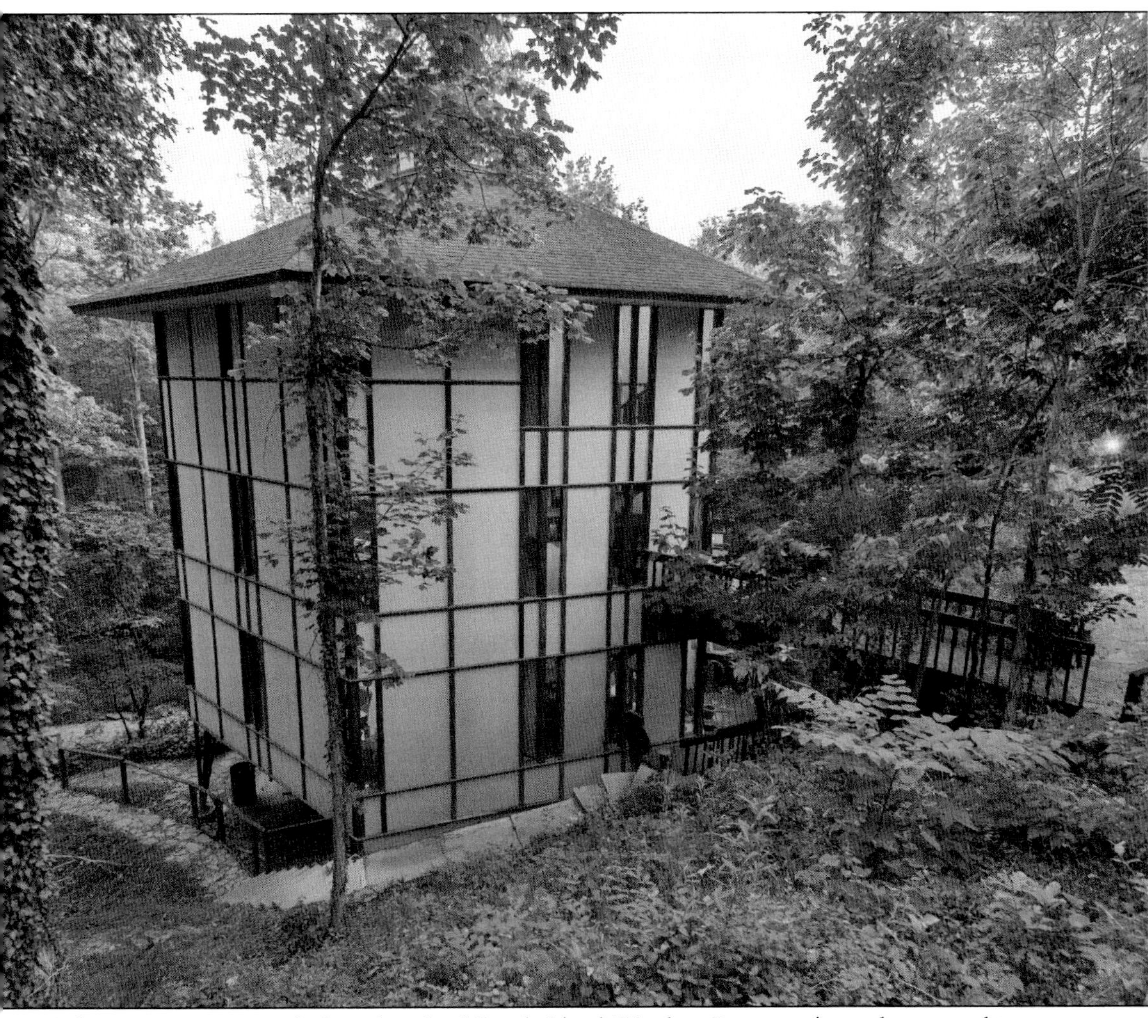

A longtime protégé and close friend of Frank Lloyd Wright, Cincinnati's modernist architect Benjamin Dombar designed and constructed this four-story, hexagon-shaped home on a steep slope along Galbraith Road in Finneytown. He purchased the property next to Congress Run Creek in 1958. For several years, the successful local architect picnicked and camped with his family on the property while he plotted out how to construct the house. He placed the home below the road to lower traffic noise, but high enough to catch the sun. The Dombar family moved into the exotic house in 1968. Benjamin and his wife Shirley lived there until 2006. "When I come home at night, it's like suddenly being on vacation," he told the *Cincinnati Enquirer*. After the home had fallen into disrepair, Beth Johnson purchased and restored the house in 2017. Through her efforts, the house, a wonderful example of Wright-inspired "organic architecture" mixed with mid-century modern features, is in the National Register of Historic Places. (Mark Evans.)

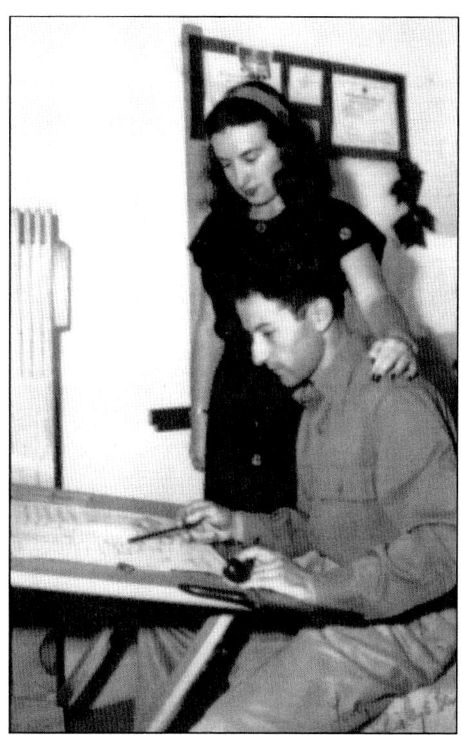

A young Benjamin Dombar is at his design table with his wife, Shirley. Shortly after graduating from Hughes High School in 1934, Benjamin, then 17, joined his older brother Abe, an architect, at Frank Lloyd Wright's home in Wisconsin. Benjamin stayed there for seven years and became a valued apprentice of Wright. Later, Benjamin managed dozens of projects for Wright. Benjamin and Shirley began their 54-year marriage in 1942. (Beth Johnson.)

On the wall of Benjamin Dombar's hexagon-shaped house is an art piece made from his drawings of the house. After serving in the military during World War II, Benjamin worked with local architect Woodie Garber. In 1948, he opened his own practice. A prolific architect with a thriving private practice, Benjamin designed more than 1,000 residential and commercial buildings from the 1940s into the 1980s. (Beth Johnson.)

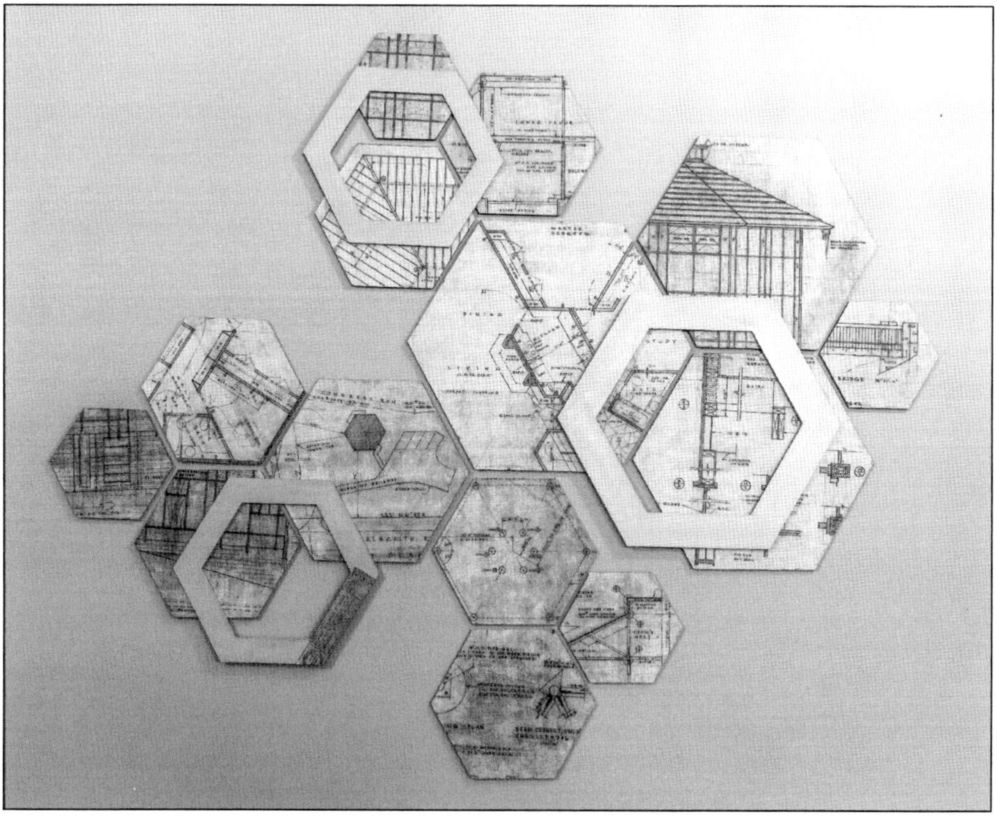

Benjamin, pictured in 1967 working on his family residence, not only designed the Finneytown building, but also did much of the carpentry and masonry himself. Similar to many Frank Lloyd Wright designs, this house incorporates modular constructions, including asbestos panels with baked-in color. Even though the Dombar family lived in the house for decades, the third floor was never completed. (Beth Johnson.)

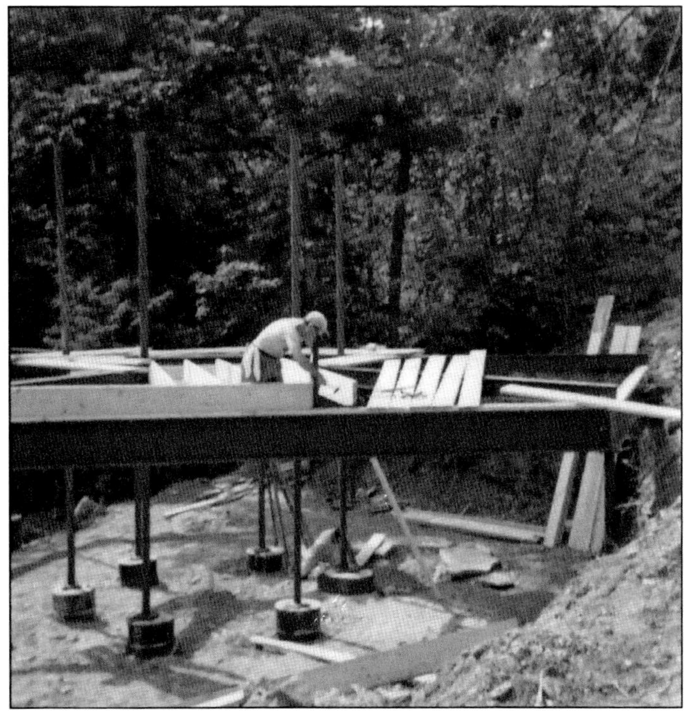

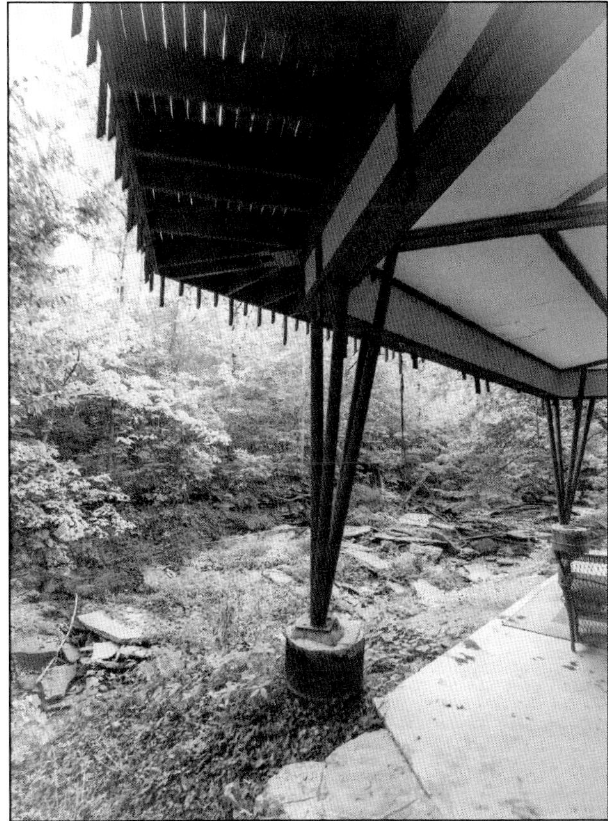

Welded steel braces support much of the Dombar house. The basement is 48 feet below Galbraith Road. As a result, the house is barely visible in the warmer months when the trees are full of leaves. However, from inside the house, there are four levels of panoramic views of the neighboring creek and surrounding woods. (Beth Johnson.)

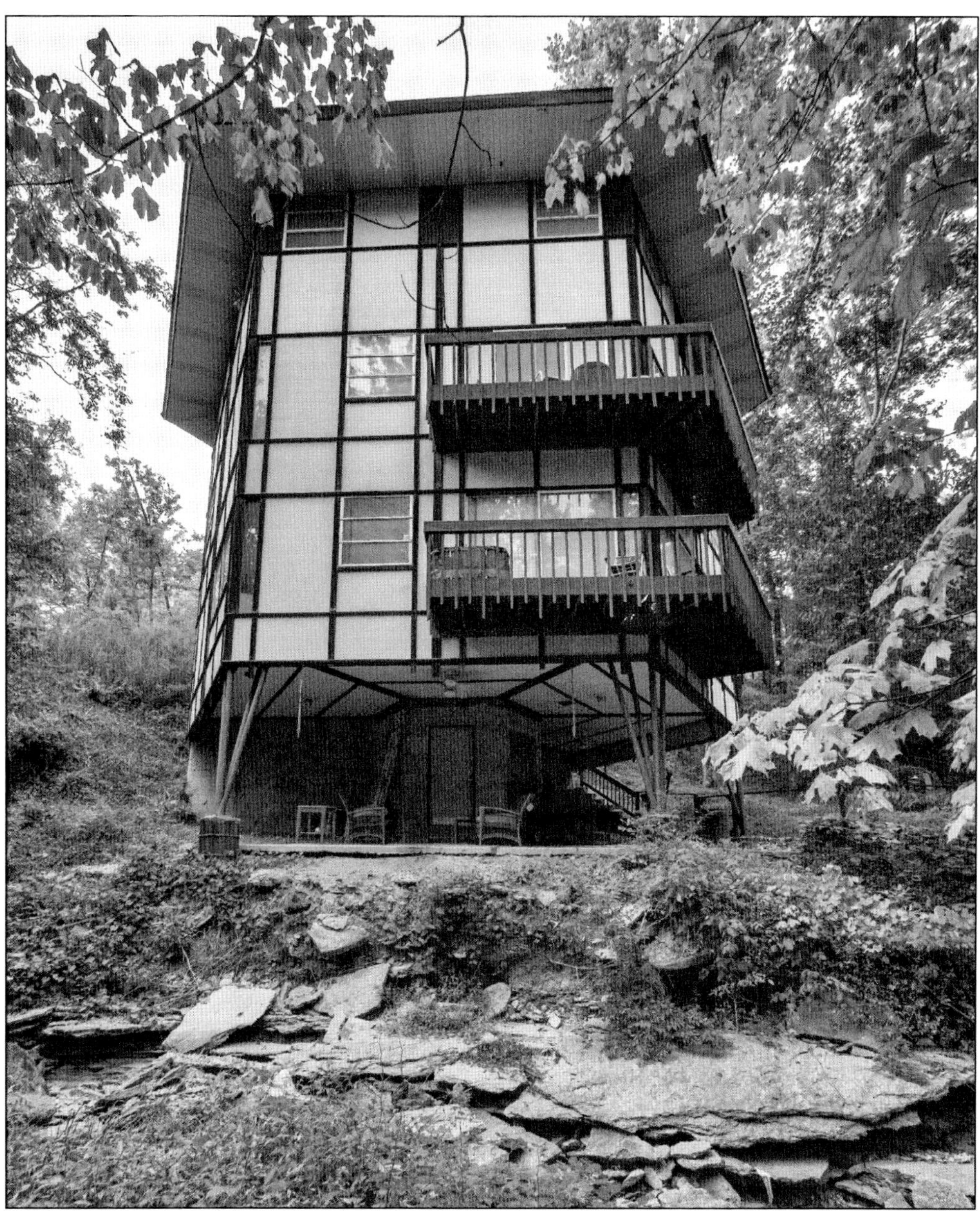

The Dombar house celebrates the philosophy of "organic architecture" espoused by Frank Lloyd Wright. The desire is to create harmony between human habitation and the natural world, which is achieved with designs and materials that integrate the surroundings. Benjamin used bed stones from the creek to create a floor in the foyer, a backsplash in the kitchen, and a large fireplace. He also built stone flooring near the windows. The Dombar house is one of a dozen unique homes along Congress Run Creek and tucked below Galbraith Road on the border of Finneytown and Wyoming. Benjamin designed three of them. The Dombars sold the hexagon home after Benjamin died at age 90 in 2006. Shirley died at age 92 in 2014. By 2016, the house was in foreclosure and disrepair. "The property is now much the same as it was in 1968," said Beth Johnson, who restored it. "But the surroundings have changed dramatically," she added with the sound of nearby Ronald Reagan Highway behind her. (Mark Evans.)

Ten

NOTABLES

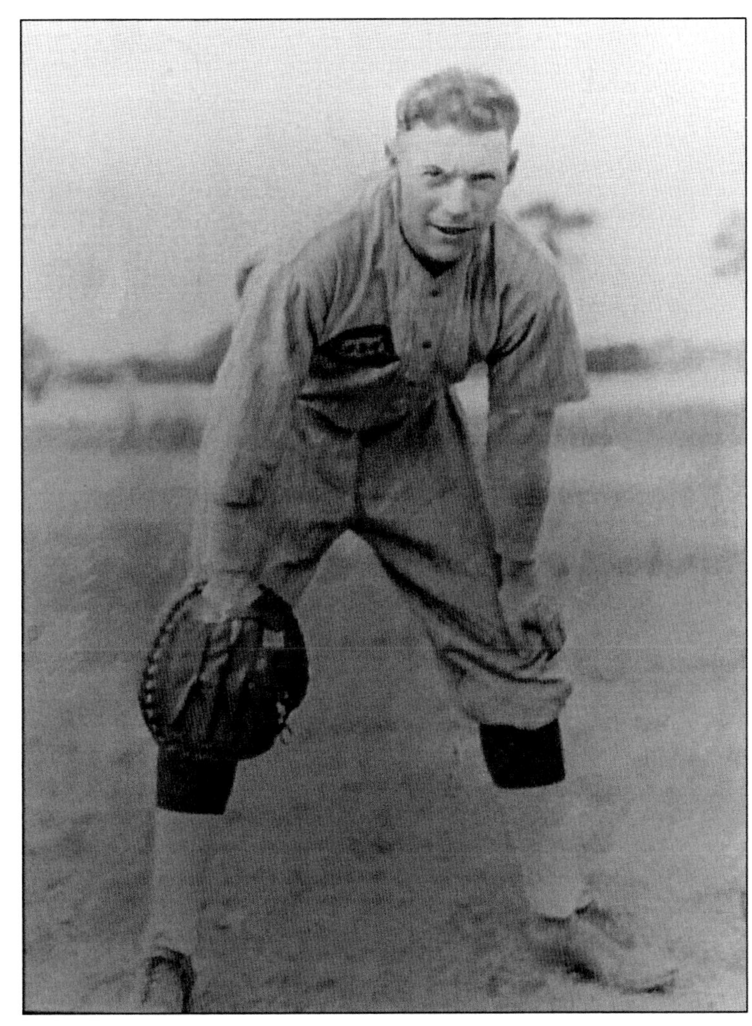

Eugene "Bubbles" Hargrave was one of the best-hitting catchers in Cincinnati Reds history. After retiring, he and his wife, Hester, lived for two decades at 859 Northern Parkway in Parkview Heights. He played eight seasons with the Reds. He hit .353 in 1926 to win the National League batting title. While living in Finneytown, he worked for a valve company. (Author's collection.)

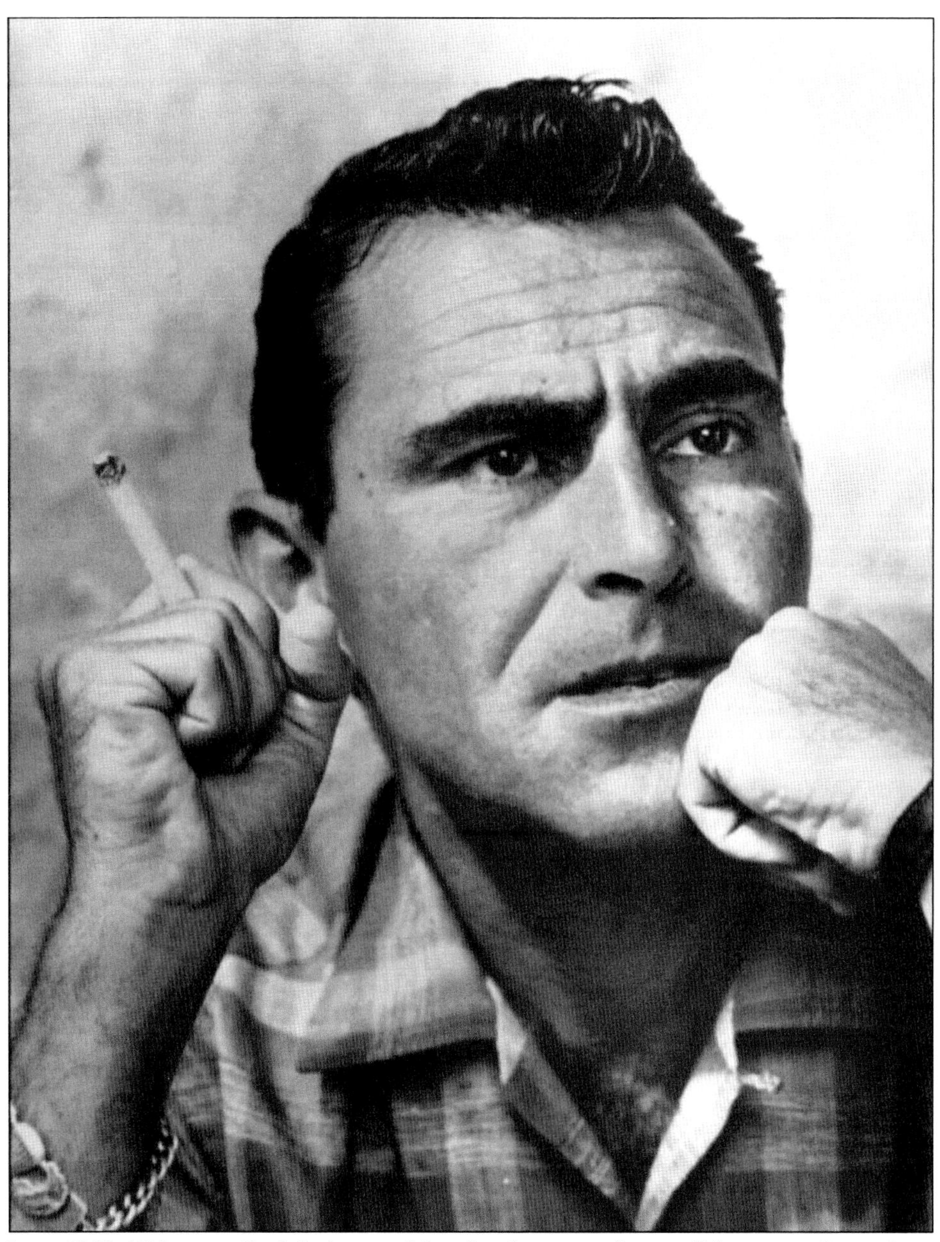

In June 1952, TV writer Rod Serling and his family acquired a small house on Long Lane in Finneytown. A decorated World War II veteran, Rod and wife Carol graduated from Antioch College and moved to Cincinnati in 1950. He first wrote for WLW's radio and TV stations. The Serling family moved to Finneytown shortly after WKRC-TV canceled his local TV drama series, *The Storm*, which was broadcast during 1951 and 1952. However, during his two years on Long Lane, his career blossomed. "Serling sold scripts to the *Hallmark Hall of Fame*, *Kraft Television Theatre*, *Studio One*, and other live TV series in New York," wrote John Kiesewetter, retired *Cincinnati Enquirer* TV critic. Living in Finneytown, Serling also wrote a teleplay called *The Time Element* as a local TV drama. It is now considered the pilot for his iconic *The Twilight Zone* TV series, which debuted on CBS in 1959, five years after the Serlings had moved from Cincinnati to New York. (Author's collection.)

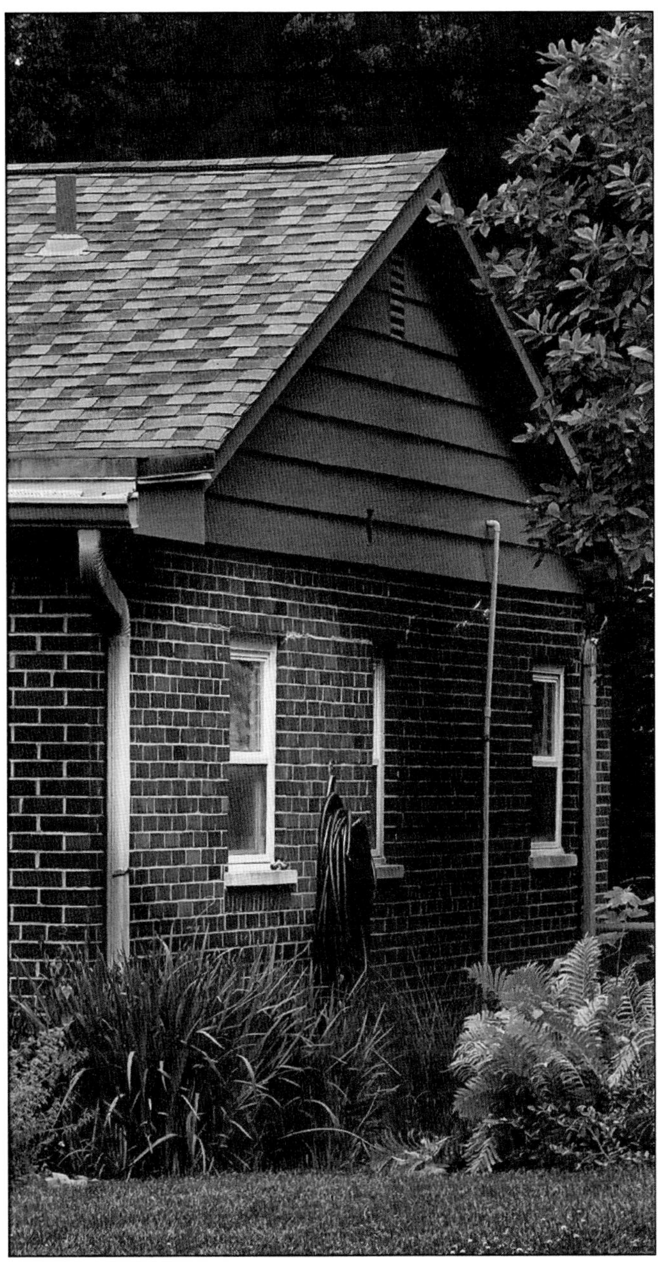

Rod and Carol Serling raised two daughters while living in Finneytown. Neighbors recalled him as a friendly workaholic. One next-door neighbor recalled late summer nights hearing him work on the typewriter while his cigarette smoke and coffee emanated from the home's side window highlighted in this photograph. Living on Long Lane, Serling wrote more than 30 scripts for TV and radio programs, including *Patterns* and *The Twilight Rounds*, which both aired on national TV to great critical success. After leaving Cincinnati, he revised *The Twilight Rounds* and renamed it *Requiem For A Heavyweight*. "The teleplay confirmed his status as one of the great TV writers of television's 'Golden Age' of live dramas," wrote TV critic John Kiesewetter. Longtime owners of Serling's former Long Lane house, Michael and Carolyn Morgan, would grow used to drivers stopping to stare at the house or stand uninvited in the front yard with a camera. (Mark Evans.)

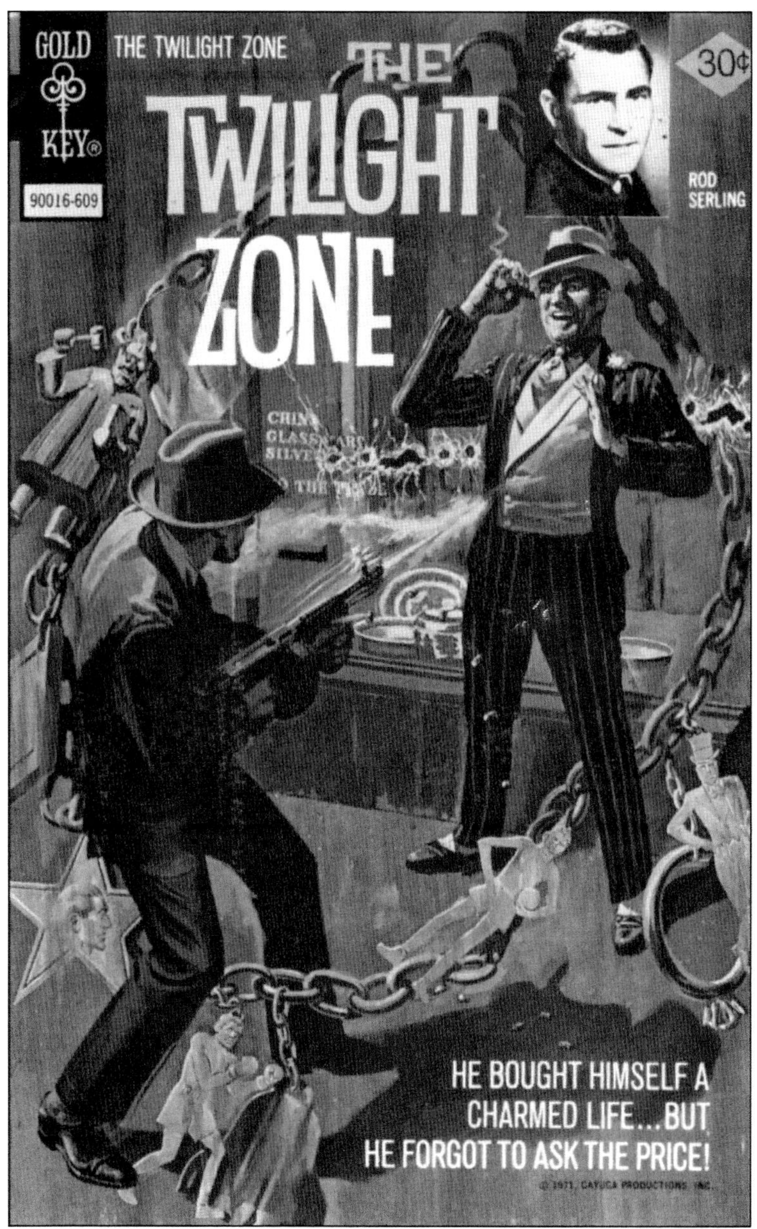

Less than a decade after leaving Finneytown, Serling's *The Twilight Zone,* which aired on TV from 1959 through 1964, had become a franchise, spawning drugstore paperbacks and comic books. In 1963, the five-time Emmy Award winner returned to Cincinnati to give a speech. Notoriously outspoken, he complained to the local audience that TV programmers were "frightened to try anything new." He also waxed nostalgic about being a young hungry writer churning out scripts for the networks while supporting a family in Finneytown. "The golden age of TV is past," he said. By the early 1970s, he also earned big money doing voiceovers for TV commercials. Near the end of his life, he taught at Ithaca College in his native New York state. He died in 1975 at age 50 of heart failure in Rochester, New York. But *The Twilight Zone* lives on in TV syndication and inspires new adaptations. And baby boomers still drive down Long Lane and yell, "There's the house!" (Author's collection.)

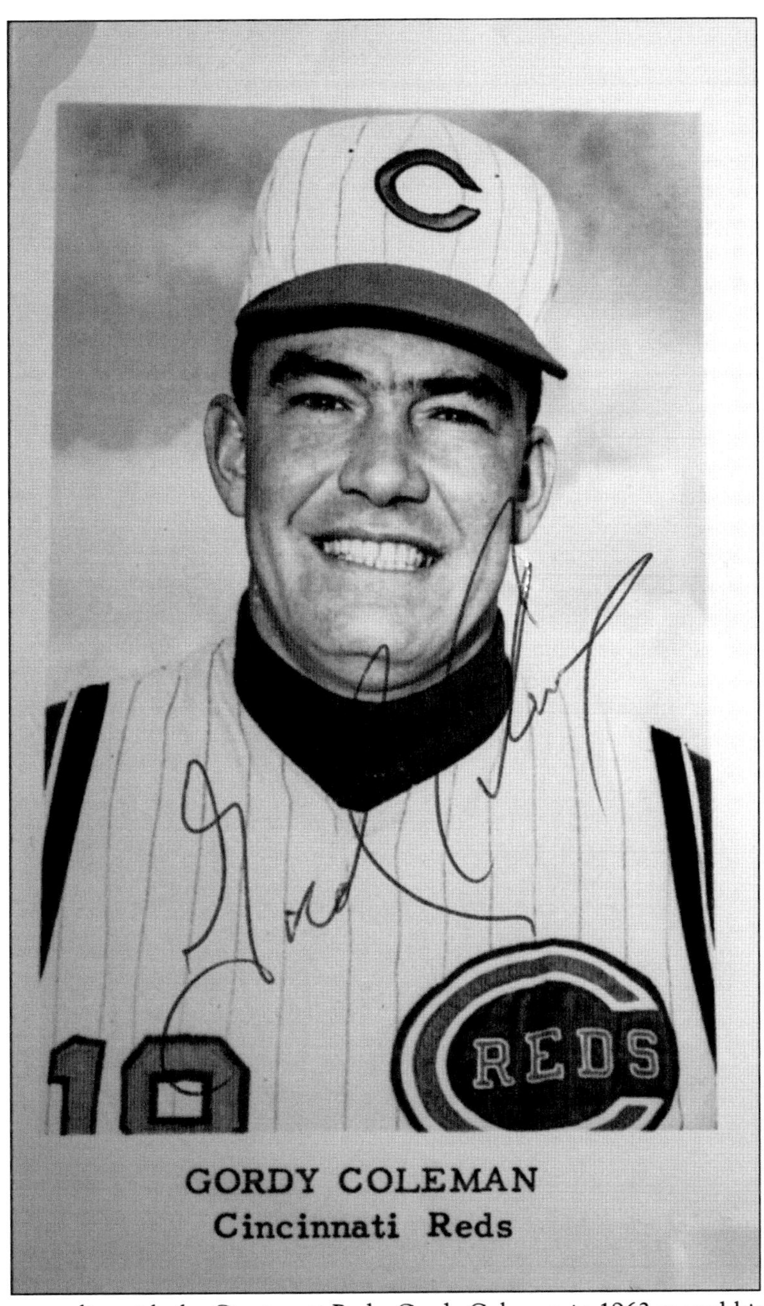

A beloved personality with the Cincinnati Reds, Gordy Coleman in 1963 moved his family into a small ranch house on Burgundy Lane. He happily handed this autographed photograph to Finneytown kids who knocked on his door. In eight Reds seasons, he hit .273 with 98 home runs (HRs). In 1961, he hit 26 HRs for the NL Champions and smacked a HR in the World Series. After his playing days, he donned a red sports coat as director of the Reds Speakers Bureau. With the ever-present cigarette in hand, he gave thousands of lively talks. Gordy and his wife, Marian, raised their son, Shawn, in Finneytown. In the 1970s, Shawn was a standout football lineman and pitcher at Finneytown High School. For five baseball seasons leading up to his death at age 59 in 1994, Gordy was a commentator for Reds TV broadcasts. (Jane Kennedy.)

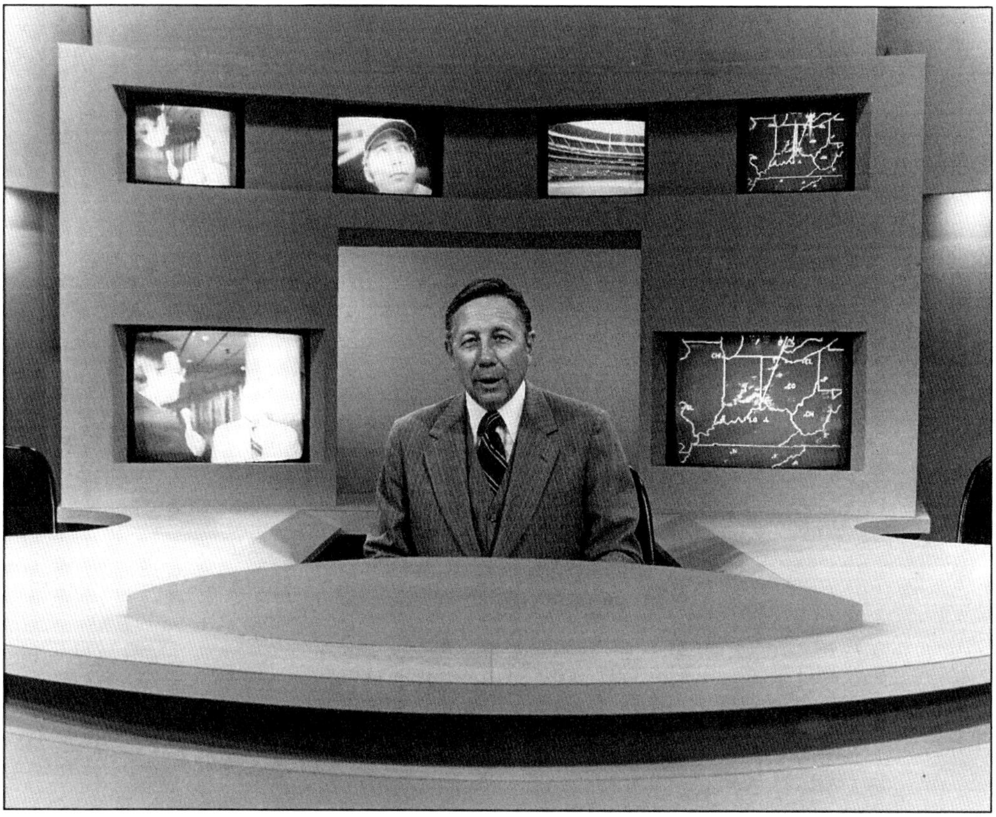

When Al Schottelkotte moved his large family to Pineglen Drive in the early 1960s, he was already a popular local newsman. A former *Cincinnati Enquirer* columnist with a radio newscast on WSAI-AM, he began anchoring WCPO-TV news in 1960. In an era when television offered only a handful of channels, his following was extraordinary. He was the top-ranked local news anchor of the 1960s and 1970s. (Cincinnati Public Library.)

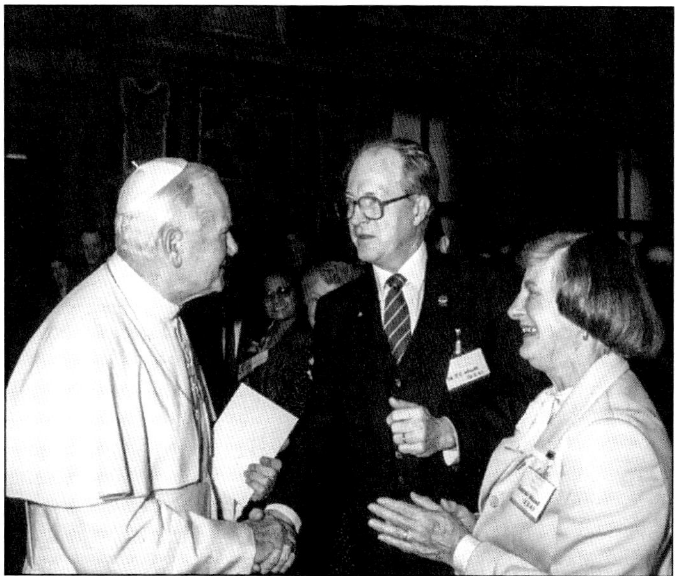

Photographed with Pope John Paul II, Dr. John Willke, a longtime family practitioner, and wife, Barbara, lived for more than a half-century on Pineglen Drive. Never shy of controversy and a former president of the National Right to Life Committee, John Willke would be credited for shaping the pro-life movement for decades. (Kate McAuliffe.)

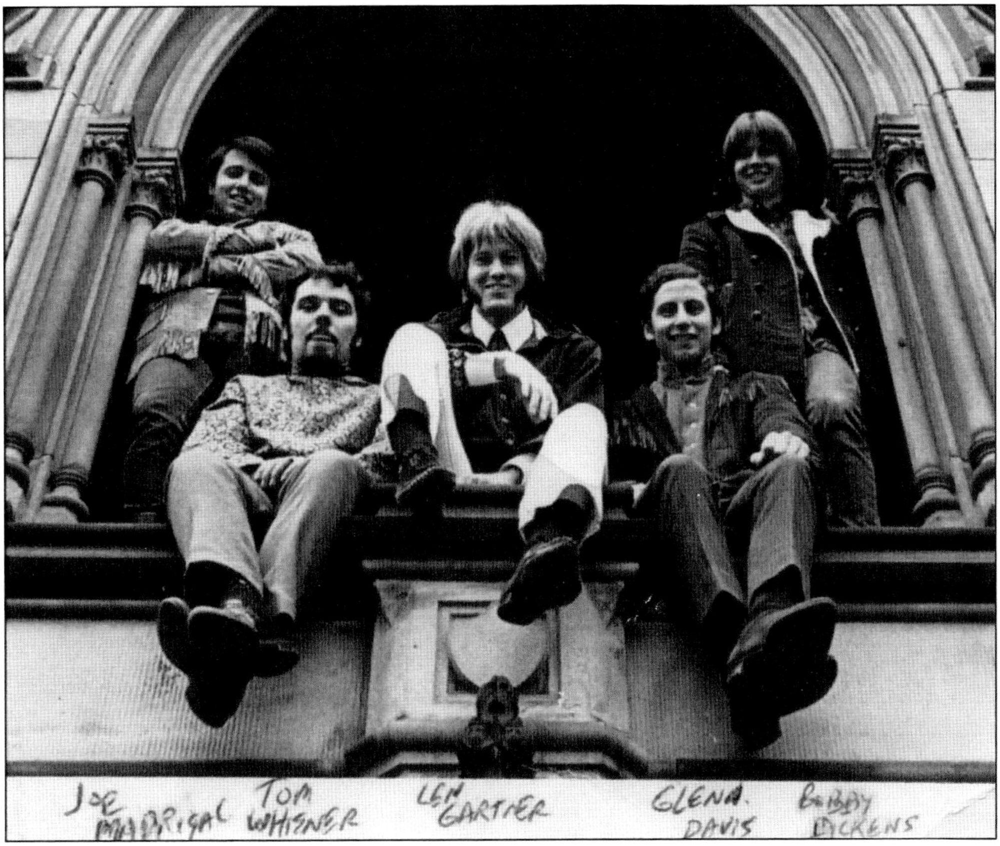

During the late 1960s era of the garage rock band, US Too Group, comprised of five Finneytown teenagers, recorded 45-rpm singles during 1966 and 1967 written by its lead singer, Len Gartner (center). His song "The Only Thing To Do" was a regional hit, thanks largely to heavy airplay on the local WSAI-AM radio. (Randy McNutt.)

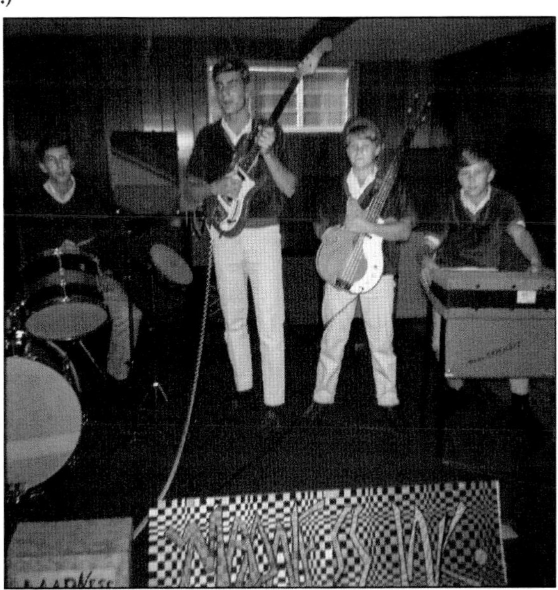

Holding an electric bass nearly his size, Mike Bany (third from left) was in grade school at St. Vivian in 1966 when he joined Madness Inc., a rock band comprised of Finneytown High School students. He later became a popular local musician with several bands, most notably Wheels. He wrote their 1982 regional hit "Amaretta." His 1995 murder after a nightclub gig shocked Cincinnati. (Matt Angert.)

Discover Thousands of Local History Books Featuring Millions of Vintage Images

Arcadia Publishing, the leading local history publisher in the United States, is committed to making history accessible and meaningful through publishing books that celebrate and preserve the heritage of America's people and places.

Find more books like this at
www.arcadiapublishing.com

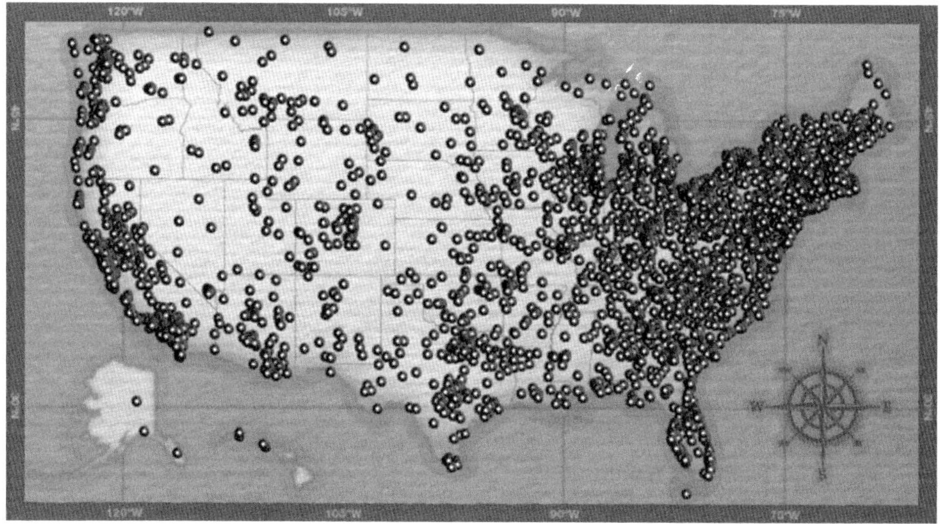

Search for your hometown history, your old stomping grounds, and even your favorite sports team.

Consistent with our mission to preserve history on a local level, this book was printed in South Carolina on American-made paper and manufactured entirely in the United States. Products carrying the accredited Forest Stewardship Council (FSC) label are printed on 100 percent FSC-certified paper.

MADE IN THE

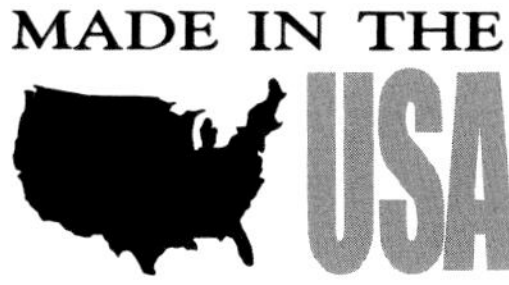